Advance Praise for

"There's combat. Then, there's the rest of your life. We need survival skills for each battle zone. This is the guide to surviving the war back here. We all need it. A hell of a book. The lucky get it."

—Max Cleland, former U.S. Senator and VA Administrator,
wounded decorated combat veteran

"I've never met a mental health professional who 'gets it' as well as Colonel Charles Hoge. He's done the research, he's been shoulder-to-shoulder with warriors, and he's woven it together in language that is real and resonant. *Once a Warrior—Always a Warrior* is a vital handbook for every leader, and a survival book for warriors-come-home."

—Nate Self, former Army Ranger Captain,
author of *Two Wars: One Hero's Fight on Two Fronts—Abroad and Within*

"Of all the victimizing crap out there regarding what real warriors experience in battle, Dr. Hoge's deeply researched work stands a breed apart from anything in this genre. He has simply written the best, most comprehensive study of not only what those at the tip of spear have endured, but what they can expect to go through as they confront the realities of combat. Just as every warrior should drink water and clean their rifle in battle, every returning veteran should pack this book as they continue their journey home."

—Staff Sergeant David Bellavia,
author of *House to House: An Epic Memoir of War*

"*Once a Warrior—Always a Warrior* provides a uniquely valuable addition to the subject of post traumatic stress in the military population because it comes from a soldier and a mental health professional who has years of real world, hands-on experience helping our warriors deal with these issues. Dr. Hoge possesses the rare gift of being able to translate the science from published research into the language of the warrior. As valuable as this book is for warriors coping with experiences that in many instances are normal responses to abnormal circumstances, it should also be required reading for mental health professionals to whom our warriors turn for assistance. It will help them strike the right chord with those they serve, even if they have not walked in their boots. Finally, it's a book for the warrior's family. It will help them to understand, participate in, and facilitate the warrior's journey, and realize that it can be a journey of growth."

—James B. Peake, MD, Secretary of Veteran Affairs (2007–2009),
40th Surgeon General of the U.S. Army, decorated Vietnam combat veteran

"Dr. Hoge has served his nation well by compiling a user-friendly guide to issues this generation faces in the long wars of Iraq and Afghanistan. Written in a language warriors can understand, he takes complex issues and delivers practical advice, tips and strategies that are the antidote to suffering. Ultimately no matter the experience, the warrior must decide which path they will choose. They can go down a negative path that leads to dysfunction and suffering or they can choose to own their experience, rather than being owned by it. This book and the skills within it can serve as a first step in a journey toward resilience and positive growth."

—Steve Robinson, SFC (Retired), Army Ranger, Veteran Advocate

"Dr. Hoge explains cutting-edge medical discoveries in plain English, and describes the psychological and physiological mechanisms underlying post-deployment transition challenges. In essence, he tells us two things: there are good reasons why it is hard to adjust to "normal" life after combat, and understanding those reasons empowers us and makes us more likely to succeed at adjusting and integrating combat experiences into a healthy psychological and emotional life. This understanding is essential for our growing ranks of combat veterans and their loved ones, mental health professionals, policy makers, and concerned citizens, and this book is the way to get it."

—Gabriel Ledeen, Former Captain, U.S. Marine Corps;
two-tour Iraq combat veteran; Senior Fellow, Vets For Freedom

"Colonel Hoge, MD, a well-known and respected psychiatric researcher and clinician, has written a smart, insightful, jargon-free book on reactions to trauma and the syndrome of post traumatic stress disorder. This book is a gift to anyone in the military or anyone who has relatives or loved-ones in the military. What was obvious to me is that Col. Hoge genuinely cares about the health and well-being of people serving in the military and of their relatives. His direct, clear language and thinking help clear up many misconceptions about reactions to combat, and provide useful tools to aid in recovery/readjustment."

—Greer Richardson, MD,
Assistant Clinical Professor of Psychiatry, Yale University;
Veterans Affairs Staff Psychiatrist, West Haven, Connecticut

ONCE A WARRIOR
ALWAYS A WARRIOR

Navigating the Transition from Combat to Home—
Including Combat Stress, PTSD, and mTBI

CHARLES W. HOGE, MD
COLONEL, U.S. ARMY (RETIRED)

life

Guilford, Connecticut
An imprint of Globe Pequot Press

To buy books in quantity for corporate use
or incentives, call **(800) 962–0973**
or e-mail **premiums@GlobePequot.com**.

GPP Life is an imprint of Globe Pequot Press.

Text design by Sheryl P. Kober
Cover photo by Teun Voeten

Library of Congress Cataloging-in-Publication Data is available on file.

ISBN 978-0-7627-5442-7

Printed in the United States of America

10 9 8 7 6 5 4 3 2 1

The material in this book is intended to provide accurate and authoritative information, but should not be used as a substitute for professional care. The author and publisher urge you to consult with your health care provider or seek other professional advice in the event that you require expert assistance.

CONTENTS

"What is grace?" I asked God.
And he said,
"All that happens."

—St. John of the Cross
(translated by Daniel Ladinksy)

ACKNOWLEDGMENTS

This book wouldn't exist without the insights, knowledge, and counsel of Herb M. Goldberg. Fundamental concepts he's developed and employed over the past thirty years were foundational to this work. Additionally, his objective feedback and precise edits of the entire manuscript were invaluable. I am grateful for his contribution.

This book would also not have happened if it weren't for the unwavering support of my wife, Charise, through the entire process (starting long before the writing began). Her review and edits to the book and contribution to the chapter for spouses and family members were wonderful. I'm filled with gratitude for her presence in my life. A heartfelt thank-you to my daughters, Alex and Amelia, my parents, Tom and Jeanne, and my brother, Mark, for their love and encouragement. Thanks to VJ for his compassion and care for my father.

Thanks to First Sergeant Michael Schindler (Retired) for the strength, courage, and wisdom expressed in the stories he shares in this book. It was truly an honor to collaborate, and I learned so much from him. Thanks to Noriko for introducing us.

I want to thank my professional colleagues, Carl Castro, PhD and Victoria Bruner, LCSW, for their suggestions, based on their wealth of experience, on important material to add or modify. Thanks to the many researchers and clinicians at Walter Reed Army Institute of Research, Walter Reed Army Medical Center, U.S. Army Research Unit–Europe, Deployment Health Clinical Center, and Uniformed Services University for Health Sciences, whom I've had the pleasure to work with over the last twelve years, and for the countless lessons I've learned from them.

Thanks to the service members, veterans, and family members I've had the privilege of treating; you have given me the priceless gift of your trust and life stories, and the inspiration and confidence to write this book.

Thanks to my agent, Celeste Fine, at Folio Literary Management, for discovering me, and for her faith and support throughout this process. Finally, I want to thank the many service members and veterans (of several wars) who reviewed the manuscript at various stages and provided critical feedback to ensure that this book is on point and relevant. I'm grateful and honored for the support that each of you has given me.

INTRODUCTION
POSTWAR "TRANSITION—
READJUSTMENT"

If you are a service member, veteran, government worker, or contractor who has ever deployed to a war zone, or their spouse, partner, or family member, then this book is for you. It provides essential knowledge on what it means to be a warrior and to transition home from war. It addresses what medical professionals call "PTSD" (post-traumatic stress disorder) and other reactions to war (e.g., "combat stress," "mild traumatic brain injury," "crazy"). It provides skills for navigating the transition no matter how much time has passed since leaving the war zone.

Society hasn't yet grasped that "transitioning" home from combat does not mean giving up being a warrior, but rather learning to dial up or down the warrior responses depending on the situation. This book will also benefit mental health care professionals who want to expand their perspective and gain greater understanding of how to connect with and treat the many great men and women who have risked their lives in a war zone in the service of their country.

There are numerous self-help books on PTSD and other problems related to combat deployment, but this one takes a different approach. It's true that like many of the other books, this one was written by a mental health professional (I'm a medical doctor with a specialty in psychiatry). However, my intention in writing this book is to cut to the chase, eliminate as much of our jargon as possible, and provide something that will bridge the vast divide that exists between combat veterans, society, and mental health professionals in understanding what we call PTSD and other war reactions.

After a twenty-year active-duty military career, I have a growing understanding of the limitations of the current health-care system in addressing the concerns of warriors back from war. My knowledge is drawn from treating service members returning from Iraq and Afghanistan at Walter Reed Army Medical Center, directing a widely recognized research program on the mental health effects of the Iraq and Afghanistan wars, investigating suicides and homicides involving soldiers after they returned home from deployment, and assisting leaders at the highest levels of the Department of Defense (DoD) and the Department of Veterans Affairs (VA) in developing mental health programs for service members, veterans, and their loved ones.

I've been involved in developing interventions for Pentagon employees after 9/11, and guiding research to validate training materials that enhance resilience before, during, and after combat. The articles my colleagues and I wrote on PTSD and traumatic brain injury, published in the world's leading medical journals (e.g., the *New England Journal of Medicine*, the *Journal of the American Medical Association*), have resulted in large increases in health-care funding to help service members and veterans. I've testified on several occasions to Congress and have appeared on national TV and radio news shows.

I also deployed to Iraq during the second year of the war, where I traveled throughout the country, assessing the quality and availability of combat stress control services. Although never in a situation where I had to discharge my weapon, I have an appreciation for what it feels like to live with danger, convoy in dangerous sectors, be shot at, have soldiers killed by indirect fire adjacent to where I was sleeping, travel "outside the wire," and cope with separation from my family.

These experiences have given me a unique appreciation for the different perspectives service members, veterans, clinicians, policy-makers, family members, and the public have on transitioning home from war.

This book is about transitioning home from a combat deployment. It includes information on PTSD—not only on the disorder that medical professionals diagnose and treat, but the more common ways in which this label is used to describe the myriad normal, confusing, and paradoxical transition experiences encountered after returning home from a war zone.

This book is not intended to provide standard mental health educational material with lists of symptoms and descriptions of the many ways in which you or your loved one may have been psychologically "injured" by war, deployment, or military service. You probably don't want to read long stories of fellow warriors or spouses struggling with transition problems, or receive laundry lists of "coping strategies" without adequate explanation of their limitations. What I believe to be important is an understanding of what to expect from postwar reactions, including PTSD, but on your terms, rather than the terms defined for you by the medical establishment or society.

The Contradictions of PTSD

PTSD is full of contradictions. Virtually every reaction that mental health professionals label a "symptom," and which indeed can cause havoc in your life after returning home from combat, is an essential survival skill in the war zone. The dilemma is that the reactions that are necessary for survival and success in combat are not easy to dial down and adapt after coming home. Society believes that a warrior should be able to transition home and lead a "normal" life, but the reality is that most of society has no clue what it means to be a warrior. Those who have worked in a war zone understand that their warrior responses—including responses doctors may label "PTSD"—could be needed again in the future—for instance, if they mobilize for another deployment, someone tries to break into their home, or they take a job in a dangerous profession (e.g., law enforcement, security, emergency services). *Once a warrior—always a warrior.*

PTSD means different things to different people. To mental health professionals, it's one of nearly 300 diagnoses detailed in the American Psychiatric Association's *Diagnostic and Statistical Manual of Mental Disorders* (DSM). To others it's a catchall phrase for the various ways that service members and veterans react to things after coming back from war, synonymous with terms from past wars, such as *battle fatigue* and *shell shock*. PTSD as a result of combat is almost always associated with various physical reactions, emotions, and perceptions that do not conform to a neat diagnosis.

For this generation of warriors from the Iraq and Afghanistan battlefields, PTSD has even become confused with concussion, now being called "mild traumatic brain injury," or "mTBI." This means that getting a concussion on the battlefield has special significance it didn't have in earlier wars. A concussion is a brief period of being knocked out or disoriented from a blow or jolt to the head ("getting your bell rung," "seeing stars"). Concussions are very common from military training, such as combatives, as well as contact sports and motor vehicle accidents; concussions also occur during combat from blasts, falls, accidents, or other injuries. Most service members who experience a concussion can expect a full recovery, generally in a matter of a few hours or days, but the wars in Iraq and Afghanistan have created the fear that concussions/mTBIs (particularly blast-related) may lead to lasting health effects in a large percentage of service members. Many warriors and veterans have been told that their postwar problems, such as anger, sleep disturbance, fatigue, concentration problems, memory problems, or PTSD symptoms, are likely due to untreated concussions from exposure to blasts. The reality is that these problems occur for many reasons. Concussion/mTBI has been overdiagnosed, underdiagnosed, and misdiagnosed in Iraq and Afghanistan veterans, leading to unwarranted—and, in some cases—harmful treatments.

There is controversy over when normal reactions to combat or stress become PTSD. Everyone has a "breaking point," and warriors sometimes reach this in reaction to severe combat events or complete physical or mental exhaustion. These "combat stress reactions" (also called "acute stress reactions," or "operational stress reactions") are expected to occur on the battlefield, and good leaders prepare their units for this inevitability. Combat stress reactions are treated with rest and reassurance, and rarely turn into PTSD. They are not a mental disorder.

Reaching a "breaking point" in combat does not mean that a warrior is broken. It just means that the warrior needs to regroup and recharge in order to be able to go back into the fight. Most warriors, even after going through extreme stress and trauma, do not develop PTSD. But they are also not the same person after deployment as they were before, and this is part of what it means to be a warrior. They react differently after deployment. There is a strength of character that is sharp and direct, but one that may at times make others feel uncomfortable. There is maturity, but combat also takes its toll and can make one feel older. It's not uncommon for service members to feel as if they've aged one or two decades during a single deployment. Warriors are more independent, but this may make it difficult to tolerate authority at work.

Many warriors have a hard time reconnecting with loved ones, despite their demonstrated ability to form lifelong bonds with unit peers. This is not only because of how they've changed, but also because their loved ones and society don't necessarily understand these changes, or view these changes as "bad" or as an "illness." Unfortunately, PTSD has become confused with various normal reactions that warriors experience.

PTSD is in many ways indistinguishable physically from prolonged severe stress. Under prolonged stress, the stress "thermostat" is reset to a different level. Prolonged stress causes numerous changes in the nervous system and endocrine (hormone) system that affect the entire body. These can include increased heart rate and blood pressure, changes in hormone levels, elevation in adrenaline, changes in concentration and memory, and reduced immunity to fight infection. Studies suggest that cells in the body that are under prolonged stress may undergo accelerated aging, validating the perceptions of combat veterans that they have aged more rapidly than their peers back home. Deployment to a war zone, which is a form of prolonged and severe stress, can change the way in which the body adjusts to or responds to normal everyday levels of stress. These physical (physiological) changes in the body are double-edged. Warriors develop remarkable observational skills and reflexes. However, post-deployment, they sometimes overreact to things in a way that leads to strained relationships and problems at home or work.

Coming Home

Coming back from a combat deployment is like returning to the three-dimensional world after experiencing a fourth dimension. It's hard to sort out who is really crazy—you, or the rest of the world. The rest of the world can't comprehend the concept of a fourth dimension; they can't relate to it, and may not even be interested. Service members and veterans often feel they're wasting their time dealing with people who can't relate to their perspective, and many actually feel more at home in the war zone. One infantry soldier, several months after returning from Iraq, said: "Through all the hell and anguish I've experienced fighting a war, I'd still rather be fighting at war than wake up everyday to the bullshit I have to deal with and overcome here at home in what I call my job and life."

A marine who had been in Iraq said, "Truth is, many marines are lost when they get home; there is a gap between us and civilians, which is having an effect on each other understanding one another."

In this book we'll examine why the soldier quoted above feels like he'd rather be back in combat, and why the marine feels a split between his peers and civilians. We'll explore the contradictions and paradoxes of PTSD, and untangle what PTSD is from what it's not. Most important, you'll be provided with concrete guidance toward a goal of living life with greater joy and meaning, embracing your warrior spirit and using skills you already have to successfully "transition" or "readjust" after combat, whether that's within a few months of coming home or decades later. It's never too late. The "transition" and "readjustment" process doesn't mean you give up being a warrior, but rather learn to dial up or down your warrior responses depending on what's happening around you, always adapting to the environment you find yourself in.

"Transition" and "Readjustment"

The "transition/readjustment" time frame that is the focus of this book is ill-defined and full of hazards. Depending on who you talk to, it seems to span the time from getting off the plane (or boat); completing the reintegration process (including the post-deployment health assessment for veterans of the Iraq/Afghanistan wars); the "honeymoon" period (for all of you who had a spouse or partner waiting for you through the long deployment); block leave; the first three months home; deactivation (if in the National Guard or Reserves); post-deployment health re-assessment (for veterans of Iraq/Afghanistan); the next nine months or so of the first year home; and then perhaps for a long time thereafter (years), depending on your wartime experiences, whether or not there was another intervening deployment(s), whether your previous job was waiting for you upon your return, whether or not your marriage or relationship broke up, how much pain you were in due to physical injuries, whether you got embroiled in a custody battle for your kids, and various other factors. In short, there's no clear definition of what the normal "transition/readjustment" period is, and the extent to which this book is going to be helpful has nothing to do with how long or short a time it's been since you came home.

How warriors and family members describe the transition experience often reflects a gap in perspectives. Married service members just home from a tour of duty in the sandbox or jungle can't possibly understand what could be worse than being shot at every day or living constantly under that threat, while their spouse feels that it was they who had it worse—waiting, worrying, single-parenting, running the household alone, juggling life back here, and so on. The two experiences seem incongruous, and the reality is that each person has matured individually during the deployment period and is not the same person he or she was when they parted. There is a similar split with friends and family.

Each generation of warriors considers their war to be unique, and indeed, in many ways, every war is. World War II and Korean War veterans faced high-intensity combat over extended fronts. They were welcomed home as heroes, but there was minimal or no public discussion of the potential impact of their experiences. Vietnam veterans faced yearlong tours involving high-intensity conventional and guerrilla warfare. They faced a hostile public upon their return that had little understanding or compassion for the impact of their combat experiences. PTSD was not yet recognized, and many Vietnam veterans were told that their war-related reactions were the result of alcoholism or drug abuse, implying that their problems were their "fault." Gulf War I veterans faced enormous uncertainties during a yearlong buildup to combat operations, including a high threat of chemical and biological attacks, followed by a brief high-intensity conventional ground operation.

Over the past twenty years there have been multiple operational deployments involving combat, security, and humanitarian missions to Panama, Somalia, Haiti, Bosnia, Kosovo, and other locations. Veterans of the Iraq and Afghanistan wars (Operation Iraqi Freedom—OIF and Operation Enduring Freedom—OEF), the post-9/11 generation, have experienced the lack of a clear front line, other than the concertina wire at the perimeter of the FOB ("Forward Operating Base"), and missions involving simultaneous and overlapping duties—combat, security, humanitarian, training of local nationals—going on in the same sectors of the battle-field. They have also faced multiple deployments, in-theater extensions in deployment length, recalls to active duty, stop-loss (the "hidden draft"), single parents deploying, and dual military families (with deployments of both partners), along with many other challenges.

However, the day-to-day experience of war, from the perspective of the average line infantry "grunt" and anyone supporting them "outside the wire" or far forward (in convoys, logistics, supply, medical, intelligence, aviation, etc.), has huge similarities from one war to the next—namely, working 24/7 in a hostile operational environment where people are trying to kill you using tactics and weapons that in many ways haven't changed through the years (ambushes, sniper fire, mortars, roadside bombs, grenades, rockets, etc.); where you may well find yourself helpless to respond because the enemy looks like non-combatants; and where you're hampered by whatever rules of engagement exist at the moment (and they change frequently), or whatever other nonsensical orders may be raining down from higher up during moments of chaos.

Unique Challenges for Modern Warriors

In recent years the military has considered the "resetting" of a warrior's health after combat in much the same way that it considers the resetting or refitting of equipment and vehicles. The protracted duration of the Iraq and Afghanistan wars and the reality of multiple deployments have led to the unrealistic expectation that warriors (and their family members) can "reset" physically and mentally for another combat tour in less than twelve months. Numerous Active Component Infantry Brigade and Regimental Combat teams have deployed multiple times since the start of these wars, with "dwell" times between deployments of not much more than the time spent in-theater. Service members in some Reserve or National Guard units have experienced more than one mobilization, each lasting up to twenty months including training prior to deployment. Warriors have put life plans—such as college education, family, and civilian careers—on hold for extended periods.

Modern warriors have faced the cumulative emotional toll of not being available to raise their children, missing numerous milestones in their children's lives, missing funerals of close relatives or friends, or not being able to assist in the care of an aging parent. Women have for the first time been involved in direct-combat operations in substantial numbers. Single parents have faced the challenge of having to arrange extended child care, and there is evidence that parental absence as a result of deployment has been associated with increased conduct and academic problems in military children, and in some cases child abuse. Dual military couples have faced many of the same stresses.

Warriors and their family members are often surprised at how difficult the transition period is after coming back from a combat deployment. Many expect that they'll just need a little time for things to go back to "normal," but find that "normal" is elusive and time is relative.

> *The government is awesome at getting men ready for war, but they can't quite get them back to civilian life and a humble heart.*
> —**JUNIOR ENLISTED MARINE, POST-IRAQ**

> *After we came back, many of us were only back in body. Our souls stayed over there.*
> —**ARMY COMBAT ENGINEER, POST-IRAQ**

> *Transition can mean the big picture of how a warrior has to try to adjust back into society, but the short term is very critical, from when a warrior leaves the battlefield to when they hit the streets at home. If there's one thing I learned from my experiences, it was that there was no transition at all.*
> —**VIETNAM VETERAN**

I want to express my gratitude for the many soldiers, marines, sailors, airmen, and family members I've encountered during my years of research and clinical work, and whose quotes and stories from their Iraq and Afghanistan deployment experiences I drew from to bring this book to life. (Names have been changed, and some of the stories have been modified to protect the individuals involved.)

I also want to thank my collaborator and friend, First Sergeant Michael Schindler (Retired), who helped to bring alive the experience of transitioning home by sharing his story, stemming from two tours in Vietnam (1970 and 1971) and a twenty-eight-year career in the Army Infantry (Ranger-qualified, two combat infantryman badges), in both the Active and Reserve Components. First Sergeant Schindler's transition and the process of wrestling his demons of war didn't begin until 2002, after he had retired from the Army, and more than thirty years after his combat experiences. No matter how much time had passed, his transition was no less direct and immediate than if he had begun the process the day he'd returned from the war zone. His words add to the many quotes and stories from Iraq and Afghanistan warriors and highlight the opportunity these warriors have to address transition issues much earlier than warriors from prior conflicts.

Enjoy the reading, and please feel free to send me any feedback at onceawarrior.com.

Charles W. Hoge, MD
Colonel, U.S. Army (Retired)

HOW TO USE THIS BOOK

Chapter 1 will get into what PTSD is all about, including a discussion of the physiology of stress, and when normal responses and normal "transition" issues become PTSD. The chapter explains the PTSD paradox—the fact that what medical professionals label *symptoms* are also combat survival skills—and how this paradox can create misery after coming home. The chapter will help you understand that PTSD is not an "emotional" or "psychological" problem, but a physiological condition that includes physical, emotional, psychological, and behavioral reactions; this is of vital importance in understanding how to address it. "PTSD" is a catchall term used to describe many reactions to combat that go beyond the medical diagnosis; PTSD is also strongly linked to a wide range of physical health effects (e.g., endocrine, adrenaline, cardiovascular, and immunity).

Chapter 2 will cover the topic of combat mTBI (mild traumatic brain injury, i.e., concussion) and it's relationship to PTSD and various physical, cognitive, and behavioral symptoms experienced after coming home from deployment. There is a lot of confusion about mTBI, even among medical professionals, which this chapter will address.

Chapters 3–11 will cover specific skills to help with the transition process, including one chapter for spouses, partners, and family members of warriors. When I was thinking about the content of these self-help chapters, I found myself struggling to find the best term(s) to describe what I wanted to write about. My wife suggested the term *navigating* instead of words like *coping, overcoming, healing, recovering, surviving, understanding, transcending, improving,* or *self-helping;* a term that is active and engaged, with you firmly in the driver's seat, and with no suggestion that something about you is broken. There might be something that needs adjusting or dialing up or down, but there's not something personally wrong with you.

The subjects of PTSD and transitioning from combat are not about illness, per se. They are also not about growth—although there is a whole body of literature on "post-traumatic growth." Yes, we grow from all of our life experiences, but we don't ask for the "growth" experiences that get thrown our way. We have little or no control on the nature of any divine plan, luck, fate, or random disturbance life may send our way.

The word *navigating* is very much the spirit of this book—finding your own way to a healthy, meaningful warrior existence, with help along the way, but understanding that no one has the answers for you or a magic pill. As warriors, land navigation (LANDNAV) is an essential skill that you hone, to ensure that you know where you are at all times, where you need to be, and what coordinates you want rounds dropped on. There are many ways to get off track, lost, or call in rounds on the wrong target if your LANDNAV skills falter. A small mistake can cascade into mission failure. But if you stay focused on this skill, it will help get you through. "Navigating" (LANDNAV) became the framework that this book is built upon.

In addition to covering individual LANDNAV skills, this book includes in chapter 8 information on how to navigate the mental health care system, should you want or need to seek professional help. It addresses several hard facts regarding treatment of PTSD, mTBI, and other war-related reactions. This can help you to advocate for yourself or your loved one and find the formula that best suits you.

The first hard fact is that many mental health professionals are hampered by the existing structure of medical practice and/or don't have sufficient training or experience in providing treatment to combat veterans. They are likely to be knowledgeable about the diagnosis of PTSD and other mental health problems, but don't necessarily have the vocabulary for the unique military experiences, or an understanding of the range of what's normal. Most combat veterans need to feel that the person listening to their story understands, appreciates, and relates to it. This doesn't mean that every therapist needs to have deployed to a combat zone, but it does mean that every therapist needs to know their own limitations concerning the extent of their knowledge of military culture. The health professional's knowledge or experience may not be sufficient to discern what is normal or abnormal for a particular combat veteran, but if they remain open and honest regarding their own limitations, it can go a long way toward making the veteran or family member feel like it's worth talking with them.

The second hard fact is that even the best treatments for PTSD fall far short of being 100 percent effective; they are closer to 50 percent. The confusion that the medical community has regarding the treatment of mTBI-related symptoms adds to problems with treatment effectiveness. There are many factors that play into this, including the nature of health care, as well as the current state of science and practice for the various treatment approaches. Some initiatives intended to help service members and veterans actually may have the opposite effect.

This doesn't mean that you should throw in the towel and not try to get help. It just means that it's important to take the time to learn about the broad range of treatment and "self-help" options available, so you'll know how to tailor them in a way that works best for you; be able to combine them to increase their effectiveness; and prepare yourself to take charge of your health and become a better advocate for yourself or your loved one. This isn't necessarily something that mental health professionals are able to spend their time explaining.

In summary, this book is about navigating the perils, pitfalls, and "growth" opportunities in the unique terrain of the home front after you, your spouse, family member, or friend has returned from a military deployment. LANDNAV means understanding the warrior spirit, keeping track of where you are at all times, planning where you want to move next, and what coordinates you need to focus on. This ability to navigate in a treacherous environment is exactly the skill needed to get you through any situation. The military acronym "LANDNAV" was co-opted and turned into a mnemonic for the purposes of helping you learn to "cope"/"navigate" in a unique home-front environment during the ill-defined "transition" period, whether this period has lasted only a few months or has gone on for years.

Who This Book is for and the Terminology Used

For this book, the terms *warrior* and *veteran* are meant to be interchangeable, with *warrior* being most often used. "Once a warrior—always a warrior." The term *warrior* refers to anyone who has ever put their life in harm's way as a result of duty in a war zone: soldiers, marines, airmen, sailors, government workers, and contractors from the United States and other countries. This includes service members in both the Active and Reserve Components (Reserves and National Guard), and those who served in line operational units as well as support roles. Although masculine sounding, the term *warrior* is used for both men and women. *Veteran* also refers to anyone who has ever deployed to a war zone, whether or not they are still in military service or eligible for VA government benefits. The term *post-combat* is not meant to imply that this book is only for those who have experienced direct combat. The terms *post-combat, postwar,* and *post-deployment* are synonymous, recognizing that significant war-zone experiences encompass combat as well as noncombat roles. This book is just as much for government employees and contractors, and acknowledges the enormous contribution that they've brought to war efforts.

This book intends to help bring clarity and understanding to the transition period after a wide range of deployment experiences, both anticipated and unanticipated. Although most of the examples cited in this book have to do with direct combat in the deployed environment, trauma can take many forms. All personnel working in the war zone are in danger from indirect fire. Noncombat trauma, including accidents, assault, or rape, can be just as debilitating as trauma experienced during direct combat. Whether or not there were serious traumatic experiences, most people change as a result of wartime deployment, and this book is intended for anyone who wants a greater understanding of these possible changes and how to effectively navigate them.

Although I often address the writing directly to the warrior, this book is intended for spouses, partners, and family members as well. It can provide you with a greater understanding of your warrior's perspective, and they will likely appreciate the effort on your part. Chapter 10 is specifically written for you, but all the exercises in this book can be useful.

A disclaimer: This book is not intended to serve as a substitute for therapy or treatment of any specific disorder. This book includes information and advice for consideration, but ultimately, each warrior (and spouse, partner, or family member) needs to seek out and find whatever works best for them. This book is no substitute for professional help when it's needed.

CHAPTER 1

COMBAT STRESS AND POST-TRAUMATIC STRESS DISORDER

WHAT IS COMBAT STRESS AND PTSD?

Mental health professionals define post-traumatic stress disorder (PTSD) according to a specific list of symptoms. However, the medical definition does not provide any understanding of what PTSD is from the perspective of someone who has gone through combat. It does not capture the full spectrum of reactions to war, or distinguish between what is normal and abnormal in a military context. PTSD has become part of the vocabulary of modern warriors, but is sometimes misused as a catchall term for any postwar behavioral problem, such as getting in fights, driving under the influence of alcohol, or having failed relationships. The terms *combat stress*, *post-traumatic stress*, *combat stress reaction*, and *acute stress reaction* are often used interchangeably with PTSD, even by medical professionals, creating confusion over the meaning of all of these terms.

Combat stress and *post-traumatic stress* are general terms that are used to refer to any distress or symptoms, less severe than PTSD, which have resulted from stressful or traumatic events in the war zone. They are not particularly useful terms because they lack a clear definition. A "combat stress reaction" (also called "acute stress reaction" and "operational stress reaction") has a specific meaning on the battlefield, and refers to an immediate reaction to severe stress, trauma, or exhaustion. It reflects the moment when a warrior reaches a "breaking point" and needs to shut down for a while. A combat stress reaction can manifest as virtually any physical symptom (e.g., fatigue, chest pain, shortness of breath, muscle shaking, headaches, neurological symptoms) or behavioral reaction (e.g., rage, agitation, fear, panic, restlessness, bizarre behavior, inability to think clearly). A combat stress reaction is not a mental disorder. It's treated with rest and reassurance as close to the unit as possible, and almost all warriors who receive this care are back in the fight within two or three days.

The disorder of PTSD is defined according to a specific set of symptoms that have gone on for at least one month (usually much longer). If the symptoms have lasted more than a month but less than three, the disorder is called "acute"; if more than three months, it's called "chronic." If the symptoms didn't begin until at least six months after the combat trauma, this is referred to as "delayed onset," although in most cases warriors with "delayed onset" PTSD did experience some reactions close to the time of the trauma that they suppressed or avoided dealing with. The distinction between these three categories of PTSD has not proven very helpful.

PTSD has gained a much higher level of importance during the wars in Iraq and Afghanistan than in any prior conflict—not because the problem is greater in veterans of these wars, but because there is greater political interest and public awareness of the mental health effects of war. The attention on PTSD has been combined with increased attention on mild traumatic brain injury (mTBI), also known as concussion. PTSD and mTBI have been labeled the "signature injuries" of the wars in Iraq and Afghanistan, but this has unfortunately created confusion over the nature of both of these conditions.

Although PTSD is considered a mental disorder, it's actually a physical condition that affects the entire body, and is best understood through the emerging science of stress physiology, which describes how the body normally responds to extreme stress. Physiology is the science of how the body works, including how the brain and the rest of the nervous system functions (also called "neurophysiology" or "neurobiology"). PTSD is a contradiction, a paradox—a collection of reactions that are both normal and abnormal depending on the situation—and there is debate as to where to draw the line.

When I consider the question, "What is PTSD?" I don't mean only how doctors define it. What I'm considering is how each person experiences the condition, or what they perceive the condition to be. For warriors,

PTSD can be a day-to-day experience of living with memories they want to forget, staying constantly alert to dangers others don't pay any attention to, enduring sleepless nights, and reacting to things at home as if still in the war zone. It's very difficult (if not impossible) for anyone who has not been in a war zone to understand what these experiences are like. These reactions may help a warrior survive in combat, and may be needed again if they return to the war zone or any other situation where there's danger. What "normal" is in this context can't be precisely defined.

The DoD and VA acknowledged at the beginning of the wars in Afghanistan and Iraq that there would be substantial psychological costs. No prior war has had as much research conducted on the mental health impact while the war is going on. Congress and news organizations took special interest in PTSD in part because of a paper my research team and I wrote that was published in the *New England Journal of Medicine* in 2004, showing that 12 to 20 percent of soldiers and marines who had participated in the initial ground invasion of Iraq had serious symptoms of PTSD three to four months after coming home.

GOOD NEWS AND BAD NEWS ABOUT PTSD

Enormous advances have occurred in the understanding of PTSD over the last two decades, including characterizing the neurobiology, and how to diagnose, evaluate, and treat the condition. Neurobiology is the study of nerve functioning and chemical processes in the nervous system. Neurobiological research related to PTSD has included many experiments using animals subjected to stress and studies of humans who have suffered trauma. Neurobiological research has helped us to understand that PTSD is not an "emotional" or "psychological" disorder, but a physiological condition that affects the entire body, including cardiovascular functioning, hormone system balance, and immune functioning. PTSD can result in physical, cognitive, psychological, emotional, and behavioral reactions that all have a physiological basis. These studies have led to new treatments of PTSD, including psychotherapy (talk therapy) and medications that target specific areas of the brain and body responses. Successful treatment with psychotherapy and medications lead to chemical changes in the brain and nervous system, and some of these changes can actually be seen on brain-imaging studies. Numerous new types of treatment are being evaluated and will be reviewed later in this book.

The wars in Iraq and Afghanistan have led to a greater understanding of the stigma of mental health problems, not only in the military, but also in society in general. The word *stigma* literally means to be stained or marked by a shameful disease. Our article in the *New England Journal of Medicine* showed that less than half of the soldiers and marines who were experiencing serious symptoms of PTSD or depression received any help, including counseling by a chaplain. The stigma was the main reason they avoided getting help. Warriors expressed concern that they would be perceived as weak or treated differently by their leaders and buddies if they sought assistance for their problems. They also expressed distrust that mental health professionals could help them, a topic that will be discussed further in later chapters. The findings from this study contributed to new programs in the DoD and VA to encourage service members and veterans to seek help early, before problems become serious. These programs have involved screening after returning from deployment (post-deployment health assessments), resiliency training, and increased training of mental health professionals in how to treat combat-related problems. Many of these services were unavailable during prior wars.

The increased attention on PTSD in the military has had a positive effect on the way that society views mental illness. Society has often viewed mental disorders as a personal failure of character. People with these conditions have felt shame and have been stigmatized socially and occupationally. The advances in research and increased awareness of the mental health impact of war have helped to bring about a shift in the way mental illnesses are viewed. PTSD and other mental disorders are now being regarded as medical problems. Mental disorders are slowly being accepted as medical conditions that are not the "fault" of the person who acquires them, and which can be treated like any other physical illness, not something to be ashamed of.

So that was the good news; now for the bad.

The bad news is that we still have a long way to go. It's a step forward that mental health problems, including PTSD, are beginning to be viewed like other physical health problems (and PTSD *is* a physical health problem). However, we can take it a step further, especially for combat veterans, and that is to view PTSD and many other mental health problems as part of the normal range of human responses to extremely stressful experiences. Society still tends to perceive mental illness as something that you get if you're unfortunate or don't have the right genes, not something that everyone can expect to encounter in one form or another during the course of a normal life. However, the reality is that mental health problems touch everyone to one degree or another, either directly or indirectly, and are thus part of the human experience. By considering PTSD within the framework of normal reactions, it doesn't mean that we don't also consider it a disorder. PTSD is both, and the more we become aware of this contradiction, the further our understanding will evolve in how best to help each other get through difficult experiences.

More bad news is that mental health professionals don't have the answer. They can help, but their approach to understanding PTSD is far too narrow. Many mental health professionals are rigidly bound by conventional medical definitions and practices. They can prescribe one or more of the treatments that are available, but there are huge limitations as to how effective these treatments are, and many assumptions inherent in these treatments. Traditional mental health practices cannot fix the broader issues of what PTSD means for combat veterans.

HOW MENTAL HEALTH PROFESSIONALS DEFINE PTSD

Mental health professionals rely on the American Psychiatric Association's *Diagnostic and Statistical Manual of Mental Disorders* (DSM for short) to make a diagnosis of PTSD. If that diagnosis doesn't fit the client's symptoms, then there are nearly 300 other diagnoses in the manual to choose from. Although the American Psychiatric Association assembled the DSM, all mental health professionals (i.e., psychiatrists, psychologists, clinical social workers, psychiatric nurses, psychotherapists, and counselors) use the same DSM. (The distinctions between these different types of profession-als will be addressed in a later chapter.)

The DSM manual (currently in its fourth edition) provides laundry lists of all the symptoms found for each diagnosis, and the use of the man-ual creates the impression that mental disorders are well-defined condi-tions that everyone agrees on and understands in the same way. Mental health professionals memorize the specific criteria of the most common disorders, or refer to the DSM menu to find just the right one(s), in order to inform their patients of their diagnosis, often after less than an hour meeting with them.

Realities of the DSM Definition of PTSD

Although patients frequently ask mental health professionals to tell them if they're "normal," we aren't in the business of "normal," because we don't know how to define what normal looks like, and people generally don't come to us unless there's something bothering them. Plus, if we work in the civilian sector, insurance companies generally won't pay us when we use the DSM label for normal—"No Diagnosis on Axis I or II" ("Axis I" includes all diagnoses that you can acquire, including PTSD; "Axis II" includes personal-ity disorders, which are usually lifelong). That means that virtually no one walks out of our offices "normal"; everyone can expect to be blessed by one or more of the diagnoses contained in the DSM.

Most people (including many mental health professionals) don't real-ize that the diagnoses contained in the DSM were essentially created by committees of doctors sitting around conference tables. They are best guesses regarding which groups of symptoms should be considered dis-crete disorders, based on the doctors' clinical experience treating patients with mental health problems and their interpretation of published studies. Many of the diagnoses, including PTSD, have been shown to have a strong biological basis and have stood the test of time; however, the science of how these diagnoses are validated and how useful they are in deciding how to help someone remains very complex and subject to considerable error.

Although the medical establishment considers mental disorders in the same way that other medical illnesses are considered, these conditions are not like tuberculosis or pneumonia, where the offending bacteria obtained from an ill patient can be grown in a petri dish, observed under a microscope, or found in a blood test. We don't have any definitive means of making a mental disorder diagnosis other than what patients tell us about their symptoms, which we compare with the lists of symptoms in the *Diagnostic and Statistical Manual of Mental Disorders.*

This is not to knock the DSM, or any of the brilliant men and women who created it; it's just to recognize that the manual is designed merely as a way for mental health professionals to communicate with each other regarding the various types of problems patients present with. If a medical doctor refers a patient suspected of having "PTSD," "major depression," and "traits of a personality disorder" to a psychiatrist, all of the medical professionals perceive this in a similar way, and this common language is used to direct treatment. The use of a diagnosis with an agreed-upon definition helps us to feel more confident about what we're doing, including which treatment we think will be most effective.

However, one major problem is that the various disorders outlined in DSM overlap extensively with each other. They are not distinct conditions, like bacterial infections. They blur together, and it has been proven through carefully conducted studies that different mental health professionals will frequently diagnose different disorders when they interview the same patient. This fact is very important to consider when we start to talk more about how effective current treatments are.

All that aside, PTSD seems relatively straightforward for mental health professionals to diagnose, and it's unique among other DSM disorders in that it's clearly tied to one or more traumatic event. To diagnose PTSD, we ask the client about the nature of the trauma and the symptoms. If the trauma led to the development of the requisite number and type of symptoms lasting for at least one month, then we can conclude that the person has a diagnosis of PTSD. Warriors frequently look at the list of symptoms and say, "Yep, that's me." Family members also look at the list of symptoms and say, "Yep, that's John (or Jane)." When a combat veteran tries to get help for war-related reactions that are interfering in some way with life, the mental health professional will gladly oblige them with the diagnosis. The veteran might also be diagnosed with one of many disorders that frequently go hand in hand with PTSD symptoms: depression, panic disorder, generalized anxiety disorder, alcohol or substance use disorder, and maybe a personality disorder (e.g., antisocial, borderline, or "not otherwise specified").

However, the DSM approach to figuring out the problem doesn't really help the warrior understand what's going on, or why he or she got blessed with this condition while many fellow unit members seemed to be spared; nor does it necessarily help in figuring out the best course of treatment, if treatment is even indicated. When it comes to combat—as well as professions like law enforcement, emergency medicine, and firefighting, where exposure to trauma and danger is part of the job—the whole concept of normal and abnormal gets thrown out the window.

Although trauma-related reactions were recognized well before 1980, PTSD was first proposed as a diagnosis in 1980 in the third edition of the DSM (DSM-III), as a way to help mental health professionals communicate between themselves and with their clients concerning the collection of symptoms that seemed to be associated with life-threatening traumatic events. Part of the impetus for creating the definition of PTSD was the generation of veterans from Vietnam, as well as the history of conditions described after previous wars, such as shell shock. It took a number of years after the Vietnam War to recognize that thousands of veterans were suffering serious postwar reactions for which they were not being treated or compensated.

After publication of the DSM-III, there was intense debate regarding whether or not PTSD should be considered a legitimate disorder, since many of the reactions are expected after serious traumatic events. The definition changed somewhat between the third and fourth editions of the DSM, and there is continued debate regarding whether the definition is either too restrictive or too liberal in defining what should be considered abnormal reactions to trauma, and what level of functioning should be considered impaired. Another committee is working to come up with revised criteria for the fifth edition of DSM, scheduled for release in 2012.

Although the PTSD definition in DSM is considered to encompass war-related reactions, it's based largely on single episodes of trauma in civilian settings where the person is a victim of assault, rape, an accident, or a natural disaster. This is very different than the experiences of warriors who are trained to encounter trauma as part of their profession (and individuals who work in other dangerous professions like law enforcement or firefighting).

PTSD is a paradox. For medical professionals it's simply defined by the specific set of symptoms and impairment. However, every "symptom" included in the definition can also reflect normal responses to life-threatening events or the normal way the body responds to extreme stress. Reactions that mental health professionals label "PTSD" may be entirely expected for warriors who have trained and prepared themselves to deal with serious traumatic events. Warriors speak a different language than mental health professionals when it comes to their reactions to war.

Perceptions Matter

Why is this important? The answer has to do with your perception of yourself as a warrior. If you view yourself (or your warrior loved one) as having a disorder according to what a professional (or society) says, rather than someone experiencing expected reactions from combat, it affects how you feel and think about yourself or your loved one. A negative perception of yourself actually affects your body chemistry. Perceptions (usually considered in the realm of psychology) involve nerve functions that connect with virtually all organ systems in the body. The mind and body are not separate. Many therapies focus on helping to correct negative perceptions through a process called "cognitive reframing." Having a positive view of yourself is an essential starting place toward navigating the reactions resulting from combat experiences.

A positive view is one that acknowledges mental health problems as part of the normal human experience and not a personal failure of character; it recognizes that you have control only over the things that you have control over (which is much less than you might think), and that every human makes mistakes. A positive view acknowledges that perfection is unachievable; it means accepting that you did the very best you could, even if you feel (or wish) that you could have (or should have) done something differently, which would have resulted in a better outcome.

Mental health professionals can contribute to the stigma of mental ill-ness through the perception that most everyone coming into their office has something wrong with them. A therapist's role isn't typically one of a minister or coach, but rather that of an educated professional entrusted to make the correct diagnosis so that the right treatment can be prescribed. This perspective sets up an expectation that this person is the judge of what's normal or abnormal, rather than an ally helping the client navigate their own way through serious life difficulties. Some therapists fool them-selves into thinking they know what the best treatment is for each indi-vidual sitting in front of them. Good therapists understand that they don't know what's best for their client, and set the stage by helping to normalize the experience of the client by saying something like, "I don't see how you could have done anything differently at the time," or "How did you have the strength to respond in that way?"

The bottom line, coming from an insider in the profession, is that if you've read this far, you're probably "normal." Everyone who has ever deployed to a war zone is changed by his or her experiences; it would be abnormal not to be. Some reactions may seriously interfere with your life, but that doesn't mean there's something wrong with you as a person. There are things that you'll identify and want to change, but, more impor-tant, the journey of readjusting after combat is one of learning to live with your experiences, and of integrating them into who you are without blam-ing yourself for what happened or what you did or didn't do. It's a process of developing an understanding of how you react to situations now in a way that's different from how you reacted before you became a warrior.

DEFINING "NORMAL" VS. "ABNORMAL"

What is normal and abnormal when it comes to reactions to combat? When do normal "reactions" become "symptoms" of a disorder? (Note that in this book, the terms *reaction* and *symptom* are often used interchangeably.)

The answers are both complicated and simple. Making the distinction between normal and abnormal based on the level of impairment in work or personal relationships isn't sufficient. Many warriors experience high levels of symptoms that they would rather get rid of, but learn to cope with them and continue to function relatively well in their work and/or home lives. Other warriors are severely debilitated by "normal" (expected) reactions to particularly severe wartime experiences.

The simplest answer is that when reactions interfere with your happiness or your ability to do the things you want to do, then they're undesirable (you can say that they are "symptoms"), and you've identified something that you want to change or learn to dial up or down. You deserve to be happy and enjoy life. The focus here isn't on deciding what's normal or abnormal, but on identifying what it is that interferes with your life in such a way that change is warranted. You may have all the symptoms listed in the DSM after combat, or exhibit other behaviors that don't match with societal norms, but if they're not interfering seriously with your life or the lives of others, then they shouldn't be considered abnormal. An example is a combat veteran who develops a passion for gun collecting up to the limit of what the law will allow. Some people may consider that "abnormal," but if it's something that the veteran enjoys, and he isn't intending to use these weapons dishonorably, then it's not "abnormal." On the other hand, if he's barricading himself in his house, suspicious of anyone who approaches, threatening people, unable to have any close personal relationships or hold a job, then this behavior is not serving the veteran well.

DECONSTRUCTING AND UNDERSTANDING THE PTSD DEFINITION

If we take each component of the DSM definition of PTSD and break it down, we discover some of the problems with how PTSD is conceptualized from the perspective of warriors. Every "symptom" of PTSD stems from things your body normally does in response to severe danger or stress. PTSD symptoms can be manifestations of normal stress reactions to threatening situations, as well as a disorder that requires treatment. That's the paradox of it.

When mental health professionals assess PTSD, the DSM definition requires that they ask about six different criteria, A through F, all of which must be fulfilled to make the diagnosis "true."

Criterion A defines a trauma exposure as witnessing or experiencing an event involving serious injury or death. This may be an actual injury or a threat to the physical integrity of self or others. Clearly, many combat scenarios would fulfill this definition, as well as assault, rape, and other serious events. In addition, the DSM requires that the response to this trauma at the time included intense fear, horror, or helplessness.

If the person (in this case, a warrior) meets criterion A and develops symptoms as a result of the traumatic event, then the mental health professional would determine if there are a sufficient number of symptoms present according to the list contained in the DSM. The DSM diagnosis for PTSD includes seventeen total symptoms divided into three groups: Criterion B includes five symptoms related to re-experiencing the traumatic event; criterion C includes seven symptoms related to avoidance; and criterion D includes five symptoms related to hyperarousal (revved-up, hypervigilance).

The following survey will help you understand the seventeen symptoms a mental health professional looks for. This is one of the most common surveys given to veterans to identify PTSD, and you may have taken this or a similar one at some point during your service. This is not a "test"; there are no right or wrong answers. The survey will do two things: First, it will familiarize you with the definition according to DSM-IV, and second, it will allow you to assess your own level of current symptoms.

(If you're a spouse, partner, family member, or friend who has experienced a traumatic experience and want to take this survey, simply remove the words "military" or "veteran." The scale can be used to refer to any traumatic experience.)

To score this, first look at questions 1–5. If you marked a "3" (moderately) or higher on *any* of these first five questions, then this fulfills the DSM criterion B requirement for re-experiencing the traumatic event. Next, look at questions 6–12. If you marked a "3" or higher on any three (or more) of these seven questions, then this fulfills the criterion C requirement for avoidance symptoms. (At least *three* of these seven questions must be present to fulfill criterion C, but only *one* of the criterion B symptoms is required.) Finally, if you marked a "3"or higher on any

PTSD Checklist—Military Version (PCL-M)

Instructions: Below is a list of problems and complaints that veterans sometimes have in response to stressful military experiences (such as combat events). Please read each one carefully and put an "X" in the box to indicate how much you have been bothered by that problem *in the past month*.

	(1) Not at all	(2) A little bit	(3) Moderately	(4) Quite a bit	(5) Extremely
1. Repeated, disturbing memories, thoughts, or images of a stressful military experience?					
2. Repeated, disturbing dreams of a stressful military experience?					
3. Suddenly acting or feeling as if a stressful military experience were happening again (as if you were reliving it)?					
4. Feeling very upset when something reminded you of a stressful military experience?					
5. Having physical reactions (e.g., heart pounding, trouble breathing, or sweating) when something reminded you of a stressful military experience?					
6. Avoid thinking about or talking about a stressful military experience, or avoid having feelings related to it?					
7. Avoid activities or situations because they remind you of a stressful military experience?					
8. Trouble remembering important parts of a stressful military experience?					

	(1) Not at all	(2) A little bit	(3) Moderately	(4) Quite a bit	(5) Extremely
9. Loss of interest in things that you used to enjoy?					
10. Feeling distant or cut off from other people?					
11. Feeling emotionally numb or being unable to have loving feelings for those close to you?					
12. Feeling as if your future will somehow be cut short?					
13. Trouble falling or staying asleep?					
14. Feeling irritable or having angry outbursts?					
15. Having difficulty concentrating?					
16. Being "super alert" or watchful on guard?					
17. Feeling jumpy or easily startled?					

PCL-M for DSM-IV (11/1/94). Weathers, Litz, Huska, & Keane National Center for PTSD—Behavioral Science Division. This is a government document in the public domain.

two of questions 13–17, this fulfills the DSM requirement for criterion D hyperarousal symptoms.

This may be confusing, but follows the way the definition is written. The DSM-IV requires that there are symptoms in all three categories of criteria B–D; again, at least *one* of the first five questions, *three* of questions 6–12, and *two* of questions 13–17. If after taking the survey yourself, you discover that you meet this definition, don't panic. This is only a preliminary screening tool designed to give you information for consideration, and we'll discuss this in more detail.

Using another scoring method, add up the total score from the seventeen questions you already marked. For example, if you marked all seventeen questions "1" ("not at all"), your total score would be 17, the minimum value possible; if you marked all seventeen questions "5" ("extremely"), you would have the highest possible score of 85. If you marked three questions at the level of "1," six questions at the level of "2" ("a little bit"), five at the level of "3" ("moderately"), two at the level of "4" ("quite a bit"), and one at the level of "5," this would add up to a total score of 43 (3+12+15+8+5).

For the total score, less than 30 is considered low ("normal"), 30–39 indicates some symptoms, 40–49 indicates moderate symptoms, and 50 or more is considered a high score for PTSD. The higher the score, the more likely you would be considered to have PTSD by a medical professional, although this is not a perfect measure. Most warriors who experienced direct combat will have some of these symptoms. For warriors who have moderate or high scores, some continue to function very well, while others experience serious problems with relationships or work. The level of symptoms isn't as important as whether they are interfering with your happiness or ability to do the things you want to do. However, when this survey is used in a medical or mental health clinic setting, any person who has a moderate or high score or meets the DSM definition would be evaluated further by the health professional.

The last two criteria necessary to fulfill the DSM-IV definition is criterion E, which requires that symptoms have been present for at least one month; and criterion F, which requires that there is significant distress or impairment in work or relationships as a result of the symptoms.

This survey, along with my description, provides you with detailed information about how mental health professionals define PTSD, as well as information regarding your own level of reactions that you can monitor over time. If you have a moderate or high score on this survey, most mental health professionals would agree that further evaluation is warranted. There is information on how to do this in chapter 8, as well as many skills throughout the book to help you address specific reactions you may be experiencing.

The next section provides additional detail about each criterion of the PTSD definition from the perspective of being a warrior. Warriors are professionals trained in how to respond to traumatic events. There are many unique factors regarding how well (or poorly) this definition describes the experience for warriors.

Criterion A. The Traumatic Event

Criterion A concerns the definition of a traumatic event, and has two parts, A-1 and A-2. A-1 defines what type of traumatic event is considered necessary to cause PTSD, and A-2 defines an "abnormal" response to this event. The irony is that the "abnormal" reaction from the standpoint of fulfilling the PTSD definition may be a perfectly normal, expected response to a serious life-threatening event, a normal reaction to an extremely abnormal circumstance. In essence, in order to be defined as having PTSD, your normal response has to be considered "abnormal," which really makes no sense when you think about it.

More important, the medical definition of a traumatic event doesn't really capture the horrific nature of many events, nor explain why some warriors exposed to combat develop serious symptoms of PTSD, while others exposed to the same or similar events do not. This is one of the most fundamental questions, and a tremendous amount of research spurred on by the Iraq and Afghanistan (OIF and OEF) wars is being devoted to answering it.

Criterion A-1. The Definition of Trauma

The A-1 definition of a traumatic event is quite broad. Almost any event that is perceived as life-threatening can meet the definition, although lawyers or disability specialists might disagree. However, this doesn't mean that all traumas are equal. The definition doesn't speak to what a traumatic event is, but rather whether the trauma—whatever it is—is *perceived* to be threatening to life or personal integrity. For example, working in a war zone but remaining inside the "wire" (the protective perimeter of the base camp) for the duration of the rotation and never seeing direct combat could be sufficiently traumatic if one is constantly threatened from enemy mortars landing inside. Line or transport folks working constantly outside the wire might roll their eyes at this notion, but the fact remains that a threat is a threat, whether it involves episodic mortar attacks or constant ambushes and firefights.

The VA has traditionally required that veterans seeking disability for PTSD prove that they actually experienced a seriously life-threatening direct-combat event, through military records or affidavits. This policy was designed to prevent fraudulent claims. Lying about military service to gain compensation (called "malingering") does occur, but is infrequent, and the policy ended up being a significant barrier and source of frustration for thousands of veterans with legitimate claims. Change in this policy was finally initiated several years into the OIF and OEF wars to make it sufficient to have been in the war zone to qualify. This change was long overdue. Mental health professionals should not be put in a position of having to judge how much threat is sufficient for each individual. We should be meeting each of our clients where they are.

We need to appreciate that the experiences of infantry warriors operating in hostile territory 24/7 are different than warriors who mostly work inside a protective perimeter. Personnel working inside the wire (pejoratively dubbed in the current wars "Fobbits," from "FOB" or "Forward Operating Base") often don't live with the same level of day-to-day threat from direct combat as line infantry personnel. Yet, it's also important to appreciate that these warriors in support roles can experience substantial stress from indirect fire and other deployment stressors. They may also be at *higher* risk than line infantry warriors when they do go on support missions outside the wire (as most do), because of a lower level of experience dealing with unexpected combat scenarios, such as ambushes. Combat teams often have higher cohesion and combat readiness than support teams, and are therefore better equipped to handle unexpected enemy engagement. This can actually translate into lower rates of PTSD for some line units, despite much higher levels of combat, compared with some support units. Personnel in support units may also feel a sense of guilt that they are stuck in a support role when they would rather be out directly engaging the enemy, and this can take a toll. The guilt may lead them to resist seeking help for serious war-related problems because they feel that they shouldn't be having these problems in light of the relative security of their assignment.

Fundamentally, everyone's experiences are important, and we can't define what a traumatic event is for one warrior compared with another. Anyone deployed to a war zone, whether in line or support roles, has likely experienced some level of trauma exposure. Each person's experience is unique and relative, and only relevant to themselves.

While the nature of trauma is distinctly personal, there are some experiences known to increase the risk of developing PTSD or other reactions after coming home. The list of events that can occur in the war zone is sobering. Table 1, taken from one of our studies, details some combat experiences reported by warriors involved in the initial ground invasion of Iraq.

Although the level of combat has fluctuated over the course of the wars in Iraq and Afghanistan, the frequency and intensity have remained high for numerous units (both line and support) throughout the many years of war in both countries. Mental health professionals would refer to these experiences as "Potentially Traumatic Events," or "PTE" for short, implying that only a traumatic event that produces PTSD is relevant from their perspective. However, these experiences are anything but "potential." They are immediate and inescapable, not just statistics in a table. Each warrior has a unique story regarding their own experiences, and there are millions of stories just like this:

> *The vehicle in front of us was destroyed by IED [improvised explosive device]. We established security and called a medevac. As security was established a secondary IED detonated approx 20 meters from my location and directly under where I was just standing. Then a third IED detonated. Helpless feeling because I could not see them and did not know where the trigger man was.*
>
> —JUNIOR OFFICER IN IRAQ

Table 1. Percent of U.S. Army and Marine Service Members from Brigade and Regimental Combat Teams Who Reported Combat Experiences During Initial Ground Invasion of Iraq

Combat/Deployment Experiences	Army	Marines
Being attacked or ambushed	89	95
Receiving incoming artillery, rocket, or mortar fire	86	92
Being shot at or receiving small-arms fire	93	97
Shooting or directing fire at the enemy	77	87
Being responsible for the death of an enemy combatant	48	65
Being responsible for the death of a noncombatant	14	28
Seeing dead bodies or human remains	95	94
Handling or uncovering human remains	50	57
Seeing dead or seriously injured Americans	65	75
Knowing someone seriously injured or killed	86	87
Participating in demining operations	38	34
Seeing ill/injured women or children who you were unable to help	69	83
Being wounded or injured	14	9
Had a close call, was shot or hit but protective gear saved you	8	10
Had a buddy shot or hit who was near you	22	26
Clearing/searching homes or buildings	80	86
Engaged in hand-to-hand combat	22	9
Saved the life of a soldier or civilian	21	19

(From Hoge, et. al. *New England Journal of Medicine* 2004; 351: 13–22)

The worst was picking up body parts, "bagging," standing by help-lessly as the Bradley burned after we had tried to get our buddies out but were overcome by the heat. The smell sticks.

—ENLISTED SOLDIER IN IRAQ

I didn't think the old man approaching was a threat because he was holding the hand of a boy. I must have turned away just when he detonated his belt. It knocked me out and cracked my back SAPI plate [Kevlar protective plate]. Two of my soldiers were killed, along with the boy.

—SENIOR NONCOMMISSIONED OFFICER IN AFGHANISTAN

I wasn't prepared to see so many injured women and children. It was frustrating not being able to help them.

—NAVY CORPSMAN WITH MARINES, POST-IRAQ

Trauma in the war zone encompasses much more than taking direct or indirect fire, including experiencing a near miss on one's life; knowing someone who was seriously injured or killed; handling body parts; witnessing or being involved in accidents involving vehicles or aircraft; witnessing noncombatants suffering; or seeing poverty, pain, destruction, or ethnic violence. Some events are so catastrophic that there isn't anything that compares, especially losing a close buddy, but there are also cumulative effects from multiple less severe incidents.

Distinct from most traumas in civilian settings, we are not talking about single events. Warriors may encounter "potentially" traumatic events on a daily basis, and there are effects from working every day under constant threat of attack or ambush, even if nothing happens; long periods of bore-dom and waiting can be punctuated by bursts of insanity. Environmental stressors (heat, cold, carrying heavy loads), exhaustion, and sleep depriva-tion magnify the impact that these experiences have.

What distinguishes traumatic events for warriors is their preparation and the fact that they might experience multiple events in the course of their professional duties, whereas civilians exposed to trauma are usually victims of a single situation for which they were unprepared. Warriors may still be surprised or devastated when combat events occur, but they have an understanding that these things will likely happen, and have prepared for them to the best of their ability. The PTSD definition and treatment is generally conceptualized around a single traumatic event, although warriors routinely experience multiple events.

The Impact of Killing

One important event that is not addressed as directly as it should be is killing. The impact of killing is misunderstood. Killing the enemy is what a warrior is trained to do, and success in this, like any occupational success, can be gratifying. One NCO (noncommissioned officer) in Iraq said:

> *Two days ago I killed an Iraqi for the first time. He was a triggerman and had an IED 500 meters down the road. I shot his ass with 60 rounds of coax 7.62 [machine gun] and then 15 rounds of the 25MM. I have not been this happy since I've been in Iraq. This fuck was going to kill us and I killed him.*

Although killing the enemy is not something that's usually associated with remorse, warriors sometimes go back to the experience of killing and second-guess themselves. They go over events like these in their minds, wondering if some of those rounds may have gone astray and killed an innocent person. They also may ignore evidence suggesting that the person they killed wasn't really a "triggerman." There can be a nagging unspoken awareness at times that innocent people may have been killed or injured. As noted in table 1, approximately half of soldiers and marines who participated in the initial ground invasion in Iraq reported being directly responsible for killing an enemy in Iraq or Afghanistan, and 14 to 28 percent reported being directly responsible for killing a noncombatant. In Mental Health Advisory Team surveys my team conducted in Iraq, approximately 10 percent of soldiers and marines reported that they had damaged Iraqi property when it wasn't necessary, and 5 percent reported that they had kicked or hit a noncombatant when it wasn't necessary. These incidents aren't always easy to live with after coming home. If a warrior is going over and over in their mind experiences such as these after coming home, the transition can be rocky.

Military Sexual Trauma

It's important to acknowledge another serious type of trauma that also occurs in the war zone: sexual assault by fellow service members, or "military sexual trauma," as experts in the field refer to it. Sexual assault is also one of the most common causes of PTSD in civilians. Usually it involves men assaulting women, but men can also be victims. In one 2005 study conducted by the Research Triangle Institute, 7 percent of women and 1 percent of men in the military reported unwanted sexual contact.

In the military, where women are outnumbered 10:1, women may often find themselves in situations where there is male-oriented sexual banter, sexually explicit humor, or exposure to pornography, even though this is prohibited in the war zone. Women have different levels of tolerance, and different levels of comfort for when to take offense; but clearly this is an environment where unwanted advances, touching, or rape sometimes occur. Since supervisors are very often men (and may themselves be the ones exhibiting inappropriate behavior), women can find themselves in awkward situations and feel discomfort bringing accusations forward. The same thing can go on in other male-dominated professions, like law enforcement or firefighting. Strong leadership that creates integrity and cohesion in the unit is important to address this.

An element that is pertinent to the discussion of "military sexual trauma," but not addressed by military leaders (except as "zero tolerance") is the desire for escape, even briefly, through sexual intimacy in the war zone. This adds another dimension to the situation women find themselves in during deployment in the male-dominated war environment. The bottom line is that the war zone presents some unique elements in terms of interactions between men and women that are not evident in other types of work environments. Sexual trauma is very different than combat trauma, and may be even more debilitating because of the feeling of being violated and betrayed.

In conclusion, criterion A-1, the traumatic event, is very much an individual experience. What distinguishes trauma for warriors is that there may be multiple traumatic events that are expected as part of professional duties. In one 2006 study we conducted (published in the *Journal of the American Medical Association*), out of 223,000 soldiers and marines returning from deployment to Iraq, 112,000 (50 percent) reported feeling in great danger of being killed. There are vast differences in each person's experience of trauma. The important thing is not what specific trauma occurred, but whether or not there was a feeling of danger or threat, and whether or not the experience sticks in one's memory in a way that makes it difficult to cope with life after coming home.

Criterion A-2. Response to the Trauma

Part 2 of criterion A of the PTSD definition, which concerns the "abnormal" response to trauma, is more confusing. It states that the person's response to their traumatic experiences must have involved "fear, helplessness, or horror." The problem with this for combat veterans is that they don't often express "helplessness," and "fear" is something that they learn to live with on a daily basis as part of their job. While *fear, helplessness, or horror* are very common terms used by civilian victims of trauma, they are much less likely to be used by warriors to describe how they respond to combat situations, even if these situations lead to significant reactions.

In one study, we asked soldiers from line infantry units (in the U.S. Army, these are called "Brigade Combat Teams"; for marines, "Regimental Combat Teams") about their combat experiences while serving in Iraq. No more than a quarter of the warriors who reported life-threatening direct combat or who had serious symptoms of PTSD said they experienced "fear, helplessness, or horror" at the time of the events.

In other words, the criteria for how one responds to trauma in order to receive the distinction of having PTSD does not hold true for warriors. Warriors don't speak of their wartime experiences in the same way that civilians who are victims of assault, hurricanes, motor vehicle accidents, or other traumas speak of their experiences. During combat, warriors report "locking down" their emotions, falling back on their training, or feeling anger. The important difference has to do with not feeling like a victim. Warriors are professionals trained to deal with trauma; most civilians are not, and often feel like victims when they experience trauma.

Warriors who face life-threatening events as part of their job learn how to control fear, how to respond using their training (not helplessly), and how to control feelings of horror. Otherwise, they wouldn't be able to function under fire. Controlling fear does not mean that a warrior doesn't feel fear, but that they learn how to operate in the presence of it, and how to use fear as an alert signal that helps them and their buddies stay alive. The same thing holds true for firefighters, emergency medical personnel, law enforcement professionals, and others working in dangerous professions.

Although the A2 criterion used by mental health professionals lacks utility for warriors, there are a couple of important caveats. We did find that the 20 to 25 percent of soldiers who reported "fear, helplessness, or horror" fared worse than those who reported other responses. This suggests that if a warrior experiences an event where they feel overcome by fear or helplessness, they will find it harder to recover. It turns out that fear and helplessness are processed by the parts of the brain shown in human and animal studies to be most affected by severe stress, and most vulnerable in terms of the likelihood of developing PTSD. In civilian populations, rape and assault are some of the most common traumas that lead to PTSD because they are strongly associated with fear and helplessness.

There are some unique situations in which warriors will acknowledge feeling helpless, and it appears that these can contribute to them developing serious PTSD symptoms on return from combat. These are situations in which warriors are unable to respond militarily, either because the enemy is elusive or because they're constrained by the rules of engagement (ROE). Rules of engagement are policies established by leaders in the war zone to protect civilian noncombatants, but warriors often feel hampered by them. Here are some examples:

Watching IEDs go off, locking and loading but not firing due to the ROE, left me feeling helpless.

—JUNIOR ENLISTED SOLDIER, IRAQ

All we do is roll on missions and hope we don't get blown up, and then when we get hit there is nothing we can do but watch my dead friends get pulled out in pieces.

—SENIOR NCO, IRAQ

The most stressful part of my job is going out every day and waiting to get blown up. When / if someone gets hit, ROE prohibits us from doing what should be done. Everyone here is "innocent." Yeah, right. If someone dug up the road in front of YOUR house and buried a bomb there, YOU would know about it.

—SENIOR NCO, IRAQ

In the last quote, this soldier is expressing anger at not being allowed to attack or detain Iraqis living in homes close to where a roadside bomb was planted. But the important underlying emotion being expressed is helplessness. In several assessments of warriors deployed to Iraq or Afghanistan, nearly half reported being in threatening situations where they were unable to respond due to ROE. There is evidence that this may play a role in developing mental health problems after coming home. This feeling of helplessness—being unable to respond because of ROE—has also been a prevalent theme throughout multiple operations over the last twenty years (e.g., Panama, Somalia, Haiti, the Balkans), where warriors have been in situations where they've been unable to help civilian women, children, or elderly suffering in the operational environments.

Fear actually can become much more of a problem for a warrior after coming home than it is in the war zone. The fear signal, which becomes almost a sixth sense in the combat environment, and which the warrior learns to trust implicitly for survival, can remain on high alert back home, where there is no longer the same need for it. At home, "locking and loading" is not going to be useful very often, and the warrior can find himself in frustrating situations where he has no outlet for channeling the fear signals going off in his brain and body. Sharply honed combat skills that helped the warrior control fear in combat may prove counterproductive on the home front, and result in the warrior not knowing what to do when the fear alarm sounds.

In summary, criterion A of the PTSD definition regarding the trauma event and response to trauma is difficult to apply within a military context. Warriors are trained professionals operating in situations where there is constant threat and multiple traumatic events. In the military, terms like *fear* and *helplessness* mean very different things than they do in civilian environments.

Most important, the language of criterion A doesn't come close to describing the intimate and life-changing traumatic events that can lead to PTSD, nor does it address the question of why some warriors develop PTSD, while most, exposed to virtually the same experiences, do not.

Resiliency to Trauma: The Million-Dollar Question

The million-dollar question is why do some warriors develop serious symptoms of PTSD after combat, while others from the same units do not? Is there individual susceptibility to developing PTSD in some warriors (or civilians) exposed to trauma? In line infantry units that have been engaged in direct combat, the majority of warriors will experience some symptoms, but for most the symptoms are not severe enough to seriously impair their functioning. Depending on the level of combat intensity, a number of studies involving OIF and OEF warriors have shown that between 10 to 20 percent experience a sufficient number and severity of symptoms to be considered to have PTSD within a year after returning home.

Studies have shown similar rates in Vietnam veterans many years after combat, as well as veterans who experienced direct combat in Gulf War I and other operations. Rates of PTSD don't go much higher than 30 percent in units that have seen the highest levels of direct combat, which means that even under the most severe conditions, most individuals remain resilient or learn to cope with their reactions. Women in support units (e.g., transport, logistics, medical) serving in Iraq have been found to have similar rates of PTSD as men in the same units, a reflection of the fact that combat is a sufficiently severe stressor that it doesn't discriminate on the basis of gender. This is in contrast to civilian settings, where women consistently show higher rates of PTSD than men.

One reason that PTSD develops in some individuals and not in others is that there are differences in resiliency, or the ability to bounce back after adversity. For example, individuals who suffered abuse or neglect as a child, or who have close family members with mental health problems or alcoholism, may be more susceptible after a traumatic event. Genetic factors are also likely to be important in susceptibility to developing PTSD (though we have a long way to go in fully understanding this). However, individual differences in resilience are probably not the main factor in the war zone. The higher the frequency or intensity of combat—and particularly, the more personal the trauma is—the higher the likelihood of developing PTSD. Combat is a great equalizer.

If a platoon suffers a casualty involving death or serious injury, all members of the platoon will be affected in a very personal way, but most will not develop PTSD. Unit members who are likely to be most at risk to develop serious PTSD symptoms are those with the closest personal connection or friendship to the injured individual, those who felt directly responsible in some way for the health and welfare of the injured individual, or those who felt most helpless to intervene in preventing the tragedy. Anyone who has witnessed or been confronted by extremely frightening or horrific events that involved death or serious injury of someone they loved, and who felt helpless or powerless to intervene effectively, are going to be at very high risk for developing PTSD. The situation is worse if there was any perception of betrayal—for instance, poor decisions by leaders that contributed to the tragedy, or gross negligence or reckless disregard resulting in a friendly-fire casualty.

Physical assault or rape in any environment, and especially by a fellow service member in the war zone, is another example of a severe personal trauma involving betrayal of trust that confers a high risk of PTSD. Close calls on your life, particularly if there was any injury, even a minor injury, can be very personal, but probably don't have the same impact, unless there were other factors. For example, being knocked out in combat, even for only a few seconds (a concussion/mTBI), is strongly associated with PTSD; in one study we conducted, over 40 percent of soldiers who lost consciousness as a result of a blast experienced serious symptoms of PTSD when they came home. But this is likely due to the context—the fact that the blast that knocked them out also injured or killed their buddies—and that when they were knocked out they were helpless to respond.

Therefore, the development of PTSD after combat experiences has very little (or nothing) to do with the character, upbringing, or genetics of the warrior. What remains is that certain events are profoundly devastating and have a much stronger impact neurologically than others, a situation that the warrior has absolutely no control over. PTSD in these situations represents normal reactions to extremely abnormal (or extraordinary) events.

There are factors that can mitigate the risk of PTSD from combat. Studies conducted by researchers at Walter Reed Army Institute of Research have shown that strong unit leadership, high cohesion, and high unit morale are correlated with lower rates of PTSD in combat units. By contrast, poor leadership and low morale contribute to demoralization, anger, and feelings of helplessness, all of which can compound or exacerbate PTSD symptoms. Once warriors return home, one of the strongest variables that help in recovery is their level of support from loved ones.

Criteria B, C, and D PTSD Symptoms: Combat Physiology

Criteria B, C, and D concern the specific reactions ("symptoms") that constitute the definition of PTSD. Symptoms must be present in all three of these closely related categories.

Criterion B Symptoms

Criterion B includes all symptoms having to do with re-experiencing the traumatic war zone events through nightmares, flashbacks, intrusive thoughts, or memories. This can include a sudden feeling of dread, like something bad is about to happen, and physical sensations (e.g., heart pounding, sweating, pressure in chest, nausea, trembling) or strong emotional reactions (especially anger) triggered by any reminder of the trauma.

Whenever there are crowds I start feeling like I'm in Iraq and have to get out of there fast.
                        —JUNIOR ENLISTED SOLDIER, POST-IRAQ

I keep having this one nightmare where I am sleeping in one of those kerosene-soaked tents (whose fucking idea is that?) and I on the only bunk bed on top with rounds coming in.
                        —JUNIOR ENLISTED SOLDIER, POST-IRAQ

War fucked me up mentally. I have bad dreams and I see all kinds of mad ill shit. I see dead people. I sometimes get angry and pissed off and just want to kill somebody.
                    —JUNIOR ENLISTED SOLDIER, POST-AFGHANISTAN

Criterion B symptoms relate directly to how the memories of traumatic events are processed in the brain. Memories of life-threatening events are not stored in the same parts of the brain as other memories or thoughts. They are stored in deeper areas within the brain called the "limbic system," which controls survival reflexes and connects directly to areas involving all of the basic functions of the body necessary for survival, including adrenaline, breathing, heart rate, and muscle tone. Adrenaline and rage go hand in hand. They help you focus, make your muscles stronger, and help you fight. Anger helps to control fear.

The limbic system memories are not under your conscious control. Rational thinking occurs in the cerebral cortex, the part of our brain that is much more developed and larger in humans than in any other species. The limbic system, also known as the reptilian (reptile-like) part of our brain, is more primitive, more animal. It processes danger, threat, and reflexes, and expresses basic emotions necessary for survival (anger, hurt, fear). Limbic memories are not linear or logical. They are highly emotionally charged images, sounds, smells, thoughts, or perceptions that immediately connect with reflexes having to do with survival—the "fight-or-flight" reflexes. The limbic area of the brain is designed to make sure that you never forget any memories having to do with serious danger or disaster that affected you personally. These memories form the impetus that forces you to respond instantaneously when you encounter a similar situation at a future time.

Limbic memories in the form of criterion B symptoms can be triggered by any reminder of the war zone, even very minor things, like dust, the smell of diesel fuel, the name of a buddy, the sky, war movies, news, loud noises, a calendar date, an offhand comment someone makes, crowds, trash on the side of the road, an overpass, traffic, a helicopter, kids yelling, dogs barking, raw meat, smoke, a reflection from a window, going into a porta-potty, or being in an enclosed or secluded place. These memories can come flooding back unexpectedly, making you feel like you're back in the war zone again: body, mind, and soul.

Memories having to do with survival are extremely vivid, the most vivid of any of our memories: full color, sound, smells, and feelings with almost the same level of intensity as if they were actually happening now. The limbic part of the brain does not give a damn how miserable you are as a result of being overwhelmed (flooded) with these memories. The job of the limbic system is to ensure that you survive by not forgetting anything that happened during dangerous or threatening situations. These memories are not bound in time. They can be as vivid twenty years later as they were right after they happened. They have to do with immediate danger or threat—right here, right now—no matter how many months or years have passed. These memories are part of the experience of being a warrior, and also an important focus of treatment.

Many warriors describe time slowing down during combat. Soldiers who write about their combat experiences often say that they can fill pages describing events that occurred in only seconds. They remember every tiny detail. The reason for this is that during times of danger and high personal threat, the limbic area compresses much more information into a shorter period of time than the brain normally processes. When there is high threat, the body shunts blood to limbic neurons, which is like shifting into overdrive, so that suddenly there is awareness of everything going on at the same time in the environment in order to identify and neutralize the threat. Warriors recognize this as "high situational awareness." All of this happens in seconds, but from the perspective of the more advanced, slower thinking, and time-conscious cerebral cortex, the large volume of information could only have happened over a "longer" period of time. The whole thing can feel surreal, like being in a movie or video game. It can also feel like the most alive you've ever felt.

Understanding how the limbic system in the brain helps you survive is important for identifying ways to ensure that these memories don't intrude on your life so much that they prevent you from sleeping or doing things you want to do, like being with your friends or family. The goal is not to erase these memories (that's impossible), but rather to be able to get to the point where they are not so intense or frequent, are tolerable, and don't cause anxiety or strong reactions every time they occur. How to do this will be explored later on in this book.

Criterion C Symptoms

Criterion C symptoms have to do with withdrawal, avoidance, and emotional detachment, and are often the most difficult to address and the ones that can most seriously affect a warrior's life. In some ways, these symptoms are reactions to criterion B symptoms—an effort to avoid any situation where wartime memories may come flooding back.

I don't talk much about my stress or personal matters. I don't like to discuss them.
> —NCO, MARINE, POST-IRAQ

To whom this may concern—my thoughts are my thoughts. I sometimes wish I would just forget things.
> —JUNIOR ENLISTED SOLDIER, POST-IRAQ

If I'm having a bad day, I try to withdraw.
> —JUNIOR ENLISTED SOLDIER, POST-IRAQ

I used to love to go to the beach, but after Iraq, I can't stand sand and don't go anymore.
> —JUNIOR ENLISTED MARINE, POST-IRAQ

When I came back from Iraq, I didn't care about anything, even my wife's tears.

—**NCO, post-Iraq**

The desire to shut down, detach, and withdraw can be very strong after combat. Warriors often want to be left alone. They may avoid going out because it puts them in situations that trigger strong reactions or reminds them of their deployment. Since many little things can cause reactions or lead to confrontations, the natural tendency is to want to avoid going anywhere. They also don't want to explain to people who may not understand why they react the way they do. This can mean not doing a lot of things that the warrior used to enjoy doing, and can be extremely frustrating for loved ones and friends.

The most detrimental aspect of criterion C is emotional detachment—having difficulty feeling a full range of emotions; not being able to show love or other feelings toward others.

He was very distant after coming home—it seemed like he didn't care.

—**MILITARY SPOUSE**

Shutting down emotions is a necessary skill in combat, and it can sometimes be very difficult to turn them back on after coming home. Warriors often describe not being able to feel love, not caring about others, and feeling numb or detached. This is also essential for survival in combat. Unfortunately, these problems are the hardest for loved ones to deal with, and the ones that are most likely to end up in failed relationships, breakups, and divorce. Another problem is that once the emotions start to turn back on, it can feel like floodgates opening. Believe me, it's far better to go through the process of connecting with your emotions than keeping them bottled up forever, even though it can feel overwhelming at first. The truth is that warriors are in some ways best prepared to handle the most complex human emotions a person can endure, but it may take a while to appreciate this.

Criterion D Symptoms

Criterion D symptoms, the final set of symptoms that define PTSD, have to do with the body's physical (physiological) response to trauma or threat: feeling constantly revved up, startling easily, getting angry easily, having difficulty sleeping, and difficulty concentrating.

> *I woke up at 0100 hrs today after going to sleep at 10 p.m. last night. Do you think I really have an interest in doing anything but sleeping right now? Too many long days. Too much stupid shit going on at work. It makes me want to hurt someone sometimes; thank God I have some control.*
>
> **—JUNIOR ENLISTED MARINE, POST-IRAQ**

> *I have found that I drink more, dream less, and have more mood swings since my deployment. It is very hard to manage my anger and irritability towards others. I have little patience for repetition and get angry over menial things for no reason.*
>
> **—JUNIOR ENLISTED SOLDIER, POST-IRAQ**

> *I'm jumpy when I hear thunder, door slams, fireworks. Much like in Iraq, when I heard incoming. I drink more than I should.*
>
> **—JUNIOR ENLISTED SOLDIER, POST-IRAQ**

Body physiology plays a huge role in criterion D symptoms. Criterion D has to do with the body remaining on high alert to threat and able to respond instantly if needed—the "fight-or-flight" response. Small things can trigger large physical reactions, including rapid heart rate and breathing, heightened sense of fear or anxiety, jumpiness, irritability, and muscle tension. There may also be stomach queasiness or nausea, because during times of stress intestinal function shuts down so that blood can be shunted off for more important purposes like keeping muscles going. The increased physiological reactivity can lead to sleep disturbance, concentration problems, memory problems, and the feeling of never being able to shut down.

Mental health professionals label criterion D symptoms *hypervigilance*, but in combat this state of being revved up and on high alert is a very useful and necessary skill—what warriors call "situational awareness" or "tactical awareness."

Criteria B, C, and D symptoms can combine in various ways and have different levels of severity. In the most severe cases (which are relatively rare), the flashbacks, intrusive thoughts, feelings, and hypervigilance can progress to obsessiveness, paranoia, delusions, and even hallucinations concerning threat and safety, with the warrior checking everything repeatedly, convinced that an attack on their loved ones or themselves is imminent.

OTHER MENTAL AND PHYSICAL HEALTH PROBLEMS EXPERIENCED BY WARRIORS

Although this chapter focuses on PTSD, this isn't the only mental health concern experienced by warriors returning from combat. There are a number of other problems listed in the DSM that warriors struggle with after returning from war, which many spouses and significant others do as well. These often coexist with PTSD, or can occur independently.

Depression—characterized by a low mood, loss of interest in activities, hopelessness, guilt, sleep disturbance, appetite disturbance, concentration problems, low energy, and sometimes suicidal thinking—is one of the more-common conditions besides PTSD.

Panic attacks are also relatively frequent, characterized by a sudden feeling of fear or anxiety (such as a fear of dying or going crazy), along with a pounding heart, sweating, shaking, feeling of choking, nausea, dizziness, and other physical symptoms. Generalized anxiety—characterized by excessive worry, restlessness, fatigue, sleep disturbance, anger, and muscle tension—is common. Alcohol and substance abuse also frequently coexist with PTSD.

These conditions overlap with and have many similarities to PTSD. For example, when a warrior wants to hole up and avoid the world, this could be considered by a mental health professional as one of the hallmark PTSD criterion C symptoms, or as one of the main criteria for depression, loss of interest in activities. Symptoms like sleep disturbance, concentration problems, anger, and anxiety run through all of these conditions. It also turns out that many of the same treatments are used for these different conditions.

Service in a combat zone and PTSD are both strongly associated with physical health problems related to prolonged changes in stress hormone and adrenaline levels. These include high blood pressure, chronic headaches, concentration or memory difficulties, gastroesophageal reflux disease (GERD), cardiovascular disease, joint or back pain, sexual problems (e.g., impotence, loss of interest), and other health problems. Warriors sometimes experience flashbacks involving wartime memories or aggressive images brought on by sexual arousal, a result of physiological changes resulting from wartime service.

The bottom line is that these are all part of the larger range of reactions that warriors experience after coming back from combat, and therefore, for purposes of this book, separate chapters for each condition are not required. The focus of this book is on helping you learn to navigate the broad range of reactions that warriors experience after returning from combat, and how to most effectively make the transition back home.

SUMMARY

The physical effects of PTSD on the body are indistinguishable from what happens as a result of extreme stress, but continue long after the source of the stress has passed. PTSD is essentially a manifestation of the natural mechanisms for survival and functioning under extremely threatening situations. Everything we label a "symptom" of PTSD is an adaptive and beneficial response when there is a threat to your personal welfare or that of others, and the persistence of these reactions is the body's effort to ensure that you're immediately ready if the danger occurs again.

However, the reactions of PTSD can also seriously interfere with life after coming home. These include symptoms related to how memories of traumatic events are processed in the brain, the body's natural defense to shut down emotions and cope with what's happening, and the body's "fight-or-flight" physiological responses related to heart rate, breathing, and physical reflexes. All of these are interrelated. PTSD is also strongly associated with other conditions, including depression, cognitive problems, and physical health problems. Understanding the nature of what mental health professionals call "PTSD," and learning what is unique about a warrior's experience, is essential to learning how to address these reactions after combat.

CHAPTER 2
COMBAT MILD TRAUMATIC BRAIN INJURY (MTBI/ CONCUSSION)

The wars in Iraq and Afghanistan have led to increased awareness of the impact of traumatic brain injury (TBI) on troops. The availability of modern protective equipment and advances in battlefield medicine have resulted in many warriors surviving injuries from IEDs (improvised explosive devices), RPGs (rocket-propelled grenades), rockets, mortars, EFPs (explosively formed projectiles), and other munitions that would have been fatal in prior wars. Some of these injured warriors have experienced serious brain injuries resulting in long-term impairment in physical, cognitive, and behavioral functioning.

Unfortunately, there has been very poor education about the distinction between mild traumatic brain injury (mTBI), also known as "concussion," and moderate or severe TBI, where damage to the brain is usually apparent on clinical evaluation and brain scans (CTs and MRIs). All TBIs (concussions/mild, moderate, and severe) have been grouped together by medical professionals and in educational materials given to warriors and their families. In 2008, investigators from the RAND Corporation reported that 20 percent of all Iraq and Afghanistan war veterans (more than 300,000) experienced a "probable traumatic brain injury" while deployed, without clarifying that over 99 percent of these cases were concussions and that their study was based on an inadequately validated survey administered months or years after the warriors had returned from deployment. Concussions/mTBIs have also become entangled and confused with PTSD, and these two conditions have been described as "silent" wounds, affecting hundreds of thousands of OIF and OEF warriors.

When a warrior experiences a moderate or severe TBI on the Iraq or Afghanistan battlefields, this almost always results in rapid air transportation to one of the large military hospitals in Germany or the United States for neurosurgical, neurological, and rehabilitation services. Some of these warriors experience severe disability and require long-term treatment.

In contrast, when a warrior experiences a concussion/mTBI on the battlefield, which may involve being briefly knocked out, or getting their "bell rung" from a blast or other injury, this almost never results in evacuation from the combat theater. Concussions/mTBIs are very common in the military (as in nonmilitary settings) from sports injuries, motor vehicle accidents, hand-to-hand combatives training, and combat. Although concussions can occasionally lead to long-term health effects—such as headaches, irritability, sleep disturbance, memory problems, or fatigue—most warriors who experience concussions recover quickly. Concussions/mTBIs are clearly not the same as moderate and severe TBIs, but in the minds of many warriors, family members, the public, and even medical professionals, they have become the same condition, requiring an equivalent level of concern.

After every war, warriors have experienced high rates of physical, cognitive, emotional, or behavioral health concerns, including memory and concentration problems, anger, headaches, sleep disturbance, high blood pressure, rapid heart rate, pain, fatigue, dizziness, and other difficulties. These problems are associated with neurological, endocrine, cardiovascular, and immune system changes likely related to physiological effects of extreme stress on the body, extended sleep deprivation, environmental exposures, and other factors.

The reactions that warriors experience after coming back from war have been given different labels through the generations, including "Nostalgia" (Napoleonic Wars); "Da Costa Syndrome," "Irritable Heart" (U.S. Civil War); "Effort Syndrome," "Shell Shock" (World War I); "Battle Fatigue" (World War II); "Acute Combat Stress Reaction" (Korean War); "Agent Orange Syndrome," "Substance Abuse," "PTSD" (Vietnam); and "Gulf War Syndrome" (Gulf War 1). Some of these problems have been associated with serious environmental exposures (e.g., Agent Orange, Gulf War Syndrome).

After every war, the same mistakes are made. Rather than recognize that going to war can change the body's physiology in a number of ways and identify the best treatments for the full range of health problems that warriors experience, postwar symptoms are attributed to causes that are highly influenced by prevailing politics. After every war, veterans are told that their war-related symptoms are "stress-related" or "psychological" (which understandably infuriates them), and the medical community becomes embroiled in divisive debates as to whether the causes of war-related symptoms are predominantly "psychological" or "physical" (or environmental) in origin. While medical professionals and policy-makers get caught up in debating the definition and nature of the problems (influenced by poor quality scientific data and "turf" battles regarding allocation of resources), veterans feel that their problems are not taken seriously. Health professionals and policy-makers responsible for establishing initiatives to address the problems are well intentioned, but often become overly dependent on the advice of "experts," and myopic to any scientific evidence that doesn't support their positions. Ironically, the need to be perceived as expediently doing everything possible in the interest of veterans leads to the rapid implementation of interventions that are not necessarily beneficial, and may even prove harmful.

For the current OIF and OEF wars, the same problems have emerged. Intense debate is now going on in the medical community (and involving veterans organizations, politicians, and reporters), regarding whether or not certain war-related reactions—such as cognitive problems, rage, sleep disturbance, fatigue, headaches, and other symptoms—are best explained by a "psychological" cause (PTSD) or a "physical" cause (mTBI). Both have been labeled the "signature injuries" of these wars. There has been intense speculation, generated by a large gap in scientific knowledge, that exposure to primary pressure waves from explosions in Iraq and Afghanistan has caused "silent" mTBI injuries in hundreds of thousands of otherwise uninjured warriors that may predispose them to long-term problems. Advocates for the mTBI position, typically experts in neurology, rehabilitative medicine, or neuropsychology, have suggested that blast-related mTBI represents a new form of brain injury, and have even proposed that PTSD may be caused by the mTBIs themselves (ignoring the context in which these injuries occur).

Advocates for the PTSD position, who are often mental health professionals, frequently cite articles that our team at the Walter Reed Army Institute of Research had published in the *New England Journal of Medicine* in 2008 and 2009. These showed that concentration and memory problems, anger, sleep disturbance, fatigue, dizziness, balance problems, headaches, and other difficulties reported by soldiers returning from Iraq were much more likely to be associated with PTSD than with concussion/mTBI, and that concussion/mTBI alone was only very weakly associated with any of these problems. Several other studies have also confirmed our findings. Advocates for both positions, however, have misunderstood the most important evidence from these research studies, having to do with the optimal treatment of interrelated health concerns through collaborative care approaches.

So what is the truth about concussion/mTBI and its relationship to PTSD? What are the most important things for you to understand about any problem you may be experiencing, and treatments that are available? The remainder of this chapter summarizes the answers from a number of different studies.

CONCUSSION/mTBI: THE FACTS

Concussion/mTBI is not the same thing as moderate and severe TBI. Moderate and severe TBI are very serious medical conditions that require comprehensive treatment by neurologists, neurosurgeons, rehabilitation medicine professionals, mental health professionals, and other specialists working together. Moderate and severe TBIs are usually seen clearly on brain scans and result in health problems that can be detected on physical, neurological, and neuropsychological examinations. There have been remarkable advances in the treatment of moderate and severe TBI, and even after severe injuries, there is hope for recovery to high levels of functioning. However, recovery can be slow, and the warrior may not be able to get back to full functioning even after long-term treatment. This is very different than concussion/mTBI, and only concussion/mTBI is addressed in this book.

The term *concussion* is preferred over the term *mTBI* (*mild traumatic brain injury*) to clearly distinguish this from moderate and severe TBIs. Concussion/mTBI is defined as a blow or jolt to the head that briefly knocks you out (loss of consciousness); causes a temporary gap in your memory; or makes you confused, disoriented, or "see stars" (change in consciousness). This is also known as getting your "bell rung." Most warriors who experience a concussion during hand-to-hand combatives training, during sports, as a result of a motor vehicle accident, or after blast explosions on the battlefield are only temporarily confused or disoriented. If they experience memory gaps or are knocked out, this usually lasts for a few seconds or minutes. When brain scans are performed, they are usually normal. Injury to some nerves in the brain may be able to be seen with newer brain-imaging technologies, but these are very subtle, difficult to detect, and these technologies are not useful yet in directing treatment.

Concussions can result in headaches, irritability, dizziness, balance difficulties, fatigue, sleep disturbance, ringing in the ears, blurred vision, cognitive problems (including concentration or memory difficulties), as well as other symptoms. These almost always clear up soon after the injury, but in some warriors may persist for a longer period; there is poor understanding of why they persist in some individuals. The newer brain-imaging methods often show healing of damaged areas, but they don't always match with resolution of symptoms. When symptoms persist after concussion in combat, they are indistinguishable from symptoms warriors experience as a result of other injuries, or physiological effects of working in the war environment.

If you experienced one or more concussions during deployment or during your military service, and you're experiencing any of the above symptoms now, they may or may not be related. These types of symptoms are common after combat. Their presence likely does not mean that something is persistently wrong with your brain, as implied by the term *brain injury*. While they might be related to concussions that you had during your service, this is only one of many possible causes.

The best time to make a diagnosis of concussion/mTBI is at the time of injury, and it becomes progressively more difficult to diagnose the more time has passed. The treatment prescribed at the time of injury is to rest until symptoms resolve, which generally occurs in a few hours to a few days. Once weeks or months have passed since the injury, there is no way for a doctor to accurately determine the exact cause of your symptoms, no matter how well trained they are. There is no blood test, brain scan, or neuropsychological test that can determine with certainty whether physical, cognitive, or behavioral symptoms and reactions that persist after combat—such as headaches, concentration/memory problems, anger, or sleep problems—are due to physiological changes from combat, the physiological effects of PTSD, the effects of exposure to chemicals or environmental factors, lingering effects of concussions or other injuries, the result of chronic sleep deprivation in combat, or various other potential causes. Also, knowing the likely cause doesn't help very much with treatment, since treatment for these problems is exactly the same whether or not concussion is responsible. There are a variety of treatments that your doctor can prescribe to help with specific symptoms, such as persistent headaches.

Full recovery is expected even if you've had more than one concussion during deployment. The brain has a remarkable ability to heal itself through growing new connections between nerves, a process called "plasticity" that goes on continuously in the brain. Areas of the brain that are damaged can be replaced or reconnected through growth of other neurons. Things that help with healing include good sleep and avoidance of alcohol or drugs (both of which will be addressed in chapter 4). The brain is a living organ that can show remarkable healing capability even after very serious injuries, and certainly after concussions or mTBIs from any cause.

Although concerns about the health effects of blast waves are legitimate and are being actively researched, most injuries that warriors experience from explosions in Iraq and Afghanistan are due to fragments, shrapnel, or being thrown against something. It's very unlikely to have effects on the brain from the primary pressure wave of an explosion without other serious injuries. Fragment dispersion in explosions usually extends out much farther than the pressure wave, particularly if the explosion goes off in an open space. If an explosion penetrates a vehicle or building, the primary pressure wave can get amplified inside the space, causing greater damage, but this is usually accompanied by very severe injuries that are not "silent." This is an area that requires further research, but it's not beneficial for you to worry excessively about possible long-term brain effects because you were injured from or close to one or more explosions while deployed. Worry itself has been tied to physiological changes in the body that can contribute to symptoms or hinder healing. Even if there were some lingering effects from the blasts you were exposed to that the medical community hasn't fully identified, there's no reason to think that the brain can't heal itself as effectively after blast-related concussions as after concussions from sports, motor vehicle accidents, or combatives training.

Concussion/mTBI is *not* the same thing as PTSD, and having an either/or perspective isn't helpful. Concussion is the injury event itself. PTSD, as explained in the last chapter, refers to a specific set of reactions or symptoms after trauma (that may or may not have included physical injury) persisting for at least one month, and usually much longer. Although persistent symptoms after concussion can overlap with those of PTSD, they can also overlap with hundreds of other medical conditions, and it's not helpful to focus only on these two conditions. If you experienced a concussion during deployment, you may be at higher risk for PTSD because of the context in which the concussion occurred. If you were knocked out or temporarily disoriented from a blast on the battlefield, this was a very close call on your life, and you may also have had buddies who were injured from the same explosions. It's understandable to experience PTSD symptoms after these types of experiences.

Screening for concussion/mTBI is now routine for veterans returning from OIF and OEF. However, this is leading to concussion/mTBI being underdiagnosed, overdiagnosed, and misdiagnosed because of the lack of any definitive way to make the diagnosis so many months or years after injury. Many warriors who had concussions during deployment have not been evaluated or treated. More important, many warriors with serious postwar symptoms, such as headaches, rage, memory problems, and sleep disturbance, have been mistakenly told that their symptoms are due to the lingering effects of a brain injury, when they're actually due to other reasons. Widespread screening for concussion/mTBI may actually be causing warriors who are not brain-injured to believe that they are.

Some health professionals (and warriors) consider that it's better to be diagnosed with a brain injury than with a mental disorder (PTSD), and the mTBI label is sometimes being used instead of PTSD. This is problematic, since the treatments are completely different. Many warriors are undergoing complex neuropsychological evaluations of memory, concentration, attention, and other cognitive abilities. However, these tests are often inconclusive, even when baseline measures have been obtained for comparison. Neuropsychological tests cannot distinguish concussion from other potential causes of cognitive complaints, such as sleep disturbance, coexisting medical problems, fatigue, anxiety, depression, or PTSD. The physiological effects of PTSD have been shown in several studies to be a much more likely cause of long-term concentration, attention, and memory problems after combat than concussion. Making an incorrect diagnosis can lead to the use of potentially harmful treatments or medicines that have side effects.

Here are the key things you should know about treatment:

TREATMENT FOR CONCUSSION/mTBI

- The one treatment proven to be effective for concussion/mTBI is rest immediately after the injury combined with education on what to expect. Once weeks or months have passed after the injury, treatment becomes focused on alleviating specific symptoms, such as sleep difficulties, headaches, or cognitive problems.

- Many postwar symptoms, including those related to concussion/ mTBI, are interconnected. Problems with anger, sleep disturbance, cognitive problems, being revved up physiologically, pain, and other symptoms go hand in hand. For example, if you're experiencing memory or concentration problems, the most important initial treatment may be to ensure that there is good sleep and control of physiological symptoms related to being revved up, irritable, or angry. However, if headaches, nightmares, or pain are partially responsible for the sleep disturbance and irritability, these problems may need to be addressed first.

- Although treatment is available for your postwar health concerns, including those related to concussion, there are some caveats that you should be aware of. Many war-related health problems, including persistent ones after concussion, are probably best addressed initially by your primary care provider, who has the most experience in treating a wide range of health concerns. That being said, sometimes primary care providers don't have enough time during brief appointments to address all concerns, and may be inclined to refer you to a specialist for further evaluation or treatment. Some debilitating problems— like fatigue, cognitive problems, and pain—can be very difficult to treat, and are best addressed through collaborative approaches involving several professionals coordinated through primary care. However, evaluation by specialists can be a double-edged sword. Although specialists are skilled in the latest modalities of evaluation and treatment for their particular area of expertise (which can be of benefit to you), they often have little or no knowledge of effective treatments from other fields of medicine that may be relevant for the types of problems that you have. When the diagnosis is uncertain or involves multiple potential causes, specialists are more inclined than primary care professionals to attribute them to a disorder that they have the most expertise in, which may not be the right answer. Many specialists in concussion/mTBI have ignored evidence on effective collaborative treatments based on lessons learned from past wars and from studies conducted in primary care of how best to treat overlapping conditions when symptoms have more than one possible cause.

- Being referred to specialists for war-related symptoms can sometimes feel like being thrown around like a Ping-Pong ball, which can contribute to high distress, frustration, and worsening health problems. When you visit multiple specialists, there is a higher likelihood of being given several medicines that may not interact well with each other. If you're on several medicines, you could be at risk for complications unless your primary care provider is coordinating the care, monitoring the potential interactions, and isn't reluctant to change medications recommended by specialists. This may be difficult for your primary care provider to accomplish in the time allotted for your care. Visiting different specialists can also consume a lot of your time, which may affect your work or other aspects of your life.

- Sometimes the key to successful recovery is actually to do less. There are no easy answers. This is a product of the system that we operate in, and the only thing you can do is be aware that this is going on and ask questions about your care at each step along the way.

- There is *no* distinction between "psychological," "stress-related," and "physical" symptoms related to war. All symptoms have a physical and physiological basis involving neurological, endocrine, and other systems in the body. They need to be addressed if they are causing functional impairment sufficient to interfere with your life. All have to be addressed simultaneously, which is why multidisciplinary and collaborative care approaches involving primary care professionals is so critical. There is no split between the body and mind. Medical professionals need to learn how to communicate this better so that warriors don't feel like their debilitating symptoms are being dismissed as "stress" or "psychological" problems. In turn, warriors can help by gently reminding the medical community to stop splitting up symptoms into convenient groups and labels, stop arguing about their causes, and focus on finding the best treatment approaches for the full range of overlapping symptoms, regardless of their causes.

- Chapter 4 will present more discussion on the physiological processes associated with war. Many of the exercises and skills in the remainder of this book can be beneficial to your overall physical and cognitive health by reducing the degree to which your body may be physiologically revved up as a result of your wartime service.

- The VA has established regulations for disability concerning problems associated with concussion/mTBI that do not appear to be based on validated medical criteria. However, this is not necessarily bad for warriors. Because there is no definitive way to prove that postwar cognitive problems or other symptoms (e.g., irritability, sleep disturbance, fatigue, dizziness, headaches, etc.) are *not* due to concussion/mTBI, it would seem difficult to deny a disability claim under the current regulations as long as there's a history of concussion/mTBI during military service and a medical provider who makes a determination that your current symptoms might be related to this. However, don't consider yourself "brain-injured" if you apply for a concussion/mTBI disability. Just because you had a mild brain injury on the battlefield doesn't mean that you're brain-injured now. What you're likely experiencing are the expected physical, cognitive, or behavioral symptoms that warriors have experienced after every war; concussion may have contributed, but is probably not the only factor. The brain can heal even after very serious injuries, and there are many things that can be done to alleviate these concerns. It's important for your health to have a good understanding of these issues and to have a positive outlook. Positive expectations actually improve the physical health of the body.

SUMMARY

In summary, don't get caught up in the mTBI versus PTSD debate. Recognize that combat in itself, as well as combat-related injuries of all types, can lead to a variety of physical, behavioral, and cognitive reactions, and these are closely connected to each other. There is no mind-body split, and all postwar health concerns need to be addressed together. Have confidence that there are many things that can be done to alleviate these reactions to promote a healthy and fulfilling life despite injuries or other traumas that you may have experienced during your service in the war zone. You deserve to receive the very best care available.

CHAPTER 3

NAVIGATING THE HOME-ZONE AREA OF OPERATIONS: INTRODUCTION TO "LANDNAV"

I was less prepared returning home than when I deployed; **wooden** *was the word my wife used to describe me, reflecting the emotion that I had maintained downrange, the "put your mind on the tasks at hand and drive on" emotion, the "throw your shit at your feet and buckle in" emotion, the emotion that is embodied in the moment when the convoy commander, who only seconds before was joking around with the crew, gives the signal to move out, that split-second switch on the faces of the whole team as we move from lightheartedness to the business at hand, the business of going "outside the wire," the business of statistics, where no matter how well you prepare, no matter how many good-luck charms you carry, or how many people you have in your life to pray for you, you are simply at the mercy of "Randomé," the goddess of surreal, the feline beast that distorts time as it maims or kills in a slow-motion deafening wave.*

MEDICAL OFFICER, POST-IRAQ

WELCOME HOME

The acronym "LANDNAV" provides the framework for learning objectives and skills that can help you make a successful transition home from combat, however long since your return. Each of the following chapters corresponds to one of the letters. The chapters include objectives, information to enhance your understanding and knowledge of specific topics, exercises, and skills that you can practice and apply in your daily life as you navigate your transition experience. Each chapter builds on the material in previous chapters, toward the ultimate goal of helping you learn to become an enlightened warrior at peace with yourself in an insane world.

Chapters 4 through 9, corresponding to the letters L, A, N, D, N, and A, are mostly for warriors. They're best read in order, but don't have to be, if you're interested in a specific topic. For spouses, partners, and family members, these chapters provide an opportunity to learn a great deal about the warrior spirit that could help in your relationship with your warrior, as well as developing your own inner strength and resilience. Although the exercises are designed specifically for warriors and emphasize combat examples, anyone can use them. Stress and trauma are universal, and all of the exercises in this book can be generalized. As a spouse, partner, or family member, you've been immersed in the warrior spirit and made your own sacrifices. Chapter 10 is written for you. The closing chapter uses the final letter "V" as a springboard toward the goal of discovering meaning and purpose in your journey.

In addition to the learning content or skills, each of the LANDNAV chapters includes a brief addition by my friend and colleague, First Sergeant Michael Schindler, a two-tour Vietnam combat veteran who retired from the Army in 1999, but who did not begin his transition process home until 2002, more than thirty years after his direct-combat experiences. His experience adds depth to the learning material, along with the stories, examples, and quotes from OIF/OEF veterans who have the opportunity to navigate the transition much earlier than he did.

These chapters provide insights into the inner workings of mental health care in a way that makes it readily understandable, so you know exactly what's going on and can participate fully in directing your own transition process. Some of the material may look like "coping strategies" you've seen elsewhere, but on closer examination, you'll find the information to be more useful because the underlying assumptions and limitations of these strategies are explained. The chapters also contain many new concepts that I believe need to be more widely considered in addressing war-related reactions and transition. Because this book doesn't contain the standard mental health educational material found in most self-help books, a sense of humor and an ability to be flexible in your thinking might prove helpful.

All questionnaires and surveys used in these LANDNAV chapters are based on instruments available in the public domain. The primary source for these instruments was the Walter Reed Army Institute of Research Land Combat Study. You're free to photocopy or scan any of the surveys or questionnaires in this book for your own purposes (for example, if you'd like to repeat exercises over time and leave the original questionnaires in the book unmarked).

CHAPTER 4

LIFE SURVIVAL SKILLS—
WARRIOR REFLEXES AND SLEEP

There is no substitute for the experiences of combat and the excitement of a war zone. Combat is an adrenaline-fed, high-speed, whirlwind, tiger-on-the-loose, exhausting daily dose of life and death. To think that you won't react, feel, behave, and think differently than before your tour of combat duty is, of course, incorrect. Your experiences in combat will forever be part of you. Allow those combat experiences and knowledge to become your strength.
FIRST SERGEANT MIKE SCHINDLER

On a fundamental level, life is about survival, and the place to start the journey of transitioning home from combat is to understand how deployment to a combat zone shapes a warrior's survival skills.

LANDNAV LEARNING OBJECTIVE: LIFE SURVIVAL SKILLS—UNDERSTANDING YOUR WARRIOR REFLEXES AND IMPROVING SLEEP

The goal in this chapter is to develop a better understanding of how your body reacts to extreme stress, how your reflexes take over to help you survive as a warrior, and what you can do to improve your sleep. Combat requires that you hone your survival skills and reactions so they become ingrained reflexes. These reflexes are innate to who you are as a warrior as a result of your training and experience in the war zone, and can cause you to act as if you were still in the war zone after coming home. Understanding why your body reacts the way it does provides the foundation for all future exercises in this book.

HM3 J (Hospital Corpsman 3rd Class), a navy medic who had returned home from deployment with a marine unit in Afghanistan, kept startling or throwing himself to the ground whenever there was a loud noise. This embarrassed him in front of his friends and family. He became increasingly frustrated at not being able to control himself. Startling would lead to a rush of anger, which made his jumpiness worse. He had trouble sleeping, would wake after a couple of hours, and be unable to fall back asleep. He also experienced nightmares, and would sometimes try not to fall asleep to avoid them. Whenever he went places where there were crowds, he felt tense, edgy, and his heart pounded. As a result, he stopped going out much, which affected his relationships. He started drinking more alcohol to calm down and help with sleep.

SSgt L (Staff Sergeant), back from his second tour in Iraq, found himself becoming furious every time things didn't go the way he expected. If his fiancée, Sally, moved any of his things, he would become enraged. During one incident, while running an errand, he came storming into her house angry that he had been unable to reach her by cell phone. He had mixed up the directions she gave him and had taken a wrong turn. When she failed to pick up his calls, he lost his temper. Sally's sister, who was visiting, was stunned by the intensity of his rage, and Sally's five- and seven-year-old nieces cowered at the edge of the room. Sally felt humiliated at being yelled at in front of her relatives. She also felt helpless, confused, and angry. Finally, her sister stepped in and told SSgt L to take his anger outside, which to his credit, he did. Sally's sister then turned to Sally and told her that she was making a big mistake being involved with this guy. It took about an hour for SSgt L to calm down, after which he was apologetic; however, Sally's family continued to feel uncomfortable around him.

If either of these stories sounds familiar, then this chapter will provide context and offer some useful advice. Both of these warriors were continuing to feel physically revved up and hyperalert after returning home. They were reacting to situations back home as if in the war zone, and these reactions had become reflexes that they were unable to control. Both of these men were experiencing high levels of anger—for HM3 J, toward himself; and for SSgt L, toward his fiancée. Both were having problems with control. HM3 J was angry at being unable to control his own reactions; SSgt L was angry at his fiancée if she moved his things or if she wasn't available for him when he thought she should be. The reactions for both of these warriors were affecting their relationships. In SSgt L's case, his anger didn't make a good impression on his fiancée's family. It embarrassed his fiancée, scared her nieces, and resulted in her sister advising her to call off the engagement.

To understand the experience of these warriors, the most important thing to realize is that their reactions were products of their combat survival skills—protective reflexes that were not well controlled after coming home. For HM3 J, the speed with which he reacted to dangerous situations during deployment saved him many times and was ingrained in his reflexes. After returning home his body remained on high alert to threats and reacted instantly to loud noises. It sent him danger signals, such as his heart pounding, whenever he entered a crowded mall. He found it difficult to relax and sleep. His sleep pattern was similar to what it had been in Afghanistan, where he would catch two to three hours of sleep before going out on a night patrol. Nightmares, often involving combat, also kept him revved up. He was frustrated because his conscious mind could do nothing to control his reactions. He expected to have better control over himself since he had performed extremely well under fire. His anger at himself made everything worse. He also didn't realize that his increased use of alcohol was contributing to the heightened reactivity of his reflexes.

For SSgt L, getting angry at his fiancée was also a result of his combat survival skills. If she moved any of his things, he reacted in almost the same way he would if he couldn't find an important piece of gear before going on patrol. Not answering her cell phone triggered a reaction similar to being lost and "out of communication" on the battlefield. SSgt L's navigation skills failed him on one of his errands, and his inability to make contact with her after finding himself in an unfamiliar location caused him to feel revved up, as if he were back on the streets of Iraq. Finding his way and dealing with traffic back home seemed more stressful than driving in Iraq. His body had not yet decompressed. He also had very little sleep during his deployment, was still not sleeping well, and his temper was short-fused.

He expected Sally to be available, and he reacted to her failure to pick up her phone like he would react to one of his subordinates who failed to follow proper communication procedures.

For both HM3 J and SSgt L, their bodies were reacting as if they were back in the war zone. In PTSD terminology, these kinds of reactions are called "hyperarousal" and "flashbacks," and are very normal after combat. For both of these warriors, their bodies took over to protect them. They did exactly what they had been trained to do and had done for months during deployment, and would need to do again if they returned to the combat zone, or if they faced other types of danger.

HM3 J and SSgt L were experiencing reactions common during the transition period after returning home from deployment. Medical professionals may label reactions such as startling easily, sleep disturbance, anger, being hyperalert, and avoidance of going out as symptoms of PTSD if they interfere with work or relationships. However, these postwar reactions can also be considered normal. It's not always clear where to draw the line between normal and abnormal.

How the Brain Reacts to Threat

Extensive research has characterized the neural (brain) processes involved in responses to high threat or danger. The "limbic system," the part of the brain that acts as the alarm signal for the fight-or-flight reflex, consists of neuronal pathways deep inside the brain (beneath the rational cerebral cortex) that connect to the brain areas responsible for various physiological functions of the body, including heart rate, blood pressure, circulation, breathing, and hormone balance (e.g., adrenaline and the stress hormone, cortisol). The limbic system takes over whenever there is high threat, ensuring that the body responds rapidly. This system is critical for ensuring that the body's reflexes will kick in when needed. The limbic neurons trigger the release of adrenaline through the "autonomic" nervous system—the system of nerves that control unconscious physical processes in the body, including breathing and heart rate. Adrenaline tenses muscles; increases alertness, attention, heart rate, and blood pressure; and changes the way a person scans the environment for threats. The limbic neurons also cause the release of stress hormones, which increase endurance, as well as chemicals, similar to morphine, that dull awareness of pain. The limbic alarm system of the brain "hijacks" the conscious rational areas in order to ensure that the person's entire attention and focus is directed toward survival.

The primary emotion of the limbic system is anger. Fear is also present, but warriors learn to control this by falling back on their training. Anger helps to control fear. Emotions other than anger are generally shut down. While the speed of processing information increases, the ability to be self-reflective or consider things in a rational sequence diminishes. In times of danger, a moment of reflection may make the difference between life and death.

As an example of how the limbic system works, imagine walking through a forest and encountering a snake just where you're going to step. You instantly jerk your foot away to avoid stepping on it and save yourself from being bitten. You do this without thinking. Only after this reflex has kicked in do you notice that there was no snake in your path after all; it was just a vine shaped like a snake. You may feel like an idiot for overreacting to a vine, and your friends may laugh, but the bottom line is that you had no control over your reflex. Your body did what it needed to protect you. If there really had been a snake, you'd be very happy to have this reflex. The reflexes honed during military training and combat are some of the strongest reflexes that a person can ever develop—reflexes that become a way of life for a warrior.

The limbic alarm system is regulated by another part of the brain called the *medial prefrontal cortex*. The medial prefrontal cortex is front and center, literally and figuratively. It's located in the front part of the brain inside the midline groove separating the right from the left sides. It's an important part of the cerebral cortex that connects with the deeper limbic neurons involved in the fight-or-flight reflex. One of the most important jobs of the medial prefrontal cortex is to provide control over the limbic area. This part of the brain is what allowed SSgt L to accept the advice of Sally's sister and cool down outside rather than make things worse. This part dampens or controls the fight-or-flight reflex and tries to keep it from indiscriminately firing when there is no real threat. The medial prefrontal cortex is critical in planning, decision-making, and thinking through actions. It's important for anticipating what you're going to do next and thinking through the sequence of things.

In summary, the limbic system ensures that you can react immediately to threat, and the medial prefrontal cortex helps to keep this in balance.

The problem for combat veterans is that the medial prefrontal cortex, the part of the brain that helps to balance out the protective reflexes, may not work well when there is sleep deprivation, high-intensity combat, or other very stressful experiences. Brain-imaging studies show reduced functioning in this part of the brain as a result of both extreme stress and sleep deprivation. This means less control of the limbic system, which means you're more likely to overreact with anger or other fight-or-flight responses to situations that aren't particularly dangerous. Reduced prefrontal brain functioning as a result of combat experiences and sleep deprivation is a common reason why veterans complain of poor concentration, memory problems, cognitive dysfunction, and bad decision-making after returning from deployment.

Sleep Deprivation

During continuous military operations, it's not uncommon for warriors to go for extended periods with reduced sleep. Traditionally, military leaders have considered four hours' sleep an acceptable level in the war zone, and indeed, warriors can learn to adjust to this amount of sleep (sometimes catching micro naps to compensate). Over time the cumulative loss of sleep takes a toll on the ability to think clearly, and makes it difficult to sleep restfully after returning home. The problem isn't only the limited amount of sleep, but also the fact that most operations in the war zone happen at night. Trying to catch up on sleep during the day doesn't match with the human biological clock, known as the *circadian cycle*, a complex process in the brain that's regulated by daylight and involves secretion of the sleep hormone melatonin at night and suppression of this hormone during the day. Melatonin helps to bring on sleep and make it restful, which is one reason why nighttime sleep is more restful than the same amount of sleep during the day. After learning to function on less sleep and repeated night shifts, it may be very difficult to retrain the body and return to a normal cycle of sleeping throughout the night. Sleep deprivation, as well as combat stress, trauma, and high immediate threat to life, can all impair the medial prefrontal cortex of the brain, which then causes the limbic system to take over and rational thinking to be diminished. The medial prefrontal cortex is a part of the brain particularly susceptible to dysfunction after trauma and sleep deprivation.

Five to six nights with only four hours of sleep each night has been shown to have the same effect on cognitive ability as a full night of no sleep or a blood alcohol level of 0.1 percent—legally drunk. After this level of sleep deprivation, a person doesn't have coordination problems and can still walk a straight line; however, their ability to think is impaired. There is also a vicious cycle that veterans can fall into: Sleep deprivation reduces the ability of the medial prefrontal cortex to keep the limbic system under control. This can lead to feeling irritable and revved up, which in turn causes the medial prefrontal cortex to not function well, making things even worse. Many veterans feel like they live constantly in a state of either fight or flight, with little rest in between. Rational thought and reason get compromised.

Studies have shown that sleep deprivation significantly increases levels of anger, impulsivity, and aggression, as well as quicker and more forceful reactions to any provocation. The ability to be self-reflective and consider options is decreased, which causes decision-making to be impaired. There is increased risk-taking, decreased empathy, and decreased consideration of the long-term consequences of actions. There are also important misperceptions of thinking, termed *cognitive distortions*, which result in perceiving things as more threatening than they really are.

A Vicious Cycle of Prolonged Stress

For HM3 J, his body wasn't able to decompress, meaning that he stayed revved up and reactive to loud noises and crowds. As a result, he drank more alcohol. Although this seemed to help him calm down, it actually made things worse. Alcohol affects the quality of sleep, and it's very common after drinking to experience very poor sleep or wake up in the middle of the night or early morning and not be able to get back to sleep. The increased use of alcohol and increased anger resulted in HM3 J being caught in a vicious cycle of worsening sleep, increasing withdrawal from everyone, and being angrier at himself—a pathway toward depression and PTSD.

In SSgt L's situation, when he mixed up his directions while driving, he didn't have the ability to stop what he was doing, consider the options (other than calling his fiancée), and avoid getting angry. His body was flooded with a sudden adrenaline surge, and he became hyperalert to threat, using all the skills he had used during deployment. He expected his fiancée to be available, and when she wasn't, he reacted with rage. All of this was also compounded by sleep deprivation.

Working in a combat zone, combined with sleep deprivation, results in a number of physical changes in the body. During times of stress and danger, the body is revved up due to adrenaline and other chemicals; the heart rate is increased, breathing becomes more rapid and shallow, muscle tension increases, and the mind becomes hyperalert. As a result, warriors are able to maintain high situational awareness, which is a very useful skill. This includes scanning the environment for anything that might be a threat, using their own fear or anxiety as a warning signal, and ensuring that there are always escape routes. All of this involves activation of stress hormones. However, if the warrior is unable to decompress after deployment, or develops PTSD, this sustained level of stress can progress to hypertension (high blood pressure) and cardiovascular problems. The increased adrenaline and stress hormone levels also affect the digestive system—stomach and intestines—causing them to slow down, which can lead to gastroesophageal reflux disease (GERD), stomach ulcers, and feelings of queasiness or nausea. Prolonged stress can also affect the immune system, as well as sexual function.

Anger

The prominent emotion of prolonged stress for warriors during combat is anger. The other common emotional condition is feeling no emotion at all, or, in warrior's terms, "emotional control." Emotional control, through numbing or detachment, is necessary under extreme stress. In combat, a warrior learns to turn off emotions other than anger. Anger/rage is the "fight" part of the fight-or-flight reflex, which helps the warrior neutralize the enemy. Anger masks other emotions, such as fear or sadness, allowing the warrior to do what needs to be done under fire. Even if a unit loses a team member, right after the casualty is removed or the memorial service is finished, the grief has to be put on hold when the unit goes back "outside the wire." The warrior learns to control anger itself through training, so that anger doesn't completely take over and impair the mission. Buddies help with this, and seasoned combat warriors learn how to monitor each other. After coming out of a combat environment, it can take a long time before a warrior can express a full range of emotions again.

Cognitive Problems

Warriors often complain of having difficulty concentrating or problems with memory, attention, or thinking after leaving the war zone. These cognitive problems are some of the most common complaints of veterans after returning from war. Warriors also complain about having a hard time concentrating and maintaining focus on one task. On a neurological and physiological level, these problems are due to chronically elevated adrenaline and stress hormone levels associated with overactivation of the limbic system and reduced functioning of the medial prefrontal cortex of the brain. However, of more immediate concern, these cognitive difficulties result from essential survival skills related to the ability of a warrior to maintain control under fire. Memory, attention, and concentration all become oriented toward survival, and this can make it difficult to stay focused on other things after returning home.

Control

Control is an essential survival skill. Survival in the combat zone depends on the ability to react instantaneously with the correct sequence of combat tasks under fire. You depend on your equipment, your training, and your buddies, and if any one of these fails, then the mission can fail. The key is having all your equipment in the best working order exactly where you need it, doing exactly what is required under fire based on your training, and relying on your buddies to do exactly what is required of them. A warrior lives and breathes what they're required to do, and a good unit leader will continuously train the unit to ensure that each team can execute combat tasks collectively without hesitation. The success of the mission and the ability to respond on enemy contact in a flexible and effective way requires that everyone on the team perform their tasks instantly and in the correct way, according to their training and experience. This starts with memorizing common tasks, which after intensive training become reflexive actions. This is how the warrior maintains control under fire.

However, after returning home, the warrior continues to utilize all of these skills, including high situational awareness, scanning for threats, monitoring escape routes, controlling emotions, and keeping thought processes focused on survival, both for himself and others. This can result in the warrior experiencing difficulty tolerating someone moving their things unexpectedly, or difficulty with loved ones, friends, coworkers, or anyone not following through with what they say they're going to do. When the warrior gets stressed, which is common in daily life, his body can suddenly feel like it's back in the war zone.

What Can You Do?

What are the essential navigation skills and knowledge to learn from this chapter? The most important thing is to recognize how your body has changed as a result of being a warrior, and to make things better by cutting yourself some slack, not getting angry with yourself, and not blaming yourself. Getting angry with yourself magnifies the problems. Having a good understanding of how the body responds to stress on a physical, emotional, and cognitive level is the foundation for skills in this and subsequent chapters.

HM3 J was getting angry with himself for his inability to control his reactions when he heard loud sounds. He felt embarrassed and ashamed when he hit the ground in public, and this fueled his frustration and anger. His body was constantly revved up, and the anger made everything worse. This went on for months until he decided to seek help. One of the first things that he learned to do was to stop blaming himself for how his body reacted. He learned to accept that his warrior body was reacting according to its reflexes, and that these reflexes were attempting to protect him from danger. HM3 J let go of his blame for his body's reactions to loud noises and accepted them. Controlling his anger reaction gradually had the effect of making him less jumpy. He also got help for his sleep problem, which included changing the way he used alcohol.

SSgt L, whose behavior was straining his relationship with his fiancée, had to learn to let go of his need to control things. He started a regular physical training program, and found it helped to control his reactions. He set up a small space in his house where he could put things he needed (e.g., wallet, keys, cell phone), so he could find them easily. His fiancée learned not to move his things without first asking him. If he felt frustrated when he couldn't reach his fiancée by cell phone, he would remind himself it wasn't something that he could control, and his fiancée was not a unit member who had screwed up communication procedures, but the woman he loved and wanted to marry.

Everyone adjusts differently after coming home from a war zone, but there are similarities in experiences that can be addressed. There are five skills to learn in this chapter:

SKILL 1: BECOME MORE AWARE OF YOUR REACTIONS BY WRITING ABOUT THEM

Start by getting a notebook that's small enough to carry around, and use it for exercises in this book, notes, and journaling. Putting words to your reactions and writing about your experiences can help develop understanding and insight into your feelings, thoughts, and physical sensations.

Write down the positive and negative ways you've changed as a result of your deployment. Positive changes could be increased self-confidence, greater appreciation for what's important in your life, greater appreciation for loved ones and friends, greater maturity, increased spirituality, ability to demonstrate leadership, improved knowledge and expertise, closer bonds with unit members, improved perception of what's going on around you, faster reflexes, etc. Next, write down how things have changed negatively as a result of your deployment experiences. This could include difficulty coping with wartime experiences, strain in your relationships, physical injury, work stress, etc. Finally, compare how you react to things now to how you reacted to things before deployment.

Think of a specific stressful event since you returned from deployment; write down how you reacted, what emotions you experienced, and what you did in response to the situation. Focus on the details of this event and your reactions; don't judge yourself, or justify what you did, or defend yourself by explaining why things happened the way they did. Don't judge your reactions. You can ask yourself if your reactions resulted in doing something stupid, and if the answer is "yes," write down what you would do differently if this happened again. But don't beat yourself up for how you reacted at the time. The purpose of the exercise is to gain greater understanding and awareness of how you react to things without becoming more critical of yourself.

As an example of how to organize your writing in your notebook, please answer the following questions:

How have I changed as a result of deployment?

Positive ways: _____
_____
_____
_____

Negative ways: _____
_____
_____
_____

How do I react to things differently now than I did before deployment?
_____
_____

_____

_____

How does my body react to stressful events now, and what emotions do I experience?

Body reactions: _____

_____

_____

Emotions: _____

_____

_____

SKILL 2: LEARN TO ACCEPT YOUR REACTIONS WITHOUT JUDGMENT OR ANGER

Accept how your body reacts now and how it's changed because of your deployment. Acceptance means not blaming yourself, not judging yourself, not defending yourself, and not being angry with yourself. This isn't easy, and takes some practice, so give yourself a break. Rome wasn't built in a day.

Practice not getting angry when your body reacts like it did during combat. If you suddenly throw yourself on the ground because of a loud noise, don't get up right away. Lie there, feel the ground; get up only when your body and mind are ready for you to get up. This may seem weird to you and appear odd to others, but don't let it get to you. Don't get sucked into feeling embarrassed. You put your life on the line, and if others are uncomfortable with your behavior, that's their problem. Tell people this is what you do sometimes because of your war-zone experiences, and that you're fine. Make a joke and laugh about it if you want. Remember— you're not crazy. As long as you don't let your physical reactions (and your thoughts and emotions) get to you, others can learn to accept them, and if they don't, it's their issue.

You're a warrior, a fighter, a survivor, and your body is doing exactly what it's learned to do in order to take care of you. Over time, your reactions will change as your body learns that being away from the war zone doesn't carry the same threat level.

If you find yourself getting frustrated, annoyed, upset, or angry because people aren't doing what you think they should be doing, remember that you can't control what everyone else does. Appreciate how the *feeling* of anger has helped you survive, and understand that you don't have to respond right then to your own feelings of frustration or anger. If you feel your heart pounding or you find yourself looking for an escape route in a crowded location, realize and accept this as one of the ways you learned to protect yourself. Don't add fuel to your reactions by getting angry at your own reactions.

The most important thing is to let yourself experience how your body takes over sometimes. Let it do what it does, accept it, and learn from it.

SKILL 3: IMPROVE PHYSICAL CONDITIONING AND RELAX MUSCLE TENSION

There is no better and more natural antidepressant, antianxiety, or anger management medicine available than good physical conditioning. In study after study, regular exercise has been shown to positively affect mood, memory, anger, thinking, anxiety, work performance, sleep, blood pressure, cardiovascular functioning, and cholesterol. Physical exercise can help resolve depression and improve the symptoms associated with PTSD. Exercise improves circulation, strengthens the heart and lungs, and helps control weight. Exercise can help with pain. There are even studies that show regular exercise can help with memory impairment in elderly people with Alzheimer's disease.

Physical conditioning is an integral part of being a warrior and is built into the regular training that all warriors receive. There are five key components to good physical conditioning, all of which can improve mental well-being: A) stretching/flexibility, B) muscle relaxation, C) aerobic exercise, D) strength building, and E) a healthy diet.

A) Stretching/flexibility: The goal of stretching is to improve flexibility by lengthening muscles and tendons. Include the calves, thighs, hips, back, shoulders, and neck. There are four important rules to stretching that should be followed.

- Stretch when you're warmed up or after exercise. Muscles are more receptive to stretching when warm and can be injured if stretched cold.

- Don't bounce to achieve a greater stretch. Put yourself in the stretch and let yourself settle into it for about thirty seconds, remaining still without bouncing. After the first ten seconds or so, the muscles will release slightly and allow you to achieve a greater stretch. When this happens, settle into it. Don't force it, and never bounce, as this can damage muscles or tendons.

- Stretching should feel good, not painful. If you feel pain, back off to the point where you feel the stretch but it doesn't hurt.

- Breathe while stretching. Don't hold your breath.

B) Muscle relaxation: The ability to be aware of muscle tension and to relax muscles is often included in stretching and flexibility, but deserves its own category. We are often unaware of the degree of muscle tension that we carry, particularly in the upper back, shoulders, and neck, or the stress that we put on our body from certain postures. Warriors sometimes hold a combat-ready posture, even when strolling through the park or mall, characterized by general muscle tension, slightly hunched posture and elevated shoulders (as if there's a weight on the back); arms held stiffly out toward the sides like there's combat gear against the body that prevents the arms from swinging naturally close to the body; hands curled slightly in a fist position; and a purposeful stride. It's as if the warrior is always fully loaded. All of this results in enormous muscle tension that can contribute to poor sleep; chronic headaches; chronic pain or stiffness in the neck, shoulders, upper back, lower back, or hips; high blood pressure; irritability; and other problems. Warriors are often totally unaware of the amount of postural tension they're holding and the variety of problems this creates for them. Pain medicines are sometimes prescribed that can cause side effects or lead to overuse, worsening the situation.

Compounding this is today's increase in computer use and text-messaging, which often results in a slumped or hunched posture in both men and women, with the upper back and chest collapsed and shoulders pulled upwards; this puts strain on the upper back and shoulders and leads to associated postural problems. For these reasons, becoming aware of muscle tension and learning to relax muscles is an important skill.

To start, stand up straight, feet flat on the floor, and loosen each joint to release tension, starting from your head down to your feet. Begin by gently flexing and extending your neck by dropping your chin toward your chest to look at the floor and then raising it up toward the ceiling. Repeat this several times. Then turn your head all the way to the right and left several times. Then tilt your head to each side (ear toward shoulders) several times. Rotate your head around clockwise and counterclockwise several times. Do all of this in a very relaxed manner with the goal of loosening up your joints.

Once your neck is loose, next release the shoulders by lifting both of them up toward the ears as far as they'll go and then dropping them down quickly in a relaxed way. Do this several times. Do circles with your shoulders in both directions. Then let your shoulders drop down and relax so that they're simply hanging. Next, shake your arms and fingers out in a relaxed way. Extend your fingers and then swing your arms in wide circles at the shoulders to help release the shoulders and relax the arms. Then let them hang naturally near your body. Counter any tendency to push them out away from your body.

Next, become aware of your upper back and chest. Straighten the upper back by thinking of making yourself taller up through the top of the head toward the ceiling while keeping your feet flat against the floor. If your chest is collapsed slightly from being slumped, open it up. Roll the shoulders toward the back and pull the shoulder blades together for a few seconds and then release. Repeat this until your shoulder blades are relaxed, your chest is open, and your upper back is straight. Being open in the chest does not mean sticking your chest out (like some people do when standing at attention).

Next, become aware of your stomach, lower back, and hips, and let them relax. Let your stomach relax by sighing and letting it drop toward the floor. Do some circles with your hips and waist to help release the hips and lower back. Continue down the legs. Release any tension in the buttocks, thighs, knees, and feet; feel your weight against the floor through the center of your feet. Be aware of your toes against the floor.

Finally, move in any other way that helps to release any tension you feel. The best way to release tension is through movement. If necessary, hang off a pull-up bar or other object to help release the shoulders. You can also lie on your back on a bed with your head and upper back hanging in a relaxed manner off the edge of the bed to give yourself a stretch in the opposite direction from slumping or hunching forward. The way to release tension is to get more movement into each of your joints in a comfortable and relaxed way, so you end up standing tall in a natural manner with good posture.

Although movement is usually the simplest way to release tension, another technique to relax muscles that is frequently taught by mental health professionals is called *progressive muscle relaxation*. This involves lying down on your back (or sitting) and consciously thinking about relaxing each muscle group sequentially, beginning with your face and moving down slowly through your neck, upper back, chest, arms, hands, lower back, stomach, pelvis, legs, and feet (or vice versa). If you have trouble relaxing, then you can consciously tense each muscle one by one by flexing or extending it, holding it for a five-count, and then releasing it.

Get comfortable "taking off" your warrior posture whenever you're "off duty." When walking, stand tall and let go of any tension in the upper back and shoulders. Let your arms swing naturally close to your body. Don't text-message while you walk.

In addition, any activity that helps to relieve muscle tension or improve flexibility, such as massage or yoga, is beneficial. Massage therapists are readily available, and many shopping malls have chairs where you can get a brief massage of the back, shoulders, and neck. Having a massage is one of the best ways to learn to appreciate the difference between tense and relaxed muscles.

C) Aerobic exercise: Regular aerobic exercise that increases heart rate provides the greatest benefit to overall health. There are numerous ways to do this, including running, swimming, biking, rowing, dancing, and martial arts. Aerobic exercise should increase your heart rate, cause you to breathe faster, and develop at least a light sweat. You should be winded enough that it's difficult to carry on a conversation while exercising. Your muscles should feel like they're exerting themselves. A commonly recommended minimal amount of aerobic exercise is thirty minutes a day for five days a week, or three times a week if the activity is very vigorous, such as running or martial arts. However, this is a rough guide, and each person needs to find the routine that's most comfortable, practical, and beneficial for them. Obviously, more exercise has more benefits (as long as you don't overdo it), but even ten minutes a day of vigorous exercise is much better than nothing.

D) Strength building: Improvement in strength doesn't require hours in the gym. It can be achieved in three twenty- to thirty-minute weight-training sessions each week. Also, you don't have to do multiple repetitions. Research has shown that a single set of repetitions at the correct weight level achieves optimal results. Select the weight that allows you to do twelve to fifteen repetitions, with your muscles tiring enough that you're barely able to complete the final repetition of the set.

E) Healthy diet: It's important to eat regular meals and get the right balance of protein, complex carbohydrates, and fats. Eat a wide variety of foods that include plenty of fresh fruit, fresh vegetables, whole grains, fiber, and legumes. It's better to "graze" throughout the day by eating smaller meals more often than one big meal, and to snack on fresh fruits and vegetables and unsalted/unsweetened nuts, rather than sweets. This results in a more-balanced release of insulin, the hormone responsible for maintaining your blood sugar level and distributing the calories you take in, so that they don't go immediately toward building fat cells.

It's very important to limit your sugar intake, particularly candy, pastries, sodas, and other beverages that include high quantities of sugar (sucrose), corn syrup, high fructose corn syrup, glucose, dextrose, and related sweeteners. A single twenty-ounce bottle of regular (non-diet) soda usually contains 200 to 300 calories, which can rapidly tip the scales toward weight gain, obesity, and abnormal insulin regulation. There are also enormous calories in many processed, packaged, and fast food meals. Many breakfast cereals, as well as nut and dried fruit mixes, are marketed as being healthy but are actually heavily sweetened. It's much healthier to get your carbohydrate calories from complex grains, vegetables, or fruit than from simple sugars. The bottom line is that unless you read labels regularly, you're unknowingly eating many foods with high sugar content. Educate yourself about the different ways to maintain a healthy and balanced diet.

SKILL 4: IMPROVE SLEEP

It's common to experience sleep disturbance after returning from combat, both because the body's physiology may have been changed from the intensity of combat, and because your body has likely become used to functioning on less sleep. With many operations going on at night, reversed sleep cycles disrupt the normal internal human clock linked to sunshine and the hormone melatonin (circadian cycle); this can make it very difficult to reset back to normal nighttime sleep after returning home.

While warriors may experience difficulty falling asleep, the more common problem is waking in the middle of the night, either from a nightmare or for some other reason, and then not being able to fall back asleep. This is similar to the sleep patterns they experienced during deployment. The overall quality of sleep isn't as good, and warriors often don't feel sufficiently rested when they wake up.

Sleep is an essential part of good health and ensuring a successful transition home from combat. Warriors often find it difficult to readjust after months in a combat zone where they were constantly revved up and may have only been able to get a few hours' sleep each night. Nightmares are often the product of being revved up, and if you go to bed tense or angry, there's a greater chance of having one. The quality of sleep can be negatively affected by high stress or an inability to let go of stressful experiences after coming home.

To improve sleep, practice good "sleep hygiene" skills. *Sleep hygiene* is a medical term used to refer to the practical things you can do to improve sleep. The other thing often considered for sleep problems is medication, either over-the-counter or by prescription. However, it's important to be fully informed regarding these medicines, as there are many problems with limited effectiveness and side effects (sometimes serious).

A) Sleep hygiene: The following list provides the key elements of practicing good sleep hygiene, including the recommended standard information and other material that may prove beneficial. A lot of advice that's given hasn't been extensively studied, and there are many assumptions mental health professionals make about what's best for an individual that might not be helpful (and may even make things worse). Give yourself some time to try different things until you find the approach that works best for you. It can take some time to correct sleep problems after combat deployment, so take it easy.

- Have a comfortable place to sleep that's quiet, free from distractions, and a good temperature for you to sleep soundly (generally on the cooler side). The bed and bedroom should be reserved for sleeping and having sex, nothing else. You should not work in your bedroom. Having a comfortable mattress is very helpful.

- Establish a pre-sleep routine that includes going to bed at a regular time. Do something relaxing before sleep. This may include a warm shower or bath, light stretching, or a muscle relaxation exercise from this chapter.

- The standard advice is to not keep a TV in your bedroom and not to watch TV before going to bed. The rapidly changing visual images of television can be stimulating to the brain and can disturb sleep. If you're the type of person who prefers to fall asleep with the TV on, try replacing it with some other form of "white noise" (see next paragraph). If this doesn't work, or the TV provides a sense of comfort, turn the volume low and select a channel where the programming is pleasant or innocuous and won't trigger negative thoughts, memories, or feelings. If your TV has a sleep function, set it to turn off automatically so it doesn't disturb you after you've fallen asleep.

- Consider putting "white noise" in your bedroom. White noise is a background sound that causes other noises to become less noticeable. The simplest form of white noise is a floor or table fan (ceiling fans are usually too quiet for this). If you don't like the air blowing on you, point it in another direction. There are also inexpensive machines that produce white noise sounds like the ocean, a waterfall, rain, or wind. White noise helps to cancel out other types of noise around you. For example, if there are other people in your house, noisy neighbors, or outside traffic that disturbs you as you try to sleep, white noise can make the bedroom seem quieter by reducing the presence of other noises so you don't notice them as much. During deployment, generators and air conditioners are great sources of white noise, and warriors often find that after coming home, having some white noise can help them sleep better.

- Don't toss and turn for hours. If you haven't fallen asleep, or you're having trouble falling back asleep after waking up, give yourself about thirty minutes, but if you're not asleep after that, get up and leave the bedroom. The reason for this is to keep the bedroom as the place where you sleep, not a place that has a bad association where you frequently toss and turn or stay awake trying to sleep. The goal is to train your body to associate the bedroom with sleep by going somewhere else whenever you're not sleeping. That way, your body learns that your bedroom is only for sleeping.

- When you leave the bedroom after thirty minutes of trying to sleep, keep the TV, computer, BlackBerry, video games, and other electronics off. These involve visual processing in your brain and can be stimulating. Instead, find something quiet to do, such as reading, listening to relaxing music, doing a puzzle, drawing, or journaling. If you use your computer for writing, restrict its use only to the word-processor program, and don't check e-mail, send messages, or go on the Internet. Again, you want to do something that's quiet, reflective, and not stimulating. After doing this for a while, you'll probably start to feel tired again. When you feel sleepy enough, go back to bed.

- The best time to exercise is at the beginning of the day, but if you exercise in the afternoon or evening, leave enough time to wind down and cool off (at least an hour) before going to sleep.

- Eat big meals earlier in the day and limit yourself to a light snack within a few hours of going to bed. This helps avoid heartburn during the night. Drink fluids more than two hours before going to sleep so you're less likely to wake up needing to go to the bathroom.

- If you're having nightmares or waking suddenly with the feeling of dread, consider putting a small nightlight in your room (an alarm clock light works well also) to help orient you to where you are. If you're experiencing nightmares, particularly if they're repetitive and involve the same disturbing images or themes, write them down and think of ways to modify the images in your mind. For example, if you're having repetitive images of combat, think of the good things you've experienced and the people you loved and appreciated. Also, it's useful to know that disturbing nightmares are often related to stress and to the body being revved up. Any stressful situations going on in your life that cause anxiety, frustration, anger, increased blood pressure, or increased heart rate make it more likely for nightmares to occur. Don't ask why you get particular nightmare images. Dreams and nightmares are not mysterious processes, and are strongly influenced by what's going on during the daytime. For example, if you're having any conflicts at work or with your spouse or partner, you might have disturbing wartime images at night. Nightmares are common after combat; they're related to physiological changes in your body and how your mind processes disturbing memories of stressful experiences. Learning the various skills in this book can help with recurrent nightmares. One other thing that you can consider for nightmares is to ask your doctor for a medicine (e.g., prazosin) that reduces blood pressure, slows the heart rate, and helps reduce the revved-up feeling that can be associated with nightmares (see section C below for more details).

- Watch your caffeine intake. Drink caffeine beverages only in the morning and early afternoon. This includes coffee, tea, energy drinks, and many types of sodas. Read the label if you're not sure if it contains caffeine. Many popular sodas contain caffeine, and it's important to cut down on their use if you're having any sleep problems.

- Understand how alcohol or drugs affect sleep. Use of alcohol is one of the most common reasons for sleep difficulties. (See the last skill in this chapter for more details.)

- Keep a "sleep log" notebook nearby, and when you wake up, record the time you awoke, the amount of sleep you got, and any dreams or nightmares you had. Also, write down what you did to help you sleep, what worked and what didn't. Over time, this type of log can be very helpful, particularly if you go to a medical professional for sleep problems.

- Most important, feel free to ignore any of the advice above if it isn't working, or if there's something else you've found that's more helpful. Everyone has to learn what works and doesn't work for them. You want the bedroom to be a place that's comfortable and doesn't increase your anxiety every time you lie down to go to sleep. If the standard advice doesn't work, it doesn't mean there's something wrong with you; it may mean that the standard advice isn't any good. If you find that sleeping on the floor or sofa works better for you, then do that. Do whatever works for you to make yourself as comfortable as possible (within the limits of your living situation and the needs of others living with you).

As an example of the last point, a marine senior officer I worked with found himself regularly waking at 2:00 a.m. thinking of all the messages that he had to send to his subordinates. He would sleep fitfully after 2:00 a.m., finally getting up at 4:00 or 4:30 to take care of the messages before exercising and going in to work. He was chronically fatigued, and this affected his ability to keep his temper in check. Despite the advice to not get on e-mail in the middle of the night, I recommended that he immediately get up and get out of bed when he woke at 2:00 a.m. to take care of his messages, rather than just lie there. When he started to do this, he found that he could finish in about an hour and then fall back asleep for two or three more hours. This change allowed him to get additional sleep each night and improved his mood and energy.

B) Over-the-counter medicines: Over-the-counter medicines can be purchased without a prescription; however, be careful with these. If you're considering trying an over-the-counter sleep medicine, know they don't work very well, have a number of risks and side effects, and don't work any better at higher than recommended doses. Over-the-counter sleep aids include:

Antihistamines: Antihistamines are medicines most commonly used in the treatment of allergies. Newer antihistamines, such as loratadine (Claritin), cetirizine (Zyrtec), desloratadine (Clarinex), and fexofenadine (Allegra) cause minimal or no drowsiness and don't work as sleep aids. Many of the older antihistamines, such as brompheniramine (e.g., Dimetapp), chlorpheniramine (e.g., Chlor-Trimeton, Singlet), dimenhydrinate (e.g., Dramamine), diphenhydramine (e.g., Benadryl, Nytol, Sominex, Sleepinal, Compoz), doxylamine (e.g., NyQuil, Unisom, Nighttime Sleep Aid), clemastine (e.g., Allerhist, Tavist), are readily available and are a main ingredient in over-the-counter sleep medicines because they cause drowsiness. The antihistamine hydroxyzine (Atarax, Vistaril, Novo-Hydroxyzin), available by prescription, works in the same way.

These medicines are not habit-forming, but are likely to work best if used only on an occasional basis. Although widely used for sleep, there is very little research supporting their effectiveness, and they can cause drowsiness the next day. Other side effects include dry mouth, blurred vision, dizziness, forgetfulness, and urinary retention. These medicines are not to be used by people who have a history of glaucoma, are pregnant, or are taking certain types of medicines. There are obvious precautions concerning driving or operating heavy machinery because of the drowsiness. It's best to check with your doctor before taking these, and to read the labels and package inserts to ensure that you're informed.

Herbals and supplements: These include melatonin, tryptophan, L-tryptophan, and herbals, like valerian. Studies have produced mixed results as to their effectiveness, but in general, if they do work, they only help with falling asleep, not with staying asleep. They generally have minimal side effects, the most serious being an allergic reaction. Melatonin is a natural hormone that increases in the body at night, helping to bring about sleep, and then decreases when daylight returns. Unfortunately, taking this hormone as a pill has not proved to be very effective, although some people report it helps with falling asleep and with jet lag. Tryptophan or L-tryptophan is a basic amino acid that's important in the production of a chemical in the brain called serotonin. Some people have found it helpful for getting to sleep, but studies have been mixed. Valerian has also shown mixed results, although it's a common sleep aid used in Europe. At high doses, valerian can cause vivid dreams, blurred vision, changes in heart rhythm, and excitability.

In summary, if you choose to try an over-the-counter medicine to help with sleep, understand the risks. Side effects are higher with medicines that include antihistamines. Supplements or herbals have fewer side effects, but if they show any effectiveness, it's generally only with falling asleep, not with staying asleep. These medicines don't work any better at higher than recommended doses.

C) Prescription medications: If you experience ongoing sleep problems despite good sleep hygiene, and over-the-counter medicines have given you no relief, then it's wise to go see a medical professional. The easiest way is to see your primary care doctor, and then if further evaluation is necessary, your doctor can provide a referral. Your doctor should evaluate if there are any underlying medical conditions that explain the sleep problems before considering a prescription medicine. Medical conditions that can cause sleep difficulties include sleep apnea, pain, restless leg syndrome, periodic limb movements, narcolepsy, alcohol abuse, depression, anxiety, PTSD, and side effects of medications. If a decision is made to prescribe a sleep medication, there are several different choices, and your doctor should inform you of the options and risks. However, don't agree to take a prescription medication that may be addictive unless absolutely necessary. There are five types of prescription medicines commonly used to help with sleep.

Antidepressants: Some of the older antidepressants caused a lot of drowsiness and proved to be more useful for sleep than depression. One medicine that's commonly prescribed for sleep is trazodone (Desyrel). This is often prescribed in doses ranging from 25 to 100 mg, much lower than doses necessary to treat depression. Side effects can include dizziness, tiredness, blurred vision, gastrointestinal side effects (nausea, diarrhea, constipation), headache, dry mouth, muscle aches, and changes in weight, among others. Trazodone is not addictive, which is a distinct advantage over other prescription sleep medicines. Although it's widely used in both men and women, there is one note of caution regarding its use in men. Very rarely, trazodone can cause priapism, a condition where the penis gets a prolonged and painful erection unrelated to sexual stimulation. If this happens, it requires prompt medical intervention in an emergency department to prevent long-term problems such as impotence. Fortunately, this is a very rare event, and the only thing that's necessary is to be aware of it so if it happens you'll know what to do. Trazodone also has potential interactions with other medicines, and additional precautions and contraindications. Get as much information as you can by speaking with your doctor and reviewing the package insert.

Melatonin-like prescription medication: One medicine called ramelteon (Rozerem) acts on the same nerve pathways in the brain that melatonin acts on. This medicine is not addictive and has minimal side effects, so it's worth considering before trying other medicines. However, it's only been shown to be effective for falling asleep. If you tend to wake in the middle of the night and not be able to fall back asleep, then it's unlikely this medicine will be helpful.

Blood pressure medicine to help control nightmares: Medicines designed to reduce blood pressure have nothing to do with sleep, with one exception. An older medicine called prazosin (Minipress), which reduces blood pressure and slows heart rate, has been shown to have benefits in reducing the degree to which a warrior's body is revved up at night by adrenaline. For warriors, nightmares are often associated with increased blood pressure, pounding heart rate, and being revved up. Prazosin helps to reduce these physiological reactions, which in turn can help with the nightmares. Some warriors find that this medicine alone is sufficient to give them more restful sleep by reducing the number or intensity of nightmares. Side effects can include low blood pressure and slow heart rate, but there is a wide range of doses that can be used, and the medicine quickly leaves the body, so this usually isn't a persistent problem. The blood pressure medicines called beta-blockers also may be of use in the same way as prazosin.

New antipsychotic medicines: There are several new medicines for treating schizophrenia and bipolar disorder that are being used for purposes not approved by the U.S. Food and Drug Administration, including depression, sleep problems, and nightmares associated with PTSD. The problems with this include potentially serious side effects and a lack of evidence for effectiveness of this class of medications for these purposes. One medication in this group that is gaining widespread use, quetiapine (Seroquel), has been prescribed to warriors for sleep problems unresponsive to other medications. Although used in doses much lower than required to treat schizophrenia or bipolar disorder, there have been many concerns with this medication, including the possibility that it may contribute to diabetes, heart problems, and weight gain. For these reasons, it's important to carefully consider the risks and not rush into a decision to take this medication unless there are no good alternatives.

Sedative or hypnotic sleep medicines: These are the strongest medications for sleep and the ones with the most side effects and potential for addiction. These medicines work on specific nerve endings in the brain, called *benzodiazepine receptors*, which act by slowing down the nervous system.

These medicines should be avoided unless absolutely necessary. They can quickly cause dependency because in many ways, they act just like alcohol. Some warriors find that these are the only medicines that seem to help their sleep, but in the long run, these medicines can make the sleep problems worse.

There are two classes of sedative-hypnotics: benzodiazepines and non-benzodiazepines. Benzodiazepines include medications marketed specifically for sleep, like estazolam (ProSom), flurazepam (Dalmane), quazepam (Doral), temazepam (Restoril), and triazolam (Halcion), and medicines marketed for anxiety that also may have effects on sleep, including alprazolam (Xanax), clonazepam (Klonopin), lorazepam (Ativan), and diazepam (Valium).

Benzodiazepines have a high risk of dependence and generally should be avoided at all costs by warriors. They're also sold on the street as downers, tranks, V's, Z bars, roofies, and various other names. Their use can lead to drug tolerance (the need to use increasing amounts to achieve the same effect), drug dependence (inability to sleep without the medicine, or inability to stop the medicine), and withdrawal symptoms (worsening of sleep or other physical effects, such as nausea, sweating, shaking, or seizures when you try to stop the medicine).

Non-benzodiazepine sedative-hypnotics are a newer class of sleep medicines that include medications like zolpidem (Ambien), eszopiclone (Lunesta), or zaleplon (Sonata). Although they also act on benzodiazepine receptors in the brain, they're more specific for sleep (they don't have antianxiety properties), and are considered to have a lower potential for dependency and fewer side effects. Nevertheless, they still have the potential to become habit-forming, and many warriors who start using them for sleep find it very difficult to quit and sleep without them.

Sedative-hypnotics have many side effects, contraindications, and interactions with other drugs (sometimes life-threatening), and it's important to discuss all concerns with your doctor, take them only as prescribed, and read the package inserts. Side effects can include daytime sleepiness, trouble concentrating, memory problems, dizziness, unsteadiness, headache, muscle aches, constipation, dry mouth, impaired judgment, and rebound insomnia (increased sleeping difficulty if you try to stop the medicine). Don't increase the dose to try to achieve a stronger effect without consulting your doctor. Increasing it on your own can carry very serious risks. The medications should never be used with alcohol, or while driving. Some of these medicines have been associated with nighttime behaviors, similar to a blackout, in which the warrior may do dangerous things while under the influence of the medication (including getting in a car and driving), when they have no conscious awareness of doing this and retain no memory of it.

The sedative-hypnotic sleep medicines are generally prescribed for short-term use (a few days), and should be used sparingly, only when needed. However, once a warrior has started using one of these medicines and finds it helpful, it can be very difficult or impossible to come off of them. Doctors will often continue to prescribe them despite the fact that they are generally only recommended for short-term use.

Warriors frequently find themselves between a rock and a hard place regarding these sleep medicines. If sleep hygiene practices or over-the-counter medicines haven't worked, then doctors will frequently prescribe one of the sedative-hypnotics. The non-benzodiazepine sedative-hypnotics are preferred over the benzodiazepine forms, but warriors need to understand that extreme caution is warranted for all of these. There's a high likelihood that the medication will help initially, particularly with falling asleep, much like alcohol can help initially. But over time, the medicines can lose their effectiveness and become habit-forming. In the end, if they're used long enough, they can lead to more sleep difficulties.

If you use one of these medications, pay attention both to how quickly you fall asleep and how long you stay asleep. The medicines may help you fall asleep quickly, but not help with the problem of nighttime awakening and not being able to fall back asleep. Sometimes this is related to the medicine having a short-term effect in the body. Several of these medicines are cleared out of the body very quickly. If this happens, doctors can switch you to one designed to stay in the body longer. However, this may lead to drowsiness the next day. The bottom line is that if you use any of these medicines, give yourself time to test them out first in the safety of your home—for instance, on a weekend—when there is sufficient time to see their effect the following day. It's also wise to let a friend or family member know you're trying this out.

If you choose to use a sleep medicine, understand the risks and the potential for dependence. If it's necessary and nothing else has worked, you can certainly try one of these sleep medicines under the supervision of your doctor, but use them sparingly, only when most needed. Try to use them only occasionally. Don't use them every day.

One more thing: Never use these medications at the same time that you're consuming alcohol, and make sure you check with your doctor about using these in combination with other medications, particularly pain medicines. These medications don't mix with anything else that can make you drowsy.

SKILL 5. LEARN HOW ALCOHOL OR DRUGS AFFECT YOUR REACTIONS

Some warriors drink heavily or use drugs after returning from deployment for reasons including relaxing, socializing with friends, helping with sleep, coping with wartime memories, enjoyment, or just because it's there. However, many warriors don't realize the degree to which alcohol or drugs can affect their ability to successfully transition home from combat. This section focuses on alcohol, since that's the most widely used recreational "drug," but any drug use (illegal, or misuse of prescription medications) can have similar effects on the body, and the advice in this section concerns drugs as well. Like alcohol, most drugs have some combination of stimulating and sedative effects that can seriously affect wartime reactions, worsen sleep, and make the transition process difficult.

Alcohol has a calming effect, can seem to help with sleep, and goes together with socializing and partying. However, it's a trap. Alcohol also has a strong stimulating effect on the body, which is why conversations get louder and more spirited with alcohol, and why risky behaviors and aggression are common while under the influence. After the stimulating effect there is a sedative effect, and alcohol can result in falling asleep or "passing out." Over time alcohol actually worsens sleep. There's a rebound effect that makes it more likely that you'll wake up after only a few hours of sleep, and more difficult to fall back asleep after waking.

Sleep is characterized by periods of dreaming (rapid eye movement [REM] sleep, which happens even if you don't remember your dreams) and periods of deeper sleep without dreams. During a night of sleep, you normally cycle through REM and deeper sleep a number of times, with very brief periods of waking between cycles (not usually remembered). Feeling rested the next day requires the right balance between these different periods of sleep. If the sleep cycle is disrupted in some way, the overall quality of sleep, or the ability for sleep to restore your energy and make you feel rested, is negatively affected.

Alcohol can cause you to initially fall asleep; right after falling asleep, it reduces the amount of time spent dreaming. For warriors who experience nightmares, this may seem like a good thing. However, within two to four hours (and sometimes after only an hour), alcohol begins to clear out of the body, and the brain tries to "catch up" on the periods of dreaming sleep. This can result in increased dreams and nightmares, which may be accompanied by feeling revved up and coming out of sleep and waking up. It's common in the second half of the night to toss and turn fitfully or wake up and not be able to fall back asleep.

After drinking alcohol the normal sleep cycles and quality of sleep are disrupted, which results in being much less rested when you wake up. This may lead to the temptation to take a bigger "dose" of alcohol the next night, which would only make things worse. People may not realize that alcohol use, even in modest amounts, is the most common cause of sleep disturbance. Alcohol also fuels irritability and anger, and worsens the cognitive effects of stress. It's also a common cause of high blood pressure. People may not realize that a person can have an alcohol problem even if they don't drink every day. People who can stop drinking easily may still have a significant problem.

The quantity or frequency of alcohol use isn't what defines the problem, although higher use is obviously worse. Research shows that five or more drinks for a man, or four or more for a woman, on a single occasion is probably too much. If you hold your liquor well, meaning that you can drink five or more drinks without feeling much of an effect, your liver (which clears alcohol out of the body) has gotten used to working overtime; this is probably a sign of an alcohol problem. Definite signs of a problem are getting a DUI; a work problem caused by alcohol; a loved one often telling you that you're drinking too much; blackouts (people telling you about things you did under the influence of alcohol that you don't remember doing); or drinking before noon to get yourself going. If you have any of the problems just described but are convinced that you don't have an alcohol problem, then you probably have an alcohol problem, because denial is the number-one defense when alcohol is involved.

Take the following short survey and assess whether or not you may benefit from further evaluation for an alcohol problem:

In the past month:

1. Have you felt you wanted or needed to cut down on your drinking?	Yes	No
2. Have you used alcohol more than you meant to?	Yes	No
3. Have you had five or more drinks on any one occasion (four or more for women)?	Yes	No
4. Did you drive after having several drinks?	Yes	No
5. Have you been late or missed work because you were drinking or hungover?	Yes	No
6. Have you used alcohol to get to sleep?	Yes	No
7. Have you been told about things you did while drinking that you don't remember doing?	Yes	No
8. Has a friend or family member told you that you're drinking too much?	Yes	No
9. Have you gotten into any fights while under the influence of alcohol?	Yes	No
10. Did you ever have a drink in the morning to steady your nerves or help with a hangover?	Yes	No
11. In the past *year,* have you used any illegal drugs/substances?	Yes	No
12. In the past *year,* have you been charged with a DUI or other alcohol- or drug-related offense?	Yes	No

If you marked "yes" to any of questions 1 through 3, particularly if you also checked "yes" to any of questions 4 through 12, then this suggests that you should get a more-thorough screening. Having an alcohol problem is a medical issue, not something that you can control through willpower, and it's important to get assessed if you have these indications. If you have problems cutting down on your alcohol use or experience jitteriness, the shakes, or an inability to sleep when you stop drinking, then you need medical help. You can find out more through Alcoholics Anonymous (AA) (go to www.aa.org to find a meeting near you, including information for online meetings), or looking up information at the National Institute on Alcohol Abuse and Alcoholism (NIAAA) Web site (www.niaaa.nih.gov). You can also speak with your primary care doctor.

Even if you don't have an alcohol problem, but like to drink from time to time, make sure that you drink responsibly. This means not drinking excessively alone or with others, not driving after drinking any amount, and not allowing others to drive after drinking. If you're having any ongoing sleep problems, consider that alcohol is contributing to this. Stop drinking to see if the problem improves, but don't expect improvement quickly. If you've been using alcohol (or drugs) regularly for any amount of time, it can take weeks or months for the normal sleep cycle to restore itself.

SUMMARY

To summarize, the first letter, "L," of the LANDNAV acronym refers to life survival skills—learning how the body responds to stress, and how your reactions have been influenced by combat. There are five skills recommended, including keeping a journal of your reactions, accepting your reactions without making them worse by judging or becoming angry at yourself, exercising regularly, improving your sleep, and learning the effects that alcohol (or drugs) may be having on your reactions.

First Sergeant Schindler provides some further advice based on his experience:

> *Combat skills don't adapt well to the "real" world, and are the hardest skills to keep control of when home from the battlefield. Without help I would never have understood the reasons why I did not like crowds or standing in lines, why I ducked when I heard loud noises, got angry because my beer*

was served warm, felt a sense of dread on a dark rainy summer night ("I can feel the pricks sneaking up on my ass from a click away"), or freaked out when I heard mosquitoes buzzing around me.

These feelings, images, and noises triggered my combat skills automatically and caused great anxiety, which in turn made me want to hide from the world. Hyperawareness, rage, hate, fear, and hiding your emotions are the combat skills we warriors need every second of every day to survive.

In 1972, after returning from Vietnam, I moved to Maui, a small, quiet, beautiful laid-back island about 3,000 miles away in any direction from the rest of the world, where I tried (unsuccessfully) to not feel, see, or hear anything that would remind me of war ever again. However, no matter how far I went or what I did, my inner demon white tiger seemed always ready and willing to rip somebody's heart out. Time passed, and it wasn't until 2002 when I really began my "transition" back.

Sometime in 1974 or '75, after a couple of years of coming and going between Maui and Michigan, I moved back to my hometown of Ann Arbor, Michigan, and attempted to live a "normal" life. I rejoined the active U.S. Army Reserves in 1976, and in 1977 managed for the second time in my fledgling Army career to become a "buck" Sergeant E-5.

A pattern of repeating ranks went on for the next twenty-plus years, during which time I held several ranks more than once. My lack of respect for military authority, regulations, and other "minor" military requirements stemmed directly from my combat experiences in Vietnam. "If one more rear echelon motherfucker (REMF) tells me how to act, I swear I'm gonna shove my fist up his left nostril and pull his REMF brains out." This attitude caused great consternation for my immediate bosses, ranking NCOs, and officers, who knew I could have been an outstanding soldier if I wasn't so damn stubborn or stupid—usually both.

I eventually met a single mom with a son, and began to love them both very much. This connection felt good. I had an instant family, which seemed to fill a void. We married in 1978. I adopted our son and welcomed a baby daughter into our wonderful life. My job as a construction inspector was okay, almost tolerable. I had a truly outstanding family, and life was good—or so it seemed.

From 1978 to 1988, the Army Reserves allowed me to have a buffer zone between my warrior spirit and my family. But my civilian work slowly became intolerable, and I hated my supervisor and job. I became depressed. I felt like something wasn't right inside me, and family life went down the tubes. By 1988, I was just surviving.

My wife and I separated during the summer of 1988. In February of 1989, I was fired from my construction-engineering job. I tried to work again as a construction materials tester. Didn't take, lost that job also. In October of 1989 my first divorce was finalized, and then I experienced years of mental crash-and-burn (a second marriage in 1998 also ended in divorce in 2004). The healing for me began in 2002 when I started my commitment to therapy and began to understand my combat reflexes and reactions to situations in the civilian world.

I just didn't give a damn anymore; "Fuck it—don't mean nothing, not a damn thing." I shut my emotions and most feelings down for years in order to survive another day. I felt always on guard, on the outside looking in on life. By 2002, I hadn't found much to stop my intrusive combat thoughts and was displaying a more-combative attitude (short temper) towards family, friends, and people in general. After many years I did not yet understand my feelings and hid them from all.

The single best piece of advice that I can give to any warrior who feels alone, angry, detached, afraid of crowds, suffers from lack of sleep, dislikes loud noises, or is just not feeling right, is to talk, talk, talk about how you feel with someone you feel safe with. Understanding why you react to situations will set you free and allow you to begin healing. Start by committing, forgiving yourself, and loving yourself—then later on you can work on finding some of those same feelings for the rest of the human race. When I learned that my reflex actions are directly the result of combat experiences and training, I began to see myself as a "normal" person.

The main "tool" that I use for a negative or unpleasant situation is to repeat to myself the words "frequency, intensity, and duration." I try to keep these three actions "low, mild, and short." This "tool" is now a reflex, and helps me to control my reactions in most situations. Combat skills can become a life-changing positive force that you can trust and depend on; I found that I could deal with situations much better and be a lot happier when I reminded myself to keep the "frequency, intensity, and duration" of my reactions "low, mild, and short."

What we are trying to do is not always have to "hit the dirt" and get low because we hear firecrackers that sound like a machine gun on the Fourth of July. Another of my classic at-home combat moves was to swiftly throw my best friend on his backside and begin to drive his nose through his skull with my fist if he tried to shake me awake.

Needless to say, these over-the-top reactions involving my reflexes taking over—not to mention looking pretty strange and having a lot of friends saying, "What the fuck?"—eventually subsided with my knowledge of their root causes.

My family and friends are no longer afraid to wake me up, and I set off the family fireworks on the Fourth of July—big fun. I am "supervised" by my adult son and daughter for my own safety at all family events involving pyrotechnics. They see humor in the likelihood that I will kaboom myself in some sick kind of entertaining way, which is okay. I have a well-developed sense of humor. Laughter is good medicine. I say all this because being able to find a positive in any situation, good or bad, is a vital part of the design to your survival "blueprint."

CHAPTER 5

ATTEND TO AND MODULATE YOUR REACTIONS

What I remember about combat is the feeling of hyperawareness, the ability to see and feel everything around you. I felt a kind of high, or being super-alive. My physical reactions included feeling no pain, body rushes, and a feeling of white lava running through my veins. The only two things that I gave a shit about in combat were my platoon and squad members' safety and to kill the enemy—nothing else. I did not care about myself, pain, the weather, other units, God, or country. I mean the President, my senator, my congressman, and my general were not with me in the mud and blood of combat—so fuck them all. The only thing that I could count on was my combat skills and my battle buddies.

I didn't know that my combat skills stayed on automatic for thirty-plus years after coming home. I was combat-ready and battle-alert at all times. For years my feelings fluctuated between anger, rage, bloodlust, laughing, and somewhat happy. A combat-ready lifestyle led to many not-so-pleasant situations for me personally.

FIRST SERGEANT MIKE SCHINDLER

This chapter will provide exercises to assist you in learning to modulate your reactions. Your warrior knowledge and skills are just as useful to you at home as they are during combat, but like all skills, they need to be practiced and fine-tuned depending on the circumstances. This means becoming aware of physiological sensations in your body that relate to stress or your perception of threat or danger, how angry you feel, and other feelings existing under the surface.

LANDNAV LEARNING OBJECTIVE: ATTEND—LEARN TO PAY ATTENTION TO AND MODULATE YOUR PHYSIOLOGICAL REACTIONS, EMOTIONS, AND WAYS OF THINKING

Humans are reactive beings. We react to all sorts of things occurring around us, as well as to what's going on internally. Everyone reacts to things differently. Our reactions are influenced by who we are, how we're feeling at the moment, our physical health, how much stress we're experiencing, what's happening around us, and how we've been raised and trained. If you're in pain or haven't been sleeping well, then you're likely to react differently than if you're well rested and pain-free. A comment someone makes may send one person into a tirade while someone else would just laugh it off. Being stuck in traffic can trigger anger, frustration, anxiety, fear, humor, indifference, and other emotions. Reactions are fluid and depend on a lot of different factors.

Reactions can automatically lead to behaviors, and one objective of this chapter is to increase your awareness of these automatic responses. An event or stressful situation in our life perceived through our senses (sight, sound, touch, smell, taste) causes physiological and emotional reactions. If I stub my toe on a table, I immediately feel pain in my foot, along with anger, which I may express verbally ("Ouch!"). If I immediately kick the table in response, this behavior almost certainly involved no thought. However, if the pain or anger caused me to feel upset with myself for being clumsy and I kicked the table out of frustration at my own inadequacy, then a thought (e.g., "I shouldn't be so clumsy") contributed to my behavior.

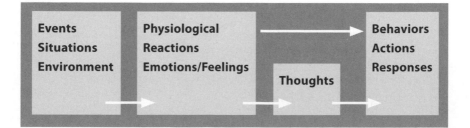

Combat experiences tend to shorten the time between stressful events and behaviors. Warriors often have hair-trigger reactions to stressful situations, and this can lead to behaviors they later regret. A stressful event may automatically result in an action without paying any attention to the feelings or thoughts inside. In addition to specific stressful events, we're also constantly reacting physiologically and emotionally to everything going on in our environment. Feelings are always present, whether or not we know what specific things are causing them.

The goal of this chapter is to become more aware of the range of physiological reactions and feelings, and how these are connected with behaviors and influenced by war-zone experiences. Specific navigation exercises are provided to help you learn to modulate your reactions.

SKILL 1: LEARN TO PAY ATTENTION TO YOUR PHYSIOLOGICAL REACTIONS AND ANXIETY LEVEL

Combat teaches a warrior how to become highly attuned to any physiological warning signs of anxiety or danger. If you feel your heart suddenly start to race; your breath quicken; the hair on your arms raise up; or your neck, chest, or upper back tense, these are all probably your warning signs of danger. You may also start to sweat or feel discomfort in the pit of your stomach. You may have a sensation that something bad is about to happen, almost a premonition, and become hyperalert, keyed up, scanning around for danger, aware of escape routes, and prepared to respond immediately. These physical manifestations of anxiety go together with anger, which is understandable, since "fight" is part of the fight-or-flight reflex, and adrenaline and anger go hand in hand. The "flight" part makes you feel a strong urge to get out of whatever situation or place you're in.

These reactions are not just about being prepared to fight an enemy or run away from danger. What they mean for a warrior is being prepared to respond to danger of any kind—for example, a fire, accident, natural disaster, or when someone is trying to break into your home. As a warrior, you're much better prepared to respond to danger than most people. This includes not panicking when something unexpected happens, and responding without hesitation in the most efficient way to protect yourself and others around you. Oddly, a sense of panic can happen when there is no danger, but when chaos breaks out, warriors often feel much calmer than non-warriors.

A warrior's body knows how to respond to threat and danger, and how to handle high anxiety, stress, and fear. Underlying many of the physiological reactions of anxiety is fear, although a warrior's perception and response to fear is different than the response of an untrained person. Warriors understand how to use fear to their advantage, to tune in to their level of fear as a warning signal, and then to dial up or down their level of alertness, tension, and awareness of potential threats. For example, in the combat zone, if a platoon drives through a sector where it was previously ambushed, all members of the team will tense up, even if they know the area was cleared and is now considered safe. Warriors don't talk much about being helpless or paralyzed by fear, but instead about how their training helps them to function effectively in the face of fear. Fear becomes almost a sixth sense.

The body's reaction to threat includes changes in alertness, mental attention, muscle tension, heart rate, and general anxiety. Being aware of these responses allows you to monitor yourself in whatever situation you may be in.

Anxiety and its associated physiological reactions are the surface manifestations of fear. It's important to be able to monitor your level of anxiety—it's the body's warning signal and protector—but having too much anxiety can lead to indecision and make it difficult to stay focused. With poor training, warriors are much more likely to succumb to anxiety (or the deeper emotion of fear), and this can jeopardize the mission and the lives of team members. Good training is designed to ensure that the warrior knows what to do in the face of fear.

The goal of this exercise is to develop greater awareness of your physiological reactions when you sense danger in relation to situations back home, and learn to monitor yourself better.

In your notebook (or in the space below) note a specific event or situation that happened recently that triggered a strong sense of danger or strong physiological reactions. Then list the physiological sensations you experienced:

Event/situation (What were you doing at the time? What happened?): _____

_____

_____

_____

_____

_____

_____

_____

Physiological sensations (e.g., heart rate, chest pressure, sweating, dizziness, nausea): _____

_____

_____

_____

_____

_____

_____

To learn to become more aware of your body's reaction to threat or danger, photocopy the following scale related to physiological reactions. Use this scale to keep track of your level of alertness, muscle tension, mental focus, heart rate, and overall anxiety distress. You can use this in three ways, to note: 1) how much anxiety you're carrying right now; 2) the highest level of anxiety that occurred over a period of time (such as over the course of a day); and 3) the highest level of anxiety that occurred related to a specific stressful situation, and how long this lasted.

Use this scale to monitor yourself over time, and when you do other exercises in this book. For example, once a day write in your notebook the highest level of physiological reactions that you experienced and how often it occurred. You can do this for any other time period as well, such as once a week.

Physiological Reactions Scale (circle)

Alertness:

1	2	3	4	5	6	7	8	9	10
Drowsy		Awake/Alert		Very Alert		Hyperalert/Keyed-Up		Super-Alert/Very Revved Up	

Muscle Tension:

1	2	3	4	5	6	7	8	9	10
Relaxed		Normal		Some Tension		Tense		Very Tense/Shaking	

Mental Focus/Attention:

1	2	3	4	5	6	7	8	9	10
Aware/Relaxed		Focused/Concentrating		Somewhat Distracted		Highly Distracted		Jumps Rapidly/Scanning	

Heart Rate:

1	2	3	4	5	6	7	8	9	10
Slow/Not Aware of Heart Beat		Normal/Not Aware of Heat Beat		Rapid/Not Aware of Heart Beat		Rapid/Aware of Heart Beat		Very Rapid/Pounding in Chest	

Distress/Anxiety:

1	2	3	4	5	6	7	8	9	10
None		Low		Moderate		High		Very High	

Date:_____

Reason for use:

_____ How I'm feeling now

_____ Highest level over course of: _____ Day, _____ Week, _____ Other

_____ Specific stressful situation, list: _____

Consider a "3" or "4" on each line of the physiological reactions scale to be generally a normal state of being awake, alert, and able to concentrate and focus with minimal distress or anxiety. At the lowest end of the scale, you feel sleepy, relaxed, or dull. At the highest end of the scale, your body is hyperalert, your muscles are tense, your mind may be jumpy or unable to focus on one thing, and you feel high anxiety or distress. Normally you should not be aware of your heartbeat, but when you're revved up, you're more likely to feel your heart racing or pounding. When you sense danger, or feel physiological reactions to a stressful situation, it's likely that you'll experience levels ranging from "5" to "10."

When there is danger, different things can happen to your focus and ability to pay attention. First, you may scan the environment around you for threats. The mind jumps rapidly from one thing to another, never settling on anything for long. You feel distracted and restless, and your mind doesn't stay still; a term that has been applied to this is "monkey mind." The second thing that can happen is your attention becomes like tunnel vision, focused *only* on one point or location where you think the greatest threat is. Both types of attention can be protective, and both can also be detrimental to your safety, depending on the situation. If your mind is so jumpy that you're unable to focus when you need to, or your head is swiveling from side to side or your eyes are darting rapidly, that can be bad; alternatively, if your focus is too much like tunnel vision, you may miss a threat from somewhere else. Warriors often shift back and forth between the more diffuse and focused attention, according to their training and the situation. For example, as warriors approach a building where there may be a target, their attention is focused not just on the building but also on scanning all sides, since they cannot be sure where the greatest threat is. When they enter the building, each member of the team becomes highly focused on the specific direction that they're supposed to cover.

There is another type of focus, which is neither jumpy nor tunnel-like. It's a wide relaxed focus, where your attention is largely oriented toward one direction—say, the building you are about to enter—but you're also tuned in to your peripheral vision and are aware of what is going on around you without looking quickly from side to side. This allows you to respond quickly to a threat in front of you and to threats from either side. The mind is also quieter and less jumpy. The wide relaxed focus is a skill that can be practiced, and will be covered later, in the section on meditation.

Sometimes after coming home, warriors lose their ability to concentrate or focus when their body sets off alarm signals, like a pounding heart. In combat, you know exactly what to do when your anxiety ramps up. Back home, when the anxiety warning bells go off it can be more difficult because you don't have a series of combat tasks or procedures to fall back on.

Most warriors are already in the habit of monitoring their environment for threats, but may not be in the habit of monitoring their own internal perceptions of threat. The physiological reactions scale is one tool for self-monitoring reactivity and anxiety, and if you find it helpful, keep track of where you fall on average throughout the day. Over the course of any day your level of alertness, attention, muscle tension, and heart rate will fluctuate, but on average you should not remain at the highest levels for too long. Obviously, during combat it's normal to be at the highest end of all of these scales, and it can be very difficult to wind down after combat missions.

Exercises will be presented in this and other chapters to help you modulate anxiety and physiological reactions. However, if you're experiencing a "10" on most or all of the physiological reactions day after day, then your body is acting like there's high danger or threat 24/7, just as it did in the war zone. This is a sign that you probably need to see someone for help. Being on high alert for a long time takes a tremendous amount of energy. Sleep is disrupted, and as discussed in the last chapter, poor sleep leads to being more revved up and irritable. There may be a strong urge to try to calm the body down with alcohol or other substances, but this just makes things worse. If the body stays on high alert for weeks or months, then it can become very difficult to reset, and over time this can lead to more chronic health problems, such as high blood pressure, cardiovascular disease, and memory difficulties.

In summary, the objective here is to develop an ability to be aware of how your body registers danger signals, and what sensations you can expect when you're revved up or when you perceive high threat or danger.

SKILL 2: LEARN TO PAY ATTENTION TO YOUR FEELINGS AND EMOTIONS

This skill involves learning to pay attention to your emotions and being aware of how many different emotions you may be feeling and how they fluctuate, shift, and change. Emotions are always changing in response to all the information coming in through our senses. Take a look at the following scale that includes common emotions and feelings, and mark how you feel right now. Make photocopies of this scale and paste them into your notebook, or refer to it to keep track of how you're feeling over time. There are no right or wrong answers. All emotions are equally valid. Learn to recognize them, whatever they are, and pay attention to how they change. You can experience various emotions over the course of a day and different emotions in the same moment. After stressful events, you can look back at what emotions you experienced at that time and how they changed after that. Be aware of your level of anger, and the fact that anger is often connected with other emotions; look deeper than anger to see what other emotions may be present.

The terms *feeling* and *emotion* are used interchangeably in this book. Some therapists distinguish between these two terms, with *feeling* representing a more internal process, and *emotion* being the outward manifestation of the feeling, but for our purposes, they mean the same thing. Additionally, there are no "positive" or "negative" emotions. Emotions are emotions. Only the behaviors that stem from them are "positive" or "negative."

Feelings/Emotions Scale
Ask yourself, "How am I feeling right now?" or "How have I been feeling overall today?" (circle the best answer)

	None		Low		Moderate		High		Very High	
Happiness/Joy	1	2	3	4	5	6	7	8	9	10
Love	1	2	3	4	5	6	7	8	9	10
Anxious/Stressed	1	2	3	4	5	6	7	8	9	10
Worried	1	2	3	4	5	6	7	8	9	10
Irritable/Angry	1	2	3	4	5	6	7	8	9	10
Afraid/Scared	1	2	3	4	5	6	7	8	9	10
Frustrated	1	2	3	4	5	6	7	8	9	10
Disgusted	1	2	3	4	5	6	7	8	9	10
Sad	1	2	3	4	5	6	7	8	9	10
Grieving	1	2	3	4	5	6	7	8	9	10
Depressed	1	2	3	4	5	6	7	8	9	10
Lonely	1	2	3	4	5	6	7	8	9	10
Hurt/Pain	1	2	3	4	5	6	7	8	9	10
Guilty/Ashamed	1	2	3	4	5	6	7	8	9	10
Contented	1	2	3	4	5	6	7	8	9	10
Grateful	1	2	3	4	5	6	7	8	9	10
Amused	1	2	3	4	5	6	7	8	9	10
Tired/Exhausted	1	2	3	4	5	6	7	8	9	10
Detached/Numb	1	2	3	4	5	6	7	8	9	10
Other (list) _____	1	2	3	4	5	6	7	8	9	10
Other (list) _____	1	2	3	4	5	6	7	8	9	10

Keep track of how your feelings change throughout each day. If your body is physiologically revved up a lot of the time, then the predominant emotion is likely to be anger. However, there are probably other emotions present along with the anger, and exploring them will help to reduce the effects of anger.

Feelings are fluid; they change and shift. For example, someone may be feeling lonely and depressed, but then suddenly feel happy when a friend calls. Sadness can change to amusement with humor, and laughter is one of the best coping strategies for difficult times. It's also perfectly reasonable to feel more than one emotion at the same time, even opposites, like happiness and gratitude along with grief and sadness. The point is to become attuned to the wide range of emotions you may be experiencing.

Special attention needs to be given to the emotion labeled "Detached/ Numb" on the chart. Feeling numb, detached, or not having emotions is also an emotion, or at least an emotional state, and one that often goes along with anger. Like anger, numbness and detachment can mask (or cover up) other emotions. If you register high on feeling numb, then pay attention to what other feelings may be underneath, like sadness, loneliness, or grief. Acknowledge your emotions and don't shut anything out.

There are times when it's necessary to shut emotions out and not acknowledge them. Combat veterans in particular understand this because in order to do an effective job on the battlefield, they have to keep their emotions in check. Spouses and partners also do this when their warriors are deployed so they're not overcome with fear or worry. However, if emotions aren't acknowledged, they have a tendency to push their way to the surface or act on the warrior's subconscious, leading to behavior the warrior may later regret. Because some emotions can be overwhelming at times, it's natural to want to lock them up and throw away the key. But this doesn't make them go away; they'll usually find other less healthy ways to express themselves. The place to begin is to acknowledge them. If they're overwhelming, try to lighten your burden by expressing them to a friend, pastor, therapist, spouse, or anyone you trust who'll listen without judgment.

It's important to understand the connection between physiological reactions, anxiety, anger, and fear. Fear is deeper and more difficult to identify. You may feel revved up, anxious, or angry, but unaware that fear exists underneath. In combat, warriors use fear as a "sixth" sense, but also learn to suppress it and keep it under control through training. Anger helps with this. Controlling fear is an important part of what it means to be a warrior.

If you marked high on the line "Afraid/Scared," you've demonstrated your ability to tune in to fear. If you marked this low, but marked high on "Anxious/Stressed," "Irritable/Angry," or "Worried," then check if there's fear as well. If it's present, then ask yourself, "What am I afraid of?"

Am I feeling afraid/scared/fearful?   Yes   No

If yes, what am I afraid of?_____

The answer is sometimes surprising. For example, fear of embarrassment, fear of being ostracized, or fear of being in a place where it's difficult to escape are prominent fears, often associated with panic or anxiety. Fear of being alone (connected to fear of being vulnerable) is deep-seated, and can make us act in crazy and paradoxical ways (for example, pushing people away we love, or ending a relationship because we're afraid that the other person will leave us). Fear of death is another.

Regarding fear, there is nothing specific that you need to do, other than become aware of it and recognize what you're afraid of. Fear can also exist with other feelings, such as being "Depressed." Fear drives a lot of behaviors, and awareness of this can help to create space between reactions and behaviors, which ties in to the next skill.

There are places on the Feelings/Emotions form to write in other emotions. Write down some additional words to describe how you feel. The list is long. Here are some examples: awe, anticipation, surprise, disappointment, apprehension, contempt, desire, longing, envy, lust, relief, apologetic, suffering, sympathy, empathy, compassion, vulnerable, caring, courage, wonder, gratitude, modesty, embarrassment, horror, relaxation, respect, appreciation, indifference, hate, hope, despair, pity, insult, outrage, calm, brave, ambivalent, stunned, confused, etc., etc. This is the human condition.

This skill is meant to help you get comfortable with your emotions and to give them room to express themselves. Emotions can coexist with one another. Some emotions can be more powerful than others. Subsequent chapters on narration, dealing with situations and people, and acceptance will add more depth to this subject.

SKILL 3: CREATE SPACE BETWEEN YOUR REACTIONS TO STRESSFUL EVENTS AND BEHAVIORS

An event or situation, like getting stuck in traffic, may lead to frustration, anger, increased alertness to danger, and a rapid heart rate. These are all *internal* processes. At this point, the warrior can either step back and not let the reactions build further or can get increasingly agitated; in other words, there are options here. The warrior may not be able to prevent how they react or feel initially, but has options for what to do based on those reactions. In First Sergeant Schindler's experience, he did this through always reminding himself to keep the frequency of his reaction low, the intensity mild, and the duration short. This is like counting to ten—common advice given for controlling responses to anger.

Obviously, if agitation continues to climb to the point of rage and running someone off the road, then this is no longer an internal process. External responses, actions, or behaviors have consequences, like getting arrested. The skill here is very simple, knowing that you have options in how you respond to your internal physiological reactions and feelings. You can get more agitated and run someone off the road, or you can accept the situation and live with it.

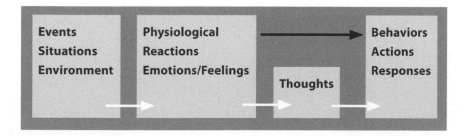

The practice of this skill involves putting space where the dark arrow is in the figure; i.e., monitor your physical sensations and feelings and realize you don't have to act on them. It's okay that your body doesn't like being penned in; that's normal for a warrior. It's okay to be frustrated and angry at traffic. Accept your feelings, but don't think you have to immediately act on the basis of these feelings. It may be hard, but the skill here is to accept and tolerate your emotions and develop patience.

Patience is a crucial skill in combat. You may have to wait out the enemy for days, weeks, or months before you strike, and it's not that different back home. However, many warriors completely forget this skill when they come home. They can't tolerate the stupid stuff people do, and instead of remembering to practice this skill (for example, in a supermarket line), they explode at relatively minor things.

Patience can be excruciating, but sometimes you don't have any other reasonable option. Maybe you can safely cut over the median strip without hurting anyone or damaging your vehicle and escape the snarled traffic, but it may not be possible. You may be stuck with the situation and have to deal with it. But as a warrior, you have the skills to do this. You may be cursing at yourself for not turning off earlier and taking a different route, but you obviously didn't have sufficient information at the time to see things differently, so what's the point of beating yourself up now? Again, the skill here is to be able to sit with your emotions and feelings and put space between them and your responses, to dial down the frequency, intensity, and duration of your responses so they are appropriate for the situation. You don't have to immediately change situations when you become uncomfortable. You can simply let your reactions and emotions exist without acting on them; eventually, they will subside or shift.

Here's another example: A friend of yours calls you up and tells you to meet at a certain time and place, but doesn't show up and then doesn't return your phone calls. This person has done this once or twice before. It would be natural in this situation to feel angry and hurt. It would also be natural to not like the fact that your friend didn't follow through on what they said they were going to do, wasting your time. In response, you can feel slighted and immediately assume that your friend has purposely betrayed you, fly into a rage, and do something you later regret, or you can have patience and weigh the options you consider possible (dial down the "frequency, intensity, and duration" of your response). The point is that there are usually options. You also may not know all the facts. Perhaps your friend didn't show up because of an accident, or perhaps you've known that this is the way your friend is but haven't accepted it, and keep expecting your friend to change. You don't have to respond to your friend's behavior immediately. At this moment you may be angry enough not to care if you destroy the friendship, but this feeling may shift over time.

Here's a final example: You're sitting in a bar with some friends and someone you don't know bumps into you, causes your drink to spill, and then doesn't apologize. Although you think it might be an accident, you can't be sure, because the person actually laughed a little as they pushed by you. You may feel angry, disrespected, and insulted that this individual wouldn't even acknowledge what they had done. So you've gone from the event (the person bumping you) to feelings (angry, disrespected, insulted). For some warriors, there would be no gap between their emotional response and further action. They would confront the person without giving it a thought, and this could immediately lead to a shouting match or fight. There might be a feeling of enjoyment in doing this. But is it worth the potential consequences of getting in a fight, such as possible injury, assault charges, and legal problems? Perhaps the person who bumped you was so drunk and out of it that they didn't realize what they did. Perhaps they actually did it on purpose and wanted to pick a fight. However, it may not be in your best interest to act in this way, no matter how satisfying it might seem to be. One of the key warrior skills is to know when it's necessary to fight and when a fight can be avoided. This is the path of the Samurai. This is wisdom. If the other person throws a punch or pulls a knife or gun on you, then all bets are off, but until that point, it may be unnecessary or undesirable to respond with force just because you were bumped and your drink got spilled. A warrior has nothing to prove.

SKILL 4: LEARN TO MONITOR AND ELIMINATE "SHOULD" AND RELATED WORDS OR PHRASES

In addition to paying attention to your feelings and emotions, another skill to learn is to pay attention to how negative thoughts may be contributing to making you feel worse or behave in ways that are detrimental. Often these happen automatically. Negative thoughts can lead directly to behaviors and can cause unhealthy physiological changes in your body. Emotions and thoughts are closely connected. In psychological terms, this skill is drawn from "cognitive therapy."

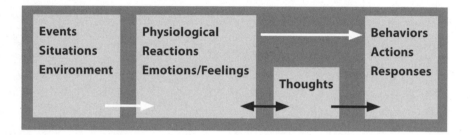

The skill is monitoring when you say to yourself: "should," "should have," "could have," "would have," "shouldn't have," "couldn't have," "wouldn't have," "what if," "if only," etc., and pick off each of these words or phrases with a cleanly targeted sniper round every time they pop up. These statements are ways we express regret, or punish, criticize, judge, blame, or place unrealistic expectations on ourselves. They refer to things in the past that can't be changed, but bother us enough to spend unreasonable amounts of energy on—sometimes a lifetime of energy.

"I *should have* been able to accomplish that goal" implies that if you *could have* accomplished the goal, things *would be* different (and somehow better). This diminishes you, sends you on a journey to the land of past what-ifs, and most important, fails to recognize the innumerable reasons why you were unable to accomplish the particular goal. Reasons like: more pressing things that needed to be done; unexpected events happening in your life; a lack of adequate instruction, training, or resources; an unsupportive family or upbringing; getting sick or injured; a family member getting sick or injured; someone not doing what they said they would do; financial difficulties; etc. The "should" statement above implies that I'm to blame for the outcome—that it's somehow my "fault" that I failed to accomplish the goal, and that somehow everything would be better *if* I had. All of this is pure projection, pure illusion.

Statements like "I shouldn't have done that" or "If only I had done that differently" express regret and blame. Even if these statements could be true, so what? It doesn't change anything, and ignores the myriad reasons why you, an imperfect and complex biological mass of cells, did what you did at that moment. Any more time spent in your thoughts going over this will only make you feel worse.

Decision-making is a complex task that involves examining what we feel, analyzing available information, and then acting on this basis. The problem is that our feelings may be mixed and unclear, and the information is almost certainly incomplete. Additionally, subconscious processes that aren't in our awareness may also affect the decision.

We can make decisions based on what we think will happen in the future or how we think we'll feel in the future, which we obviously can't know. We create stories to define who we are, and we attach some sort of rationale to whatever decision we make. However, this is rarely, if ever, the complete story. There are thousands of factors from our environment and our self (consciously and subconsciously) acting upon us that we can't fully comprehend, which contribute to the "decision" we think we ultimately make. Decision-making is incredibly complex and can't be simplified into any "should have" or "what if" statement.

This type of thinking goes on all the time as a result of combat. "*If* I had turned off earlier, we wouldn't have been ambushed." "I *should* have been able to tell that the road debris was an IED and stopped the vehicle in time." In these examples, the warrior is blaming himself for something that he most certainly had no power to change at that time. These statements express a belief that the warrior had the capacity at the time of the event to make a different decision, or *should have* been able to predict what was about to happen and avert it. It fails to take into consideration the thousands of things going on in the environment at the moment these events happened. The warrior feels like he failed and is solely to blame for any bad outcome. Holding onto and shouldering guilt and self-blame can be a significant part of PTSD and depression.

"Should haves," "would haves," "could haves," "what ifs," etc., come up all the time in daily life. When you experience reactions to stressful situations, one automatic response is to blame yourself in some way using one of these statements. "I *could have* taken a different turn and then I *would have* avoided this traffic jam." "I *should* be able to have better control over my reactions." "I *shouldn't have* come to the mall today." "I *shouldn't have* gone out with that person last night." "I *should have* taken the other job." "I *should have* spoken up." "I *shouldn't have* gotten married." These statements simplify a situation that is very complex, and support the feeling/idea that you had the power to make a different decision. These self-talk statements provide an *illusion* of control. They presume that somehow you *could have* had the same information that you have right now, and *could have* made a different decision at that time in the past. This is obviously a form of madness that only an organism with a massive cerebral cortex could come up with.

The more you attack, diminish, or punish yourself with these types of statements, the more depressed you're likely to become. Depression can be tied to sleep problems, anxiety, and anger, which is why this is so important. These self-talk statements affect behavior. The internal monologue of "shoulds" and "what-ifs," connected with emotional reactions, can lead to behavior that relates to "shoulds" that have nothing to do with what's going on now. Even if a "should have" or "shouldn't have" relates to something that happened only a few seconds or minutes ago, that's still something in the past that can't be changed. Acting on that is a recipe for disaster. As a warrior, you know that you don't want to act based on a "should" from a past event; in combat that would obviously be crazy. You want to act based on what's happening in this moment right now.

This skill is meant to help you recognize every time you say one of these "should" statements to yourself, and the degree to which you're punishing yourself with them. Think of these thoughts as pop-up targets and take them out.

SKILL 5: NOTICE YOUR BREATHING

Breathing is the most natural of processes and the simplest route to training your body to be less revved up and more relaxed; it's also a great way to
put space between your physiological/emotional reactions and behaviors.
Breathing serves to bring in oxygen and expel carbon dioxide and acids
that accumulate as a result of muscle exertion. The breath is naturally slow
and deep when we're relaxed or asleep, and increases when awake. Deep
slow breathing usually involves the diaphragm doing more of the work of
breathing than the chest, with air filling up the lower part of the lungs first.
The diaphragm is the large muscle located at the base of the lungs that
divides the chest from the abdomen. When we exercise, the rate of breathing increases, but generally remains deep to provide the oxygen necessary
to meet the increased demand. However, with high stress or anxiety, paradoxically, breathing may become very shallow, in addition to being rapid,
with muscles in the upper chest (and even neck muscles) doing more of
the work. Rapid and shallow breathing is one of the telltale signs of fear
and anxiety, and is called *hyperventilation*. Warriors often describe feeling
constricted in their upper chest or neck when they experience high anxiety or anger, which is accompanied by a rapid or pounding heartbeat.
Slowing the breath down, breathing deeper or lower, or simply becoming
aware of how you're breathing are important tools for controlling anxiety.

Contrary to popular belief, there is no "correct" or "incorrect" way to
breathe. Your body naturally breathes at the rate and depth that is most
efficient based on your level of exertion and oxygen needs. However, if
you know how to monitor yourself, you may discover that there are times
when breathing is initiated more in the chest and other times when it's initiated lower in the abdomen. Air can come in and out of the lungs because
of the actions of muscles in the chest, including those between each of
the ribs (intercostal muscles). Air can also come in and out of the lungs
because of the diaphragm beneath the lungs contracting downward into
the abdomen. You can experience both types of breathing. If you breathe
fully in through your nose with the idea of filling up your upper chest
completely, you'll mostly be using the muscles in your chest to breathe. If
instead you breathe fully in through your nose but think of the air filling

up your abdomen first, you'll probably be breathing lower down using the diaphragm. You can employ both types of breathing simultaneously by initiating the breath down in the abdomen and then expanding up into the chest. Sighing is one way for the body to increase the amount of air that is exchanged, and generally uses both the diaphragm and chest muscles.

It's common advice to "take a deep breath" when we experience anxiety, stress, or anger. This may seem like good advice, because breathing can become rapid and shallow (hyperventilation) when there is anxiety, and hyperventilation itself can increase the level of anxiety. However, the advice to "take a deep breath" isn't that simple, and most of the time people who give this advice don't understand exactly what this means. There are various ways that you can take a deep breath. You can breathe deeply into your chest or use your diaphragm to expand your abdomen. You can also experience rapid shallow breathing as a result of anxiety but think that you're already breathing deeply because the chest muscles are working so hard. Hyperventilation feels like deep breathing, and therefore being told that you should "take a deep breath" when you're already hyperventilating isn't sensible. You may get more out of smacking the person who's giving you this advice.

Better advice during times of stress is to "take a deep breath low in your abdomen," which is more specific than "take a deep breath." Anytime anyone pisses you off, you can take a deep breath low in your abdomen. If you start feeling anxious standing in a line, take a deep breath low in your abdomen. If traffic is snarled, take a deep breath low in your abdomen. If your boss or coworker comes up with some stupid plan that they think is fabulous but you know won't work, take a deep breath low in your abdomen.

Taking a deep breath from the abdomen, which is also called *diaphragmatic breathing*, is simple to do—just relax your abdomen and let the breath naturally expand it.

Here's how it works in a nutshell:

Start with sitting in a relaxed posture and place your feet on the floor. You may first want to release any muscle tension, as described in chapter 4, skill 3. Feel the weight of your body in the chair. (You can also lie on your back, and feel the weight of your body pushing against the bed or floor.)

Breathe in and out through your nose in a relaxed manner. Do this for at least a minute or two. Now place your hands one on top of the other on your abdomen and observe how it expands outward as you breathe in, slightly separating your hands apart. You may notice that after taking in a deep breath, you let it out over a slightly longer period than it took to bring the air in; relaxation occurs as you exhale. Diaphragmatic breathing simply means breathing slower and deeper from lower down in your abdomen, using your diaphragm to initiate the breath. But don't turn it into work. Let the abdomen naturally expand (get rounder) without forcing it. Don't push the abdomen out. Just let it expand on its own like air filling a balloon. You can also watch someone sleeping, especially a child, to get an idea of how this works.

It's best to practice breathing in a slower, deeper, lower, more natural "diaphragmatic" way at times when you're relaxed instead of waiting for those times when you become anxious. Once you've practiced this when you're relaxed, it'll be easier to do when you're tense or anxious.

Breathing isn't something you need to control. You can simply notice your breathing when you're relaxed without trying to change it in any way. All that's important is to observe or notice your breathing and be aware of whether you're initiating your breaths from deep in the abdomen or higher up in the chest. Get used to noticing this. As you become more practiced at observing your breathing when relaxed, then you'll be able to shift into this "noticing" mode during times when you feel stressed or anxious. This will make it easier to catch yourself breathing high up in your chest when you get anxious and shift to slower, deeper breathing to control your level of anxiety.

If you still have a difficult time doing the diaphragmatic breathing after the above description (or I haven't explained it well enough), try this exercise. Sit in a chair (you can stand or kneel if you like, but sitting is more comfortable), and imagine that you're holding a 9mm pistol (or another caliber of your choice). Now slowly raise the weapon and point it at the center of an object some distance away (use a neutral object, not a real or imaginary person). Do the actual motion with your arms, and concentrate on the target through the sights on your imaginary weapon with every intention of hitting it squarely. Now, very slowly release one round off by squeezing your trigger finger as you would in real life. Don't do this half-assed; do this just as if you had a real weapon in hand. Continue to hold the position and prepare for a second round. Now notice where you're breathing. Is your body still? In all likelihood you're breathing more quietly from down in your lower abdomen to minimize the amount of movement. You may stop breathing for a moment when you release the round, but otherwise, you'll probably find that you're breathing in a slower, more relaxed manner.

If you still find it difficult to do diaphragmatic breathing, have no worries. All you need is to become aware of your breathing without trying to change anything. Simply learning to notice your breathing without changing it can be enough to reduce anxiety levels.

SKILL 6: IMPROVE YOUR FOCUS AND ATTENTION THROUGH MEDITATION AND MINDFULNESS

Meditation, or the practice of being mindful, is an important warrior skill that can help with concentration, focus, attention, confidence building, and letting go of thoughts and feelings that may be fueling anger or anxiety or interfering with your happiness. Many books have been written about meditation, both as part of religious traditions and as secular practices to improve health and well-being. The term *mindfulness* has become popular in recent years, and is rapidly becoming part of mainstream medical treatment for depression, anxiety, pain, coping with chronic illness, and other medical problems.

What is mindfulness? It's turning your attention to the present moment without judgment, without goals, and without attachment to what's happening. It involves observing what's going on, quieting the mind, creating a sense of space, and allowing the mind to take a break from the usual chatter that characterizes mental processes involved in day-to-day activities—things like worrying about what needs to be done, keeping to-do lists straight in your head, worrying about something at work, or feeling anxious. Mindfulness means being present to what's in the "here and now," rather than thinking about what occurred in the past, or what may happen in the future. You can be mindful, or present in the moment, doing almost any activity.

The practice of meditation is one way to become more mindful, and can be very helpful in controlling anxiety, reducing worry, decreasing the feeling of being revved up, and improving confidence, focus, and attention. Meditation provides insight into how your mind works. There are two main types of meditation practices: 1) *focused meditation*, where you focus your mind on something; and 2) *open awareness meditation*, which involves observing or witnessing whatever is going on in the present moment without a specific focus. Meditation can be done sitting, lying, standing, or walking, but the most common posture is sitting. The simplest posture for meditation is to sit comfortably in a chair with your feet flat on the floor, arms in your lap (or on armrests), and your spine supported in such a way that it's as erect as possible. You can also sit cross-legged on the floor with your butt raised up on a cushion and your legs and feet resting against the floor. The cushion under you helps to lift the spine into a more comfortable upright posture. You can position your hands face up, one on top of the other in your lap, facedown with your forearms resting on your knees, or a combination of these two positions, with one hand in your lap and the other over a knee. It's good to practice meditation with your eyes open as well as closed. The time that you allow for meditation is entirely up to you, but doing a specific practice—for example, twenty minutes several times a week, or five to ten minutes every day—does help to make it become a routine skill that you incorporate into your daily life.

A) Focused meditation: A common focused meditation is to observe your breathing as it moves in and out. Close your mouth and breathe through your nose. Whenever your mind wanders, as it's prone to do, bring it back to the breath. The only goal is to keep your attention on your breathing and gently bring it back whenever you become distracted or your thoughts wander. You can silently say "inhale-exhale" or "in-out" if you want, but this isn't necessary. Don't get upset with yourself when your mind wanders, because that's exactly what the mind does, and one of the key skills is to become aware of how your mind works and allow whatever happens to occur without judgment.

You can also put an object in front of you to focus on, such as a picture, a bowl of water, a candle, a rock, a flower, or anything (even a roll of toilet paper). Alternatively, you can repeat a word, phrase, or sound (a mantra) out loud or in your head. First Sergeant Schindler's "frequency, intensity, duration" exercise is a sort of mantra that helps him to be mindful during stressful experiences or situations that may lead to anger. It helps him to be present with his feelings and not immediately act on those feelings. The goal, again, is simply to find something that you feel comfortable paying attention to. Whenever your mind wanders, just bring it back to the object of awareness. An example of mantra meditation is to select a sound/word like "Om," or any phrase that is meaningful to you. Initially say it out loud, and then gradually make it softer and softer until you're only repeating it in your mind. For all subsequent practice the word or phrase is repeated silently. To do this, gently "toss" the word or phrase into your mind. When it gradually fades away, gently repeat it. Don't focus or concentrate too much on it; make it as effortless and easy as possible. An example of a walking meditation is to walk slowly in a circle in a small area or outside in a larger area and keep your focus and attention on each step.

B) Open awareness: This practice involves observing whatever is going on in the present moment, in an open manner, without judgment, and without attaching to what's happening. For example, sit comfortably with your eyes open but not focused on anything particular. Allow all sounds, images, thoughts, feelings, and sensations that you become aware of to exist, but don't dwell on them, don't think about them, don't hold on to them, and don't follow them. Thoughts may come up like, "I have so much I have to do today" or "Oh, I forgot that I still have that thing to take care of," or "What was I thinking when I said that?", or "I better not be late," or "That really pissed me off." When thoughts like these arise, just allow them to pass on, like they are part of a movie reel or a branch floating by on a river. You're not trying to eliminate thoughts or have a "blank mind," nor are you engaging with them in some active way; instead, just allow your thoughts to exist on their own and remain in an open state of consciousness or awareness. Don't follow a thought on to the next one, or the one after that. Just let each thought pass. The same is true for feelings, or anything else that occurs during the time of your meditation. If you feel worry or anxiety, let it pass. If your phone rings, let it ring. If there is noise outside, that's okay; notice it, but don't dwell on it. There is no goal, other than to allow everything to exist as it is now without trying to change it and without judgment. Similar to the focused meditation, when your mind wanders off into a string of thoughts, then consciously let go of that line of thinking and just bring your attention back to the moment.

This type of meditation can actually be practiced in normal day-to-day situations to control anxiety, along with "take a deep breath low in your abdomen." For example, if you're in a tense meeting where opinions are being argued back and forth, you can shift into a more observing mode without judgment and with awareness of your breath. This doesn't preclude jumping in and saying whatever you need to say or taking sides. You don't have to be detached from what's happening. But neither are you *attached* to any specific outcome. You can be there, state your position, but not get caught up or angry if things don't go the way you suggest. Ultimately you may have very little control over what happens. It is what it is. This exercise, which is really just a quality of observing, allows you to recognize that most things in life that we take very seriously are, in the end, not very important, and situations that evoke conflict are often much ado about nothing. You can step back and not become so attached to any one position or outcome.

One attention skill that can be practiced as a meditation and also has applicability for combat or other stressful situations is to sit comfortably and look at a point or object a short distance away (say ten to twenty feet in front of you), but instead of focusing directly on the object, focus your eyes on an imaginary point just in front of or just beyond the object, so that the object itself is slightly out of focus. Then, without moving your eyes, notice how much you can see on either side of the object in your peripheral field of vision. The idea is to keep your eyes oriented toward the object but your awareness much wider. Become aware of everything in your full field of vision on either side of the object, as well as above and below it. Expand your awareness to the whole room, or as far as your peripheral vision will allow—again, with no goal and no judgment.

If you practice this wide relaxed focus, you'll notice how useful it can be during times of crisis or danger. During high-stress situations (and even combat), being able to pay attention to an immediate threat in front of you, while at the same time being aware of what's going on peripherally, can be very useful. This type of focus prevents you from getting pulled into tunnel vision or into a highly distracted state where your mind is jumping or scanning rapidly from one thing to another (monkey mind). This practice allows you to stay relaxed, aware of the immediate threat in front of you, and also to maintain awareness of what's happening around you.

Another great example of an open awareness meditation is to sit and listen to all the sounds that are around you with minimal thought. Simply pay attention and listen, taking in all the sounds exactly as they are. There may be birds outside, the hum of electrical appliances, a phone ringing, voices, wind, a plane overhead, the sound of a car door, a motorcycle, a lawn mower, children playing, an ambulance siren, etc. Sounds are all around you, and this meditation is simply to listen quietly and appreciate them as they are.

You can also add visualization to your meditation to deepen the level of relaxation. Sit (or lie) comfortably and close your eyes. Take a deep slow breath, take another deep slow breath, take a third deep slow breath, and as you let the air out on the third breath, allow yourself to "float" or feel lighter. Breathe naturally and imagine that you're sitting or lying next to a stream, near the ocean, or any place you'd enjoy. Use all your senses to visualize being in that location; imagine how it looks, feels, sounds, smells, and tastes. Set the temperature, time of day, and weather just the way you like it. If the sun is out, feel its warmth. If you prefer cool weather, feel the coolness. Engage all of your senses in this exercise. Literally picture yourself at the location of your choice. After doing this for as long as you would like to, then tell yourself to gradually come back to the present location. Take a couple more deep breaths, then open your eyes and return to the present time and place.

Watching a sunset, walking in the woods, looking out over the ocean, fishing in a lake or stream, hiking a beautiful trail, taking a drive in the country, listening to music, gardening, hunting, camping, playing with your dog or cat, dancing, or doing anything that brings you joy, are all opportunities for meditative moments when you can let go of the chatter of your mind, take a break from worries, and experience a sense of peace. Choosing to hang out and do nothing in particular (with no requirement that you "should" be engaging in some other activity) is another great way to enjoy the moment. The idea is to do things sometimes that aren't filled with distractions, a sense of urgency, or demands for your attention. Sometimes, simply *being* is the most constructive and beneficial thing to do for yourself.

Meditation isn't a mystery. It can be easily incorporated into your daily life. The goal of meditation is to become comfortable just being in the moment, which includes not having any goal. The goal of meditation is not to improve yourself, grow, become a better person, reach spiritual enlightenment, gain greater confidence, reduce anxiety, or anything else. The goal is to have no goal, and any results or changes that occur from meditation are gifts to be grateful for. Meditation can improve focus and concentration, and create a sense of gratitude and appreciation for the little things in life, as well as a sense of compassion or a desire to help others. It can lead to a state in which you're less self-conscious and more comfortable and accepting of yourself. But not having any goal is what opens the door to these possibilities.

SUMMARY

In conclusion, this chapter covers several training exercises to help you utilize your warrior skills in a healthy way after coming back from a war zone. The skills include learning to pay attention to your physical reactions, anxiety level and feelings and emotions, creating space between your internal reactions and actions, monitoring the use of "should" statements, noticing your breath, and practicing meditation training. These exercises are all tools you can use depending on your situation and what works best for you. You can tailor them to whatever suits your needs. You can pick the skills that seem to work, or notice how what you're doing already fits in with the skills presented here.

Additional advice from First Sergeant Schindler:

My routine for almost thirty years was that whenever I walked into a building, doctor's office, house, restaurant, etc., I mentally completed my combat-ready checklist: threat assessment, weapons check, and escape. If a store clerk didn't give me what I thought was good service, I treated the clerk like the enemy.

For nearly thirty years while in the Army and Army Reserves, anger was a constant. I had a major case of the ass, and authority was, by definition, the enemy. Attending to my physical reactions, learning why I reacted to things differently than civilians who had never gone into combat, was a challenge. Checking out the AO [Area of Operations]*, patrols, ambushes, firefights, night-guard duty, life, and death are the experiences of combat. In combat you become close to your buddies, closer than anyone in your life. If you lose a buddy, the grief and rage are off the charts. Add those experiences and feelings together with your combat skills of threat assessment, marksmanship, strength, stamina, mental toughness, detachment, and bloodlust, and you have the potential for a wide range of emotions and reactions to come spilling out of you all at once.*

In combat, in a split second you could go from telling a story and laughing with your buddies to a hellacious life-and-death firefight that possibly caused the death of your best friend in a horrible way. To top that off, you have grief, which you won't feel right away. Grief is an unpredictable emotion. If you lose any buddies in combat, there is no way to know when you will feel grief. You could be at home talking with friends, seeing a movie, or taking a shower when some small "thing" will snap your memory back into combat mode and you suddenly begin to cry, get angry, feel scared, detached, or want to crawl into a hole and shut the world out. These types of reactions and feelings are the direct result of your combat experiences. Such reactions and feelings can be so overwhelming that you feel your heart jump, you break out into a cold sweat, or you "freak out" from anxiety.

Learning how to fit back into the "real world" can be a daunting, sometimes scary, and difficult task. Learning how your reactions connect to your combat experiences is possibly the most difficult challenge. One can't just go from combat warrior to civilian overnight. After thirty years of living this way, my healing began with the "tool" that I described previously, of saying the words "frequency, intensity, and duration" over and over in my mind. This mental exercise allowed me to pay attention to and handle situations directly and with more-positive outcomes.

For years my inner demons and I had epic "battles," trying to feel normal and not feel like I was on the outside looking in. Therapy and self-determination are the tools that helped me through some evil times. I learned to apply the skills from combat to my blueprint for living a positive lifestyle. What has worked for me is to think and say to myself "frequency, intensity, duration" in respect to keeping the reactions of anger, stress, depression, guilt, and fight-or-flight tendencies to manageable, acceptable, low, mild, and short levels.

Soon after learning how to use this tool, life for me lightened up. I began to notice my willingness to be more engaged with family and friends, and to do more healthy outdoor activities and to meet new friends. This exercise is a daily habit now. Constant vigilance and determination is my path to sanity in an insane world. My personal mental exercise to think "I will keep the frequency, intensity, and duration—low, mild, and short" allows me to not strangle the store clerk, run for the hills, withdraw from life, be emotionless, or act or speak in a self-destructive manner. It allows me to be free from the burdens of anger, guilt, depression, and hyperalertness, and to allow myself to do more things that make me feel happy.

CHAPTER 6
NARRATE YOUR STORY

This chapter contains a very simple message having to do with the importance of telling your story in a way that's comfortable for you.

LANDNAV LEARNING OBJECTIVE: NARRATE— LEARN TO NARRATE YOUR STORY

It's natural for warriors not to want to talk about things that happened in combat, because they don't want to think about it themselves and they know that most people are not capable of comprehending what they went through. Warriors sometimes feel like they re-experience combat events when they talk about their experiences, including physical sensations like heart pounding, nausea, or emotions that are overwhelming. As a result, they avoid sharing their stories.

On the other hand, there's also a strong urge to tell one's story. Since the beginning of history, narration (or storytelling) has been one of the most important rituals after returning from war, and ancient war stories—such as the story of Achilles—are still relevant today. The importance of narrating one's story explains why there are thousands of books and articles written by U.S. warriors about their experiences in World War I, World War II, Korea, Vietnam, Gulf War 1, Somalia, Panama, Bosnia, Kosovo, and now OIF and OEF, as well as books by warriors from other nations recounting events from hundreds of other military campaigns. I believe that narration is essential for making a successful transition home. Telling your story doesn't mean spilling your guts to just anyone, but finding a way that best suits your style and level of comfort.

Why Narration Helps
Why does narration help? There are no clear answers to this question, but there are a lot of things that are associated with narration that seem to

be important; for instance, connecting emotions and feelings with events. When warriors wall off their emotions, it can negatively affect other things in their lives. An important component of narration is recognizing that you're not alone in your experiences. Even if the person you're sharing with has no experience with the military, they may have had other life experiences that can help them to relate to yours. Wartime experiences are some of the most profound that humans can endure. War evokes both what is most terrible and most divine about being human. War brings out the best and the worst in us. Sharing stories and feelings that are painful is a very personal experience and can bring you close to the person you share them with. Narration helps you to live with your experiences and move forward with them as part of you.

Probably the most important thing that narration does is allow you to express your emotions and feelings in words. One of the skills from the last chapter is learning to monitor your emotions internally, acknowledge how you feel, and when necessary, put space between your immediate feelings and actions. The limitation of this skill is that it's very difficult to know exactly how you feel unless you have someone to talk with. We need feedback from others. We need to struggle to come up with the right words to express our feelings, and it's very difficult or impossible to do this alone. In order to even acknowledge our deepest feelings, we need to know that there is someone who cares and who's willing to listen without judgment as we struggle to express ourselves. This is the power of narration, and the reason why ministers, rabbis, and therapists will always be able to make a living. There is something very healing in being able to put our experiences, thoughts, emotions, and feelings into words.

There are considerable data from the mental health community on the importance of narrating your story. Various studies have shown that the single most important component of therapy for PTSD and many other mental health problems is having the opportunity to speak with someone who is concerned, caring, and empathetic. Of all the different treatments for PTSD that have been tested, the most consistently effective involve narrating the story of the traumatic event(s) in some way so that the story becomes part of who you are.

Narration in Therapy

In one of the most popular forms of treatment, called *exposure therapy*, the therapist asks the client to recount the worst traumatic event(s) repeatedly until the level of reactivity, anxiety, or hurt surrounding the events becomes bearable. By revisiting the memories of the trauma in the therapy sessions, they become less intrusive, and nightmares, flashbacks, and other symptoms subside. By telling the therapist the details of the traumatic events, the memories become organized in a more coherent narrative way, and this coincides with a decrease in distressing symptoms. An important technique used in exposure therapy is called "imaginal" exposure, which is a terrible name because talking about painful traumatic memories does not in any way feel like it's "imagined." Nevertheless, mental health professionals have adopted the term *imaginal exposure* to describe a common technique used to help the client talk about traumatic memories.

Classic imaginal exposure involves the client recounting the painful traumatic event(s) in the present tense with eyes closed, as if the event(s) is going on right now. For example, a warrior in therapy might say, "I'm the gunner in the third vehicle of a convoy and we're headed back to our outpost. The vehicle in front of mine is hit with an IED on its left side. We stop and dismount and start pulling security. Just after getting out, a second IED goes off under my vehicle. I'm thrown against a wall and can't see anything for a few seconds. I hear screams. Smoke is all around me . . ." Although this warrior is talking about an actual event that he experienced months (or years) earlier, the therapist has asked him to recount it as if it's going on now. The therapist provides support and positive feedback, asks for clarification, and helps the warrior learn to cope with distressing emotional and physiological reactions. The therapist then asks the warrior to start over again and repeat the story. The warrior is asked to add in as much detail as possible, including the sights, sounds, and smells of the experience. This process is repeated over several sessions. Sometimes an audio recording is made of these sessions, and the warrior is asked to listen to the recording between sessions.

One may rightfully think that it's completely nuts to repeat combat stories over and over, much less go home and listen to a recording of yourself doing this. Indeed, those who undergo exposure therapy often feel very upset when they start treatment because the stories can be extremely painful. They often feel a strong urge to leave treatment immediately and never return, trying to avoid anything that reminds them of the trauma. There may be tears, anger, and anxiety that occur while remembering the experiences. However, studies show that the treatment reduces their symptoms and anxiety if they stay with the therapy long enough for it to be effective. One issue is that most of the research on this has been done in civilian populations, primarily with victims of assault and rape, and modifications to this treatment are probably needed for warriors.

When warriors start to tell their stories, it's common for them to describe the most horrific and painful combat events in a completely matter-of-fact, nonemotional, and neutral way. This is understandable, since shutting down emotions is an important skill in combat, which the warrior may have applied during the very events they describe. Once the story is explored in more detail, the events become better connected to the emotions.

The first time the story is told, it's common for many details to be left out; events might be presented like random photo images unconnected in any logical sequence. For example, the warrior might say, "The IED explodes. Smoke is all around me. All I hear is screams. I'm against a wall. I'm pulling security . . ." Feelings or reactions, and the fact that the story may be disjointed when first told, are expected during the narrative process. The therapist's job is to establish the environment that facilitates the warrior telling their story in a more linear way.

What happens after telling the same story in sufficient detail is that the memories of the traumatic events gradually become more organized, and the warrior finds that they can tell the story both with more emotion and connection (if initially detached) and with more acceptance and less distress in the form of guilt, self-blame, anxiety, or physical symptoms. This doesn't mean that the events become any less painful, just that the warrior becomes better able to tolerate and talk about them without reacting as strongly. Telling your story may *feel* to your body initially like being back in combat, but over time it helps to make the events part of you, rather than keeping them separate, buried, or avoided. When sessions are recorded and you listen to them (which, understandably, no one likes doing), this provides unique feedback that helps take some of the sting out of very painful stories and allows the stories to be better integrated into who you are.

It's not clear what components of talking about traumatic memories or feelings in therapy are most helpful. Although therapists utilizing imaginal exposure therapy usually encourage warriors to tell their story in the present tense with their eyes closed, as if it were going on right now, the reality is that most of the time warriors share their stories in the past tense with eyes open. How often a story needs to be told is unclear. Therapy doesn't work if the client recounts the traumatic story only once or twice. It's necessary to tell the story enough times to flesh out the details, express emotions, and integrate it.

The Narrative Experience

Although narrating the story has been shown in research studies to help, there is poor understanding of what it really means for narration to be effective, or what elements of the interaction between a warrior and the therapist listening to the story are most beneficial toward the goal of being able to live with very painful experiences. Additionally, very few studies have been conducted with warriors; most of the research on this type of treatment has involved civilian patients who were victims of trauma, such as assault, rape, motor vehicle accidents, or natural disasters. The premise underlying this form of therapy might be incorrect.

The reason this therapy may work better than others is that it most strongly emphasizes sharing your story. Therapists who do imaginal exposure therapy believe that repeatedly telling the story leads to the client's body and mind learning that there isn't a need to react to the story like it's the actual traumatic event (a process termed *habituation*). However, what's probably most important is the personal connection with someone (in this case, the therapist) who's engaged, nonjudgmental, and sincerely cares about helping you work through your very painful personal experiences. The benefit might have nothing to do with the number of times the story is repeated, but because recounting the story to someone who is supportive leads to a willingness to explore the details. Through this process, the warrior develops a greater understanding of exactly what happened, and no longer has to hold on to the guilt, self-blame, depression, anxiety, or rage surrounding the story. The story also gets connected to things that happened before and after the event and becomes part of the larger narrative of the warrior's life. The story stops having a "life of its own" and starts being one of many important stories over the course of the warrior's life.

Therapists need to have high situational awareness for how they come across in this (or any) type of therapy. If they try to administer the therapy as a "technique" in an overly neutral, impartial, or detached manner, or in a way that seems to the warrior to minimize or trivialize their story (such as making statements that reveal subtle assumptions or judgments), things are not likely to go well. If a trusting and supportive relationship hasn't been established, launching into imaginal exposure (or any other treatment for PTSD) could make things worse.

Most PTSD treatment has been tested in civilians, and there's no "off the shelf" technique that's guaranteed to work for warriors. The therapist needs to meet the warrior where they are, and do whatever is necessary to ensure that the warrior feels understood and supported while telling their story, and comfortable returning to continue their journey. Most important are empathy, compassion, and meeting the warrior where they are. There will be more on the topic of navigating the unique insanity of the mental health system in chapter 8.

In my experience, therapeutic benefit seems to come from a genuine interest in exploring the details of what happened and clarifying points of confusion in an empathetic way. For example, I remember a combat medic I treated who described a horrific event when he lost a close friend who was hit with a rocket-propelled grenade in Iraq. He attempted to keep his friend alive but was unsuccessful, and carried intense guilt for years after the incident. It wasn't until we probed deeper into the story that he began to let go of some of his guilt. I discovered that when he initially told the story, he left out the fact that he kept his friend alive all the way back to the aid station and into the operating room. We probed the specific details of why CPR would have been fruitless in this situation given how catastrophic the wound was and the amount of blood loss that had occurred. Over several sessions numerous details emerged related to this incident. For instance, the convoy commander made a command decision to send the vehicles back through the "kill zone" at considerable risk, in an effort to get the casualty back to definitive treatment as quickly as possible. The medic had been blaming himself for failing to save his buddy when the story clearly indicated that he had acted heroically as part of a team effort to save this soldier. Telling the story was painful and difficult, but after several sessions there was a sense of relief and a greater understanding that he didn't need to blame himself anymore. Narrating the story did not take away any of the grief related to losing his buddy, but it did bring this soldier closer to his grief, which was helpful.

There is a paradoxical process that happens after experiencing a traumatic event, which was mentioned in chapter 5 in the skill related to "shoulds." Often a person who has experienced a significant trauma, such as a warrior who loses a buddy in combat, will go over the event in his mind repeatedly for days, weeks, months, or years, as if the mind itself is trying to undo the event or figure out how the outcome could have been different if some small thing had been changed. Warriors who have experienced serious traumatic events will repeatedly look at the myriad ways things could have gone differently, think of things that they or others could (or should) have done to respond to the situation, and maybe alter the outcome, or ask in various ways why it happened (for example, "Why him and not me?"). These mental processes can run very deep, consume hours of time and energy (often during sleepless nights), and be tightly wrapped up with depression, guilt, self-blame, rage, and, in some cases, suicidal thoughts.

Blaming yourself for what happened and going over the event repeatedly in this way does serve a useful purpose. In the case of the warrior who loses a battle buddy, it helps the warrior to cope with and control very deep and painful emotions and thoughts related to the tragedy. Grief and survivor's guilt will be fully addressed in chapter 9.

Paradoxically, even though the warrior goes over the story repeatedly in their own mind, this doesn't automatically lead to a desire to talk about it with anyone else. The story may feel too difficult to share, or the warrior feels like no one could possibly understand what happened, or that they need to figure it out on their own. The warrior may not be ready to accept what happened, and feels that talking about it means facing very painful emotions; there may be worry about losing control. Consequently, the warrior may keep going over the event, avoid sharing it with anyone else, and stay stuck in this never-ending feedback loop. Through sharing what happened with someone else, the warrior ultimately is able to accept what happened, express the painful emotions, and begin the healing process of integrating the experiences into who they are now. This speaks directly to what narration is all about and why it's so important.

Sometimes facts change during the narrative process. As a story becomes more organized with details and a linear time line, the warrior may start to discover that they aren't really sure about the exact sequence of events. This can be incredibly disorienting because these stories take on a life of their own and become "true." One warrior told me, "What I have in my mind is so hard to put into words. It's like everything is right there, but then I go to write it down and it's completely different or not even there anymore." When the warrior realizes that they can't be exactly sure of what happened, especially after going over an event in their mind for weeks, months, or years, this can be a truly confusing moment. The moment of confusion is actually very healing because it indicates the break in the endless feedback loop that had been going on in the warrior's mind.

On a neurological level, traumatic memories are not stored in the part of the brain dealing with facts, rational thinking, or time. Traumatic memories are stored in the limbic system so they can be instantly retrieved, ensuring that protective reflexes take over immediately upon any reminder of the events. Not being connected to time is why a flashback can feel just as real as if the combat event had just taken place. As traumatic stories are narrated, these memories are connected with the parts of the brain having to do with time and sequence. This creates conflict because memories are never perfect representations of what actually happened. Memories are simply what our brains were capable of processing at the time the event(s) happened, combined with what we think happened as we look back or recount the event to ourselves or others, combined with thoughts and feelings surrounding our beliefs about what happened, including what we *would like* to have happened (which may subconsciously be tied to what we think *should* have happened differently). When time is introduced into traumatic memories, it sometimes becomes very difficult to remember exactly what the true sequence of events was. It's important for the therapist to reassure the warrior that such confusion about exactly what happened is normal.

The above description is intended to help you understand the importance of narration and how narration may occur during encounters with therapists. There are other techniques that therapists use to ask clients to share their stories, including writing about them, or focusing more on the beliefs and thought processes connected with them. These treatments will be discussed further in chapter 8.

Fundamentally, most effective therapies for PTSD involve telling the story of the traumatic events in one way or another so that they become more tolerable and bearable. Storytelling is an important part of what it means to be human, and there's nothing more powerful in alleviating suffering or distress than sharing what's happened with someone you trust and respect and you feel understands and cares about you. The important take-home message is that telling your story can help a great deal in the transition home from combat. Narration helps us to learn that we are greater than our stories, and that each story is only one of many that we carry. There is ample evidence of the value of narration from medical literature on effective therapies for PTSD, but this is also obvious given the importance of storytelling and narration related to war in rituals, literature, and history since the dawn of humanity.

TELL YOUR STORY IN A WAY THAT'S MOST COMFORTABLE FOR YOU

There is no specific exercise to learn in this chapter. Just find your own way to tell your story and express how you feel in words. You can choose to use a professional therapist, minister, rabbi, mentor/teacher, or to share your stories and feelings with a buddy, friend, or loved one who you trust. You can do this in person or write about it. You can write a journal, book, or start a Web site or blog. If you write, it's preferable to share your writing with someone in a way that allows for personal connection and feedback. There's no rule about how to do this; just find what works for you. Don't avoid telling your story or sharing your feelings with others, no matter how strongly you feel like locking them up and throwing away the key. You have many more stories than the ones from your war-zone experiences, and you are much more than any of your stories. Honor them. Trust yourself.

How you tell your story will change somewhat depending on whom you share it with. Talking with a professional, such as a therapist or chaplain, doesn't have the same feeling or quality as talking with a close friend or combat buddy. Sometimes talking with a professional can be easier, because the professional may be more neutral or less judgmental than a person you're close to. However, the professional may be too neutral, too bound up in a particular medical, psychological, or religious perspective (which can feel judgmental), or not be personable or available in the way that you need. A spouse, partner, close friend, or other family member will probably be able to give you the most sustained level of close support, but may not have the military experience, or it may feel like they're *too* close. Warriors often want to protect the people closest to them from their most difficult memories. Spouses and partners, on the other hand, generally want to know something about what happened. Whether or not the story is shared, the spouse or partner will likely *feel* it in the warrior, and it can be difficult if the warrior isn't willing to entrust them at least with how their experiences are currently affecting them. Spouses/partners need to understand that it's okay for warriors to hold on to the stories most difficult to tell; warriors need to understand that their spouses need some information, even if it's not the whole story. The best thing is to talk about this openly so that each person understands and respects each other's views and comfort level. There are no rules about this, other than to mutually support one another.

Whether it's a professional, spouse, partner, wartime buddy, or friend, there is usually someone (or more than one person) to relate to, and with whom you can feel comfortable. Whoever this is, isn't as important as finding a way to share your stories with someone in a way that works for you. Another way to give yourself some more feedback is to record your story and then listen to it. Although it can be unpleasant to listen to yourself, it can be very beneficial to hear and feel how you express yourself.

There is no experience quite like exchanging war stories with wartime buddies who all speak the same language, and who clearly understand the full range of experiences. Warriors look out for each other, whether they're in combat or back home, and it's not uncommon to feel like the only people who really can understand you are your own unit members or others who deployed to the same war zone. Also, the warrior's story is part of a collective narrative that is much larger than any individual one, and the warrior can feel very alone if they don't have contact with unit members. One warrior told me, "Even though each person on my team experienced the identical situations, they each saw them differently or remembered certain details that another had forgotten or didn't realize had actually happened. Everyone together completed the story, just like little pieces of a puzzle complete a giant picture. That is why I had a difficult time when I left my unit. Instead of being a complete 'picture,' I went to being one small piece that alone didn't make much sense."

There are some concerns with regard to sharing your stories with fellow warriors. Some things that no one wants to talk about but need to be discussed may be collectively censored by fellow warriors. When warriors get together there's often a large amount of alcohol consumed, which can be fun, but may end up being counterproductive. There may be a tendency to shift conversation away from the real issues to dark humor, or to fall into familiar unit roles or rank structures—all the things that worked well in combat. A "drive on" attitude may not be what you need. When warriors get together there may be a "ramping up" of collective anger toward the "they" of the VA, military, or society. Also, warriors can be very critical of each other if they perceive that anyone is exaggerating or bending the truth, or when differences in stories exist among those who were together in combat.

Basically, sharing your stories with buddies can be terrific, but may have limitations. It's important to narrate your story in a way that allows you to feel free of inhibitions or judgments, so you can experience whatever feelings or emotions exist, and achieve a sense that your story is part of who you are, and that you're more than your story. Talking with fellow warriors is an age-old tradition that offers the huge advantage of communicating with people who have a clue about what you went through, but make sure that your narrative experience allows you to fully address things that are personal, difficult to bring up, and are connected with the strongest emotions.

In conclusion, the bottom line here is to find a way to tell your story. Make your story a part of who you are. Don't bury it or lock it up.

The following is a brief narrative by First Sergeant Mike Schindler related to his transition home. It's his attempt to model what I am asking you to do. Enjoy his story:

The sentence that changed me and my life forever was, "Congratulations, Michael Sean Schindler—you have been selected by your local draft board to serve in the United States Armed Forces. Please report to Fort Wayne, Michigan, at 0800 hrs July 12th, 1969." From this point on I was in the U.S. Army. The white tiger was born July 13, 1969, at Fort Knox, Kentucky. The event was my first "formation" around 0430 hrs before dawn when my Army basic training drill instructor came into my barracks and rocked my world loudly and rudely by yelling at all of us newly sworn-in recruits to get our no-good, stupid, worthless asses outside in formation— music to my ears. I say that because of pure excitement and the feeling that I was at the beginning of a life-changing adventure.

Not to mention that I was away from my dysfunctional family, which included my alcoholic World War II combat veteran dad who had served in the Battle of the Bulge with General Patton (and who eventually at age fifty-seven committed suicide by drowning in Pearl Harbor), my two brothers, my sister, and my hardworking nurse mom who struggled to hold everything together. I loved both my parents and my brothers and sister. But escaping that insanity was good for me, even if that meant letting myself be "selected" by my local draft board. I was willing to do anything to get myself out of town, and I figured that the Army, even Vietnam, would be a better situation. Thus began my twenty-eight-year Army and Army Reserves career.

I arrived in Vietnam on December 12, 1969, and was assigned to Company A, 1st Battalion 27th Infantry (Wolfhounds) Regiment in Chu Chi. My first baptism by fire (firefight) happened Christmas Eve 1969. My first of many horrible combat experiences was to trip and fall face-first into a very dead and decaying Vietcong soldier. I can still smell death and decay to this day. But the more combat that I experienced the more I wanted to stay. I knew that I had found my calling, so after my first tour of duty ended in December 1970, I volunteered for a second tour. I was a warrior consumed by war and combat.

The Wolfhounds went back to Hawaii with the 2nd Brigade of the 25th Infantry Division in April of 1971, at which time I was transferred to the 101st Airborne, 1st of the 501st Geronimo's, Company B in Phu Bai. In late August 1971, while serving with the 101st off of Firebase Rifle, Bravo Company was given a mission to go into a particular valley along with Alpha Company and drive a known North Vietnamese Army (NVA) battalion up the valley into waiting Charlie and Delta companies. My job was point man for the lead platoon of both Alpha and Bravo companies. I was like a Doberman pinscher with a hand grenade in his mouth (nervous, dangerous, and in your face).

Within two to three hours we made contact with the main NVA battalion size element. That sent the NVA regulars into the waiting Charlie and Delta companies, who were supposed to catch them retreating up the valley. But what happened was carnage. Charlie and Delta companies were outmatched by the hard-core NVA Battalion and got ripped to shreds, suffering a 40 percent casualty rate. My second tour ended in October of 1971 when I caught malaria and was medevac'd to Camp Zama, Japan.

For the past thirty-eight years I have felt responsible for the carnage of Charlie and Delta companies. The battle off Firebase Rifle is but a small footnote in the larger war and means nothing to most people. However, to me and all the warriors who fought, bled, and died for each other that day, it changed our lives forever.

By the time I was sent back to the real world (home) in November of 1971, my "white tiger" inner demon was combat-ready and trained. I was pissed off, full of distrust of the system, and could not relate to my family or friends. I looked for any situation that would provide me with a feeling of danger and excitement like I experienced in combat, and I did a lot of dangerous and illegal things. I wanted to live fast and die young.

After five years, I joined the Army again as a reservist and completed Ranger training at Fort Benning, Georgia, in 1976. As a young buck sergeant (E-5) I was full of piss and vinegar and not willing to take orders from any officer, which led to many demotions during my long career.

During the summer of 1977, my reserve unit from Ann Arbor, Michigan, went to Fort McCoy, Wisconsin, for our annual two weeks of training. One particular day at Fort McCoy I went to the PX to buy some patches for my new fatigues. While shopping I noticed several soldiers wearing the Screaming Eagle patch of the 101st Airborne Division. I approached one of them and introduced myself and told him that I had served with Bravo Company of the 1/501st, 101st Airborne Division in Vietnam in 1971. The soldier said that his unit was here to help train the reservists and be the opposition force. The soldier went on to say that one of his buddies was also in Vietnam in 1971 with Charlie Company 1/501st. At that moment, a sense of foreshadowing went through me and I was instantly combat-ready. I knew for some unknown reason that this meeting between the Charlie Company soldier and me was not going to go well.

I followed the soldier over to meet the soldier from Charlie Company. I said hello and that I was in Bravo Company in 1971 in Vietnam. He introduced himself as Sergeant R and asked me if I was with the unit at Firebase Rifle. I said yes, and that I was in Bravo Company at that time. He gave me a long stare, then asked if I was in the battle off Firebase Rifle that occurred in late August of 1971, to which I replied yes. He then asked me what my job was that day. The look on his face was the same look we used to have in battle—wide-eyed and ready for blood. I told him my job was point man. Sergeant R stared at me for a few seconds and said, "So you're the son of a bitch that drove those NVA regulars into my company and got us slaughtered." I screamed "Fuck you!" so loud that everyone in the PX heard me and turned and stared at both of us. Sergeant R gave me a "Fuck you" back, at which time I slapped him so hard in the face he fell backwards onto the floor; I pounced on him.

The fight turned deadly in an instant and both of us knew it. We used every warrior skill we had learned in hand-to-hand combat and went at it. A couple of shelves and display cases were smashed as we threw each other around the PX like rag dolls. Sergeant R's buddies tried to break up the brawl. I smashed my fist in one of their faces and jammed my foot into the balls of another. My mouth filled up with blood and I loved it.

Somehow we both heard sirens; no doubt the MPs had been called. So we ran outside kicking and punching anyone who got in our way. I have always wondered what happened to the major who tried to grab me at the door and who I punched and tossed into a glass case that shattered. Once outside we brawled some more, and as the MPs (lots of MPs) arrived, we both ran into the forest in the back of the PX and concealed ourselves. The whole time we had yelled, cussed, and threatened to kill each other. For a brief moment now we both became combat buddies trying to escape the MPs surrounding us in the woods.

While hiding I asked Sergeant R why he hated me so much. He said that he'd lost a lot of buddies that day and had promised to get the fuck responsible. By his measure I was that fuck. I tried to tell him that I had also lost some buddies that day and was only doing my job. That answer seemed to infuriate him and he began to beat me again. I managed to break free and pick up a tree branch, and began to club him.

We were both oblivious to the world until I saw an MP sergeant major come with a squad of armed MPs. I tried to sidestep the sergeant major and run. He grabbed my arm with one hand and smashed the side of my head with a .45 caliber pistol in the other hand, knocking me to the ground. Before I could get up and run away, I had a loaded .45 stuck in my face. I saw that Sergeant R had about six MPs around him pointing M16s at him.

The MP sergeant major told us both in a command voice to stop trying to kill each other that second or he would do the job for us. I twitched a little and the sergeant major clicked off the safety and told me not to move a fucking muscle or he would blow my stupid fucking brains out.

Sergeant R and I were cuffed and stuffed into an MP meat wagon and transported to the Fort McCoy jail. Once there we were put in separate cells and ordered to shut the fuck up and wait for the post commander, a two-star general. We were given some medical attention for our cuts, bruises, scrapes, broken fingers, knuckles, and other combat wounds.

While waiting, the MP sergeant major came back and told us both that he had not seen such anger and bloodlust since he was in Vietnam or Korea. That's when I noticed that he was also wearing the Screaming Eagle patch of the 101st Airborne Division. He asked us what the fuck was going on. So Sergeant R and I told him the whole story. To our surprise he told us that he understood our feelings and would try to help us, but that we had caused thousands of dollars' worth of damage and the post commander was so angry he wanted our asses shot at dawn. It was a long night in that cell. I fell asleep beat, tired, and whipped, much like I felt after a firefight. I awoke the next morning so damn sore that I could not move, still tasting and spitting blood. I saw that Sergeant R was not in his cell and wondered what was going to happen to me.

The cell door opened and in walked the post commander, all six-foot-four of him (also wearing a 101st Airborne patch) along with the sergeant major. The general looked mad, mean, and serious. I thought my Army career was over, and that I would be locked up for a long time. The general ordered me to stand at attention and asked me what in the hell was going on between Sergeant R and I, and why I had assaulted Sergeant R in such a vicious manner.

I could not believe my ears; me assault Sergeant R? What a joke! We'd both tried to kill each other, but somehow it was my fault. "Bullshit," I thought. Now I really hated that son of a bitch and promised to get even.

I asked the commander and sergeant major what had happened to Sergeant R. The commander's answer completely shocked me. He told me that Sergeant R didn't want charges to be pressed against me and that he had been sent back during the night to Fort Campbell, Kentucky. The general further said that if I agreed to pay for the damages along with Sergeant R, that I could be out of jail in three to four days, and my only crime would be disorderly conduct and reduction in rank. For a brief moment I thought of *telling the general to go fuck himself. Somehow the sergeant major seemed to read my mind, recognized the look on my face, and asked the general if he could try to talk some sense into me alone.*

After the general left, the sergeant major looked at me and said, "Kid, I had a long and hard all-fucking-night-over-a-bottle-of-bourbon talk with the general to convince him to give you a break." I asked the sergeant major why I was being given a break. He said that he and the general figured that since all four of us had served in Vietnam with the 101st, that this was a "family" feud, that he and the general remembered being young and stupid once, and that any returning-home combat warrior deserved a break. So I reluctantly agreed to the deal. However, for the next three days in jail I still wanted to kick that cock-sucking, mother-fucking, piece-of-shit-for-brains Sergeant R's ass.

As it turns out, we got that chance when we met up some years later at Fort Carson and twice at Fort Benning. Both of us had remained in the Army. The first two encounters were mostly pushing, shoving, and yelling matches that led to demotions for both of us. For the third encounter at Fort Benning in 1988, where we had ended up as drill instructors, we decided to keep our distance from each other. We finally decided the Vietnam War was over for us—for now.

The fourth and last time that I saw Sergeant R was in 1990. We had managed to become first sergeants of infantry companies at Fort Benning, and we were getting our companies ready for deployment to the Gulf for Operation Desert Storm. We met at a senior NCO club and talked over some beers, and finally once and for all ended the Vietnam War between us. During that meeting I asked him why he blamed me for what happened. He answered, "I was young and stupid and still really pissed off, and no, I don't blame anyone anymore." We talked, joked, and laughed about the "McCoy Battle," and in the end decided that we were both fools and wished each other good luck in our lives and careers. I was able to move on and let go of any lingering animosity that I felt toward him.

In 1998 I left the Army, and in July of 2002 I mentally and physically crashed and burned because of PTSD. By August of 2002, I started my five-year-long, hard and painful journey back to myself and happiness through therapy. Writing this story has been very difficult for me, because I never narrated it in this way. So here we are in 2009, and I again find myself feeling somewhat withdrawn, detached, lonely, and angry at times. But I don't regret telling the story. I'll always be the combat warrior, and the reality is that my blueprint for happiness and quality of life is still a work in progress. Telling my story is an important part of that; it allows me to honestly accept my feelings, which helps me to dwell less on them. I find it beneficial to be introspective at times and think of things in different ways. Telling my story helps me to appreciate life as it is now, and all the people who are important in my life, like my daughter and son. I find that I'm able to be more empathetic, and also better able to receive the support of others.

As I was writing this, my friends noticed that I wasn't quite myself, that I was more quiet and detached compared to how I usually am; they asked me how I was doing and genuinely wanted to know the answer. I was surprised that they noticed any change at all, and it helped me to know that they cared. I told them that I was writing about some serious things that happened in Vietnam and was just going through an introspective period, which they accepted.

I hope that my story will in some way help all returning veterans to take the steps to make the transition home (hopefully in a shorter period of time than it took me) and lead a joyous life. Keep the faith, my brothers and sisters.

CHAPTER 7
DEAL WITH STRESSFUL SITUATIONS

"How are you doing Michael? Glad to see you home." This was the big question from seemingly everyone I knew when I came home from war. My response was always, "I'm okay," which is the answer most people wanted me to say. What most people do not want to hear is, "I feel like shit; my mind is gone. I've just returned from war and two years of killing the enemy and extreme hardships that you can't even imagine. I'm also angry, hate society, and wish that I could return to my unit and war right now." The "real" answer to the big question of how you are now that you're back would have most people believing that you are a cold-blooded killer, crazy, or both.

FIRST SERGEANT MIKE SCHINDLER

This chapter continues the LANDNAV training for the home front, expanding on the skills in earlier chapters to help you learn to build resilience. Earlier chapters have covered learning skills related to paying attention to your physical reactions and feelings, putting space between your reactions and actions, physical conditioning, improving sleep, noticing your breath, meditation and attention skills, and narrating your story. This chapter will help you learn additional skills to refine and add depth to your ability to respond to stressful situations and encounters involving people.

LANDNAV LEARNING OBJECTIVE: LEARNING TO DEAL WITH STRESSFUL SITUATIONS, STUPID STUFF, PEOPLE, AND ANGER

These skills focus on learning to deal with the strong reactions that you may have to stressful "triggers" in the home environment. There are many types of situations that can cause warriors to immediately shift into high alert—a crowd, a line of people, trash on the side of the road, overpasses, a hot day, someone asking "How are you?", sand, diesel fuel, traffic, a person of Middle Eastern or Vietnamese ethnicity, a loud noise, smoke, a movie image, a calendar date, a conversation about the war, a helicopter overhead, someone not following through with something they were supposed to do, being boxed in somewhere, busy intersections, certain smells, etc. Numerous things can trigger reactions of anxiety, fear, and anger, or result in the warrior suddenly being flooded with images and feelings, bringing the war zone home or the warrior back to the war zone.

What happens over time for many warriors is that they stop going out, and avoid anything and anybody that trigger reactions. They retreat as far back behind the front as they possibly can, and find the most secure bunker available. This can include not going to the mall or grocery store, not going to the movies, avoiding certain roads, avoiding social occasions with friends or family members, not showing up for work, or not getting help (because they know they'll have to talk about what's going on). This tendency to avoid things can result in numerous problems because it conflicts with the expectations and desires of loved ones, friends, or coworkers for the warrior to do "normal" things that people do.

Four skills are presented in this chapter. The first is a resiliency "inoculation" exercise designed to help you train your body to deal with particularly stressful situations that often lead to avoidance or withdrawal. The second skill involves building your resilience in dealing with the range of idiotic and stupid stuff you may encounter daily with people. The third skill addresses more serious situations involving people. The fourth skill assists in developing better understanding of anger, the distinction between anger and rage, and how to "manage" your anger.

Developing these skills doesn't imply conformity to the expectations of others. As a warrior, you're probably quite independent and satisfied with the way you are, even if others perceive your behavior as inconsistent with their expectations, or the norms of society. The reality is that most people have little or no understanding of what it means to be a warrior, and might have unreasonable or unrealistic expectations. Nevertheless, it's useful to have these skills available when you need them. These skills are not going to change your likes or dislikes, but they'll provide some useful knowledge to help cope with unpleasant and difficult situations you encounter in everyday life.

SKILL 1: RESILIENCY INOCULATION TRAINING (FACING YOUR FEARS)

This skill demonstrates how you can train your body to not react so strongly to situations that trigger high stress or anxiety. For example, if you feel your heart pound and your anxiety level jumps through the roof when you walk into a crowded mall, or you start to get a panic attack waiting in a line, or you avoid driving at certain times because you can't stand being boxed in on the road, then this training is designed to help.

The skill is to learn to "inoculate" yourself to triggers that cause you high distress or lead you to modify your life in some important way to avoid the triggers. The goal is to improve your ability to do things that you need or want to do, but avoid because they result in high distress.

Two terms that mental health professionals use to describe this "inoculation" process are *habituation* and *desensitization*. Habituation and desensitization in this context mean growing accustomed to things that normally distress you or that you react strongly to. For example, people who live in houses right next to a railroad track grow accustomed to the loud sounds and vibration of the trains. Their bodies habituate to the trains, and after a while they don't notice them. If you go to visit their house for a few days, you'll probably lose lots of sleep and feel very annoyed by the noise, but after a while you too would gradually habituate.

Your body can get used to things that initially cause you a fair amount of distress. This happens naturally, and doesn't require you to do anything, other than remain in contact with the distressing or annoying stimulus long enough for your body to habituate to it. Another term that mental health professionals use to describe this inoculation process is *reconditioning*. For warriors, this means breaking the connection between the wartime experiences and the automatic, "conditioned" reactions to things that remind you of the war environment.

This exercise is similar to what an allergy doctor does to help someone overcome severe allergies. For example, some people are so allergic to the sting of a bee that they can die from shock within minutes. A person who has such an allergy can go to an allergy doctor and be cured by receiving tiny doses of the very same bee venom that can kill them. The treatment for a severe bee allergy is to receive the bee venom that the person is deathly allergic to. Over many treatments, starting at extremely low doses and gradually increasing the amount of venom that is injected, the person's immune system gets accustomed to the venom without reacting to it. After these treatments a person can be stung by a live bee, or be injected with the same amount of venom as they would receive being stung, and have no reaction. This type of treatment saves many lives.

The resiliency inoculation skill is adapted from therapy techniques called *in-vivo exposure* and *systematic desensitization*. This means putting yourself in everyday life situations that trigger your distress or avoidance reactions and gradually increasing the "dose" until these situations don't cause the same degree of reaction. One note of caution regarding this training is that it has not been tested as a "self-help" technique, and therefore, if you have problems doing this or find that it's not helping to reduce anxiety (or anxiety is increasing after doing this), don't beat yourself up with "shoulds" (like "I *should* be able to do this"), and go see a professional. If you go to a mental health professional, this chapter can give you some valuable insights.

The first thing to do is own up to the things that cause you the most distress on a day-to-day basis, or that you regularly avoid because they trigger distress or strong reactions. In other words, identify the things that you're particularly "allergic" to. For example, if going to a crowded mall triggers high levels of anxiety, write this down on the following list under the heading "List of Triggers." Think about all the things that trigger high distress or that you avoid doing because they're associated with high distress. This could include things like "sitting in a movie theater," "going to the mall," "driving," "bridges and overpasses," "spiders," "flying in a plane," "waiting in a line of people," "elevators," etc.

After writing down several prominent triggers, circle the level of distress that this activity usually causes you. For this scale, consider a "1" to be relaxed with no distress and a "10" to be the most distress or anxiety you can imagine. After you've listed out the things that cause you high distress, pick one or two for your "inoculation" training.

List of Triggers

Level of Distress / Anxiety (circle)

	None/ Very Low		Low		Moderate		High		Very High	
_____	1	2	3	4	5	6	7	8	9	10
_____	1	2	3	4	5	6	7	8	9	10
_____	1	2	3	4	5	6	7	8	9	10
_____	1	2	3	4	5	6	7	8	9	10
_____	1	2	3	4	5	6	7	8	9	10
_____	1	2	3	4	5	6	7	8	9	10
_____	1	2	3	4	5	6	7	8	9	10

Example of Going to a Crowded Mall

For example, let's say you indicated that going to a crowded mall generally causes you to experience an "8" or a "9" level of distress or anxiety. Let's also assume that this is frustrating to you because you'd like to be able to go to the mall with your friends or family members (even if only for their sake). If this example doesn't apply to you, pick another one from your experience.

The next step is to "inoculate" yourself to the distressing trigger in a similar way the doctor would inoculate you if you had an allergy to bees— by gradually increasing your level of exposure (or "dose") to whatever causes you distress, in this case, the crowded mall. The inoculation exercise involves going to the mall on a number of occasions to gradually build up your "immunity" so you react less strongly to it.

Assume the crowded mall generally causes a "9" level of distress, but if you sit or stand in a less-crowded area close to an exit, you can keep your distress level down to a "6" or a "7"; if you sit in your car in the parking lot, the level is only a "3" or a "4."

Start by driving to the mall and sitting in the parking lot. If this causes you a lot of distress, then this is a good place to start. If this causes minimal or no distress, then walk into the mall to an area that is less crowded and near an exit, where you feel noticeable distress but not to the level where it's through the roof. The idea is to pick a place that causes you noticeable distress, but not at a "10" level (perhaps a "5," "6", or "7").

Once you've picked your location, your mission is to sit there patiently without leaving, notice your level of anxiety, and allow your body to learn that this location isn't as threatening or dangerous as it feels. What will happen is that the level of anxiety will likely increase initially, reaching a peak after several minutes. You might start to sweat or feel your heart pound. Anxiety can sometimes make you feel like there's something physically wrong with you, or like you're about to go crazy. You'll probably have a strong urge to leave right away.

Your mission, however, is not to leave, but to stay at that location until your anxiety level starts to naturally subside, which usually happens after several more minutes. If necessary, consider yourself on guard duty: You've been ordered to monitor this location, and retreat isn't an option for the duration of your assignment.

It's important not to let yourself get distracted in any way; stay focused. For example, don't talk on your cell phone, text, or check messages on your BlackBerry. Don't read, don't eat, don't try to control your breathing; just sit there and do nothing except remain aware of where you are, what's going on around you, and your level of anxiety. If it's easier to do this when you have a friend or family member with you, then ask them to be with you but to not talk or distract you.

After a while the body learns that this place isn't as threatening as you first perceived it to be, and the level of anxiety will gradually diminish. The goal isn't to actively do anything to change your anxiety level, but to allow your body to learn by itself that a high level of anxiety is no longer necessary. All you have to do is understand the process and not respond as the anxiety increases by leaving; after a while the anxiety level will start to subside. After the anxiety subsides to about half the level it was at its peak, then the exercise is over and you can get up and leave. This generally takes anywhere between twenty and thirty minutes.

It's crucial to stay there when your anxiety is at its highest point and you're feeling the greatest urge to leave. If you leave at that moment, you'll feel immediate relief, but you'll also reinforce the avoidance (retreating) behavior and actually train your combat reflexes to think that this location in the mall (and similar locations) are very high threats. That will make things worse. What you want to do is train your body's reflexes that this part of the mall is not a high threat, and that there's no need to maintain such a high level of anxiety there. Wait until your anxiety level subsides before leaving.

If after about thirty minutes your anxiety is still "through the roof" and isn't showing any signs of diminishing, then consider practicing the deep breaths and wide relaxed focused meditation to calm your reflexes down (Chapter 5, skills 5 and 6). Give it about five to ten more minutes for your body to adjust to the location and to learn that it doesn't have to maintain the high level of anxiety any longer.

After you've done this once, the next step is to set a schedule where you repeat this exercise as many times as necessary (for example, every other day for a couple of weeks), until going to this location is no longer a big deal. Then pick another location that still causes distress, like a more-crowded area, and repeat the process. If it was helpful to have a friend with you initially, then later on, practice doing the exercise when your friend is in another part of the mall, or not with you.

The only objective is a reduction in your level of anxiety. This exercise isn't intended to change what you like or dislike. It won't make you enjoy things that you find annoying or you know you won't ever enjoy doing. For instance, you may be the kind of person who hated going to malls even before your deployment. This exercise isn't going to change that. After doing this exercise you'll still find the mall aggravating and will continue to dislike being there. But you also won't be triggered so strongly or have panic attacks as a result of visiting a mall, and this allows you to go on occasion, to tolerate it for the sake of your spouse, friends, kids, or just because you need a new pair of jeans and want to go shopping for yourself.

If you find that after about thirty to forty minutes, your anxiety or distress level hasn't diminished as expected, or is increasing, then your current assignment is finished, and you can relinquish your position. But don't surrender. Try to find another location that produces less anxiety and come back the next day and work on it again. The point is to experiment with this so that your body becomes trained to react less strongly to common triggers and you retreat from things less often.

Other Examples

You can experiment with this technique for any situation that triggers strong reactions. For example, if you can't stand waiting in lines, make a habit of selecting the longest line everywhere you go until standing in line becomes just an annoying but not a threatening activity. You still won't like standing in line, but you'll be able to do it. If you don't like bridges, find a bridge that's safe to walk across and gradually confront it—for example, by standing at one end of it for twenty to thirty minutes, until your anxiety subsides, and then returning every other day and repeating this same exercise until you can move onto it and eventually cross it. If you react strongly to overpasses or trash on the side of the road, and avoid certain roads because of this, find ways to confront these things so that you can gradually resume driving on those roads. As soon as you can do the activity without getting a strong reaction, you're done with the exercise.

The example of driving brings up the fact that in certain situations, it may be difficult, impractical, or inappropriate to actually do the exercise *in vivo* (in real life). For instance, it may be unsafe to stop your car and get out and stand under an overpass or examine trash on the side of the road (you wouldn't want to anyway). Instead, you can use visualization in a safe place like your home. For example, if overpasses or trash cause you to change course or react like there may be an IED threat, visualize yourself driving on a road where there are overpasses or trash. If your anxiety level goes up from imagining this, then you can practice inoculating yourself to these images through repeatedly visualizing this and holding the visualization long enough for the anxiety to subside. You can combine this with the relaxation breathing ("deep breaths from low in your abdomen") or meditation. It's a way of preparing yourself for going out and doing it in real life.

As another example, if you have difficulty with airplane travel, close your eyes and imagine everything that has to do with taking a trip that involves flying. In particular, imagine making the reservations, packing for the trip, traveling to the airport, checking in, going through security, boarding the plane, taking your seat, taking off, in-flight service, moving about the cabin, turbulence, and then descending and landing. Imagine these things in as much detail as possible. Notice which steps in this visualization produce the most anxiety; then practice "inoculating" yourself to your own visualizations by repeatedly doing this exercise until your anxiety subsides. Start with the first step in the sequence, moving on to the next only when your anxiety level has diminished. In the event that the anxiety doesn't subside, practice breathing from deep in your lower abdomen and add muscle relaxation and/or meditation until you can visualize doing these things without anxiety. You can also "inoculate" yourself by learning more about flying from a book or the Internet. Then you can add an *in-vivo* component, such as going to a museum that has airplanes, watching planes at an airport, and then ultimately boarding a plane to take a trip, initially with a friend, and later on, alone.

The inoculation procedure can be applied to various situations, and you can experiment with it until you get the desired result. The bottom line is to face the things that cause you to feel anxiety or distress, and directly counter the urge to avoid these things. Over time, your reactivity to certain types of situations will improve. This is a path to fearlessness.

Sensitivity to Ethnicity

A delicate topic, but one that needs to be discussed, is that some veterans from OIF/OEF and Gulf War 1 find that they react strongly to any person who appears to be of Middle Eastern ethnicity (or Vietnamese ethnicity for Vietnam veterans) because they remind them of an enemy combatant. If you're one of these warriors, then you're going to have to find some way to address this. I've recommended to warriors to actually go to places where there are Middle Eastern (or Vietnamese) people, such as a restaurant that serves that type of food, and to remain there until the anxiety level subsides. Bring a buddy if you want, and make sure that you check any anger you may feel at the door and avoid all alcohol. Enjoy the food, drink some of the local coffee or tea, enjoy the belly dancers (not likely to be found at a Vietnamese restaurant), speak with the people, and show respect.

Although this may seem like a crazy thing to do (particularly if you don't like Middle Eastern or Vietnamese food), it's not as crazy as it seems, because you don't want to live your life reacting to someone's mannerisms or the color of their skin. The idea is to train your body not to react simply because a person's skin color is similar to that of the enemies you encountered during deployment. Just because your body reacts to reminders of your war-zone experiences doesn't mean that you have to remain a slave to these reminders forever. In other words, create exercises that involve facing the very thing that causes the greatest levels of distress or anxiety so that your automatic reflexes become reconditioned.

SKILL 2: DEALING WITH THE "STUPID STUFF" PEOPLE DO

This is a big topic, and the above example of going into a Middle Eastern restaurant is a perfect segue to this. Warriors frequently report problems dealing with people and intolerance to the "stupid stuff" that people do. Many warriors find themselves getting triggered during encounters with people, and situations that provoke anger can sometimes end up in a full-blown flashback or physical altercation.

This skill involves developing an understanding of the importance of *control* in combat, and how this can affect your reactions to people after returning home. Warriors learn to completely depend on their team members, respect the chain of command, take orders from no one unless that person is in their immediate chain of command, and maintain a high level of suspicion of anyone who isn't part of their unit.

There are good reasons for this perspective. In many operational environments, including the wars in Iraq, Afghanistan, and Vietnam, allies and enemies could be indistinguishable unless they were pointing a weapon at you. They may have worn the same clothes and exhibited the same cultural mannerisms. Local military or security personnel working right alongside you may have been serving as the "eyes and ears" of the enemy.

I remember walking into a dining facility (DFAC) in Mosul in 2004 during a busy lunchtime and suddenly feeling a sense of unease because all of the tables where the Iraqi National Guard soldiers usually sat at the far end of the DFAC were empty. As soon as I noticed this, a rocket landed, and then two more landed in succession, fortunately falling just shy of the DFAC and buffered by blast walls and vehicles in the parking lot. Naturally, the assumption of every U.S. service member there was that the Iraqi soldiers had been tipped off to a possible attack but hadn't warned their U.S. counterparts—an assumption that may not have been correct, but nevertheless seemed logical given the circumstances. (This facility was hit a few weeks later by a suicide bomber.)

In the war zone, it's necessary to be wary and suspicious of everyone. Your life, and the lives of your team members, depend on remaining constantly alert to threats, which includes monitoring who's approaching, what they're carrying, whether or not they are authorized to be there, and whether they can be trusted. Back home, it's obvious why warriors display similar behaviors.

The complete dependence on team members and on the chain of command is a critical survival skill. If you, or any of your unit members or superiors, fail to do your assigned jobs, or make a mistake, serious consequences can result. Warriors are trained through their experience to have a very low tolerance for any mistakes, either their own or anyone else's.

Think about how many of your warrior friends have a difficult time tolerating mistakes, and pay attention to how this causes them to act. Do they tend to be micromanagers? Do they insist on their way or the highway? Do they fly off the handle if anyone makes even the tiniest mistake? Are they unable to complete tasks because they're perfectionists? Do they have a hard time making decisions? Are they highly critical of others? This isn't to point out flaws in others, but to recognize that these kinds of behaviors are very common as a result of working in a war-zone environment.

Now rate yourself using the control scale questionnaire on the next page.

If you checked "quite a bit" or "extremely" on some of these questions, consider whether these tendencies are negatively affecting your life. If the answer is "yes," then *control* is an important topic for you. Recognize that many of the qualities related to control stem directly from skills that are highly useful and adaptive in combat. Warriors are control freaks, by definition. Their training instills this in them. They will check and recheck to make sure that their equipment is in the right place and in good working order. They do this continuously to ensure that they can collectively execute combat tasks without hesitation and without mistakes. Warriors often have as low a tolerance for their own mistakes as they have toward the mistakes of others, and can be just as critical of themselves as others. They depend on everyone in their unit doing their job correctly, and maintain a high level of distrust of others outside of their unit.

The Nature of Control and Catch-22s

With this in mind, the skill is developing awareness of the way control plays an important role in your experience as a warrior, and then learning to

Control Scale:

Check the answer that best fits how you describe yourself:

	(1) Not at all	(2) A little bit	(3) Moderately	(4) Quite a bit	(5) Extremely
I have difficulty tolerating my own mistakes.					
I have difficulty tolerating the mistakes of others.					
I feel critical of others.					
I feel like I have to pay attention to every detail.					
I feel like I have to do everything myself because no one else does things right.					
I check things repeatedly to make sure they are correct.					
I have little patience for the stupid stuff people do.					
I have difficulty dealing with people not doing what they are supposed to do.					
I have difficulty trusting people					
I have difficulty making decisions.					

dial this up or down as needed. First, answer the questions on the control scale and determine how much control is an issue in your life. If it is an issue, then being aware of it may be enough to help you. Second, learn the nature of control by asking yourself several more questions specific to each situation you find yourself in. Last, consider how many situations you find yourself in that are double-binds or absurd catch-22s, and find ways to laugh about them. The best way to illustrate this is through an example. Hang on—we're in for a ride.

I'm waiting in line at a grocery store and the person in front is holding up the line—first, by not having enough money, and then by trying to use a credit card that isn't getting authorized. The cashier is not making any moves to resolve the situation. Two men behind me are pushing into me out of their own frustration to see what's going on. This is a situation that might piss off some warriors. And of course, I have an important appointment to go to after picking up the groceries, and any delay will definitely cause problems.

1st Question

So the first question is, "Do I have any control over this situation?" The answer is, "No, of course not"; however, I do have several options as to how to respond that could give me a *sense* of control:

A) Leave my groceries and walk away (the downside being that I've wasted my time trying to get them and end up with no groceries).

B) Try to move to another line (but there may not be another line that's moving any faster, and I'll lose my place near the front of this one).

C) Stay where I am but turn around and ask the men behind to stop pushing against me. (I can do this in a nice or a hostile way, but even doing this nicely could spark a confrontation.)

D) Stay where I am but yell at the person in front or at the cashier to hurry it up. (This may feel satisfying at the moment, but probably won't actually speed anything up, and may make the situation worse.)

E) Pull out my Glock—no, never mind . . .

F) Grab an apple, pull out the stem, lob it into customer service, hit the deck, and yell, "Apple!" In the confusion, move to the front of the line. (Downside: one less apple.)

G) Pull out my clown pistol, wave it menacingly in the air, and pull the trigger, popping out the red flag that says BANG! In the confusion, move to the front of the line. (Downside: armed security guard is color-blind.)

H) Stay where I am, do nothing, and deal with my own frustration. I could get on my case for choosing this grocery store in the first place—as if somehow I *could have* known what *would* happen; or control my frustration and let the situation resolve itself, however long this takes, and delaying me further. This definitely isn't satisfying.

2nd Question

For all these options (and countless others), there's always a downside. So here's the second question to consider whenever you get into frustrating life situations where there's more than one option: "Is there any option that doesn't have a downside?" The answer is generally, "No." Get used to it. This type of situation is captured with expressions like "a no-win situation," "between a rock and a hard place," "a double-bind," "damned if you do, damned if you don't," or a "catch-22," where you feel trapped between two or more options, none of which are really any good.

There are different types of no-win situations. A "catch-22," for example, has more of a feeling of an insane and irreconcilable loop that never has any benefit to you—only to the authority who created it, whereas "between a rock and a hard place" and the other expressions reflect being stuck between two or more options, each of which has a downside, but may also have some benefit. If it's only one option that has both a downside and a benefit, then it's a "double-edged sword." For a service member facing multiple deployments, PTSD is a double-edged sword, since reactions that are beneficial in combat are unpleasant symptoms back home.

To take a brief diversion, Joseph Heller coined the widely used idiomatic expression "catch-22" in his 1961 novel by the same name. The main character, Captain Yossarian, a B-25 bombardier stationed on an island off the Italian coast near the end of World War II, requests to be grounded on the basis of insanity, per Army Regulation "Catch-22," in order to avoid flying pointless and extremely dangerous missions ordered solely for the purpose of making the squadron commander look good to his higher-ups. However, according to this regulation, an officer can only be grounded for being crazy if he requests to be grounded, which proves that he isn't crazy, since crazy people would be the only ones willing to keep flying. Yossarian's request is denied.

3rd Question

Now back to the grocery store line and the third question: "How much does this really matter?" The answer in this case could be, "It matters a lot," but more likely is, "Not much." Yes, my "choice" matters if I end up sparking a confrontation with the people behind or in front of me, ending up with a bigger problem. Yes, my "choice" matters if the appointment I'm late for happens to be to receive my father's dying words, which in this case might have been, "Why the hell did you stop off at the grocery store after I called you to come over immediately because I thought I was dying?" Yes, the "choice" might matter if standing in line is now triggering a full-blown panic attack and breathing from the abdomen isn't working. No, the "choice" doesn't matter, assuming that being punctual for the appointment isn't that important, and because in the broad scheme of life, does it really matter if I spend a few extra minutes standing in a grocery store line? Is the delay at the grocery store because of "stupid stuff" really worth getting bent out of shape (or having a panic attack) over?

The Illusion of Control and "Choice"

This may be a silly example in some ways (made more so by bringing a clown pistol and an apple into it), but it highlights the nature of *control.* The need to feel in control is both a very real pressing action on our part to prevent possible bad things from happening, as well as an illusion that is uniquely human. We maintain the feeling of control by constantly preparing and planning for the future, trying to anticipate what will happen, worrying about what will happen, checking things, setting goals and expectations (including the expectation of getting through a grocery store in just a few minutes), and believing there's a *right* choice for every situation. Our ability to ward off possible bad outcomes through our own preparation and vigilance is admirable. The problem is that most of this depends on accurately predicting the future, which is impossible. Many (if not most) things that happen in life are not under our control. Often, what we do to resolve situations, which includes pondering various apparent options, gives us the *feeling* of control through the *illusion of choice,* not true control.

The illusion of choice involves imagining other options that *would have* turned out better, i.e., the way we planned for them to, wanted them to, expected them to, or needed them to. "If I had only taken the other road I *wouldn't have* gotten stuck in this traffic and *wouldn't have* been late." The illusion is believing that the other road *would have* been okay, since we can imagine this in hindsight.

Another curious thing about the grocery store example is that it illustrates how easy it is for us to get caught up in the whole "control" and "choice" issue instead of just patiently getting the job done—in this case, picking up groceries, however long it takes. After all, we need groceries.

One thing that comes up repeatedly for warriors is dealing with situations where people don't do their job right or don't follow through on what they said they'd do. Because of how important it is in the combat environment for everyone on the team to do things exactly as they're supposed to, warriors can become highly distressed to any situation back home where someone doesn't do what they're supposed to do. This is a main source of conflict. Examples include treating the grocery store clerk, bank teller, taxi driver, waiter, etc. like the enemy; chewing someone out who makes a minor mistake; or getting extremely angry at a loved one who doesn't follow through on something they said they'd do (or you told them needed to be done).

This is also about control, and is based again on the *illusion of choice.* Since we can judge what we *should* be doing or *should have* done for ourselves, there's no reason it seems not to judge what someone else *should* be doing or *should have* done. In reality, we have very little or no control over most situations, particularly how others, including all our loved ones, behave.

Combat is the ultimate example of being in control/out of control. Every action in combat carries risk, and therefore a downside, particularly for the warrior on the ground. Everything a warrior does to be in control (through rigorous training, checking and re-checking equipment, following orders, remaining vigilant to threats, and performing all tasks in proper sequence) ultimately can break down in a few seconds of pure chaos that no one saw coming or had any control over. You round up enemy combatants after a pitched firefight, turn them over to the "authorities," and two weeks later they're out on the streets trying to kill you again, and you're powerless to change this repetitive cycle because of the rules of engagement imposed by the "authorities." (That's a catch-22.) The ones who lose aren't usually the senior leaders or politicians who wrote the orders.

Bad things happen, no matter how good a job the warrior does. The enemy wins some battles, even when it loses the war. Sometimes you lose no matter what you do. These are situations you have very little control over.

The Avoidance Option

There's another option that a warrior can take in relation to the grocery store line: Never go grocery shopping because it causes too much aggravation (except maybe in the middle of the night when there aren't any lines). Avoiding the situation completely also has downsides, like not being able to go when it's convenient, or upsetting a loved one who doesn't want to get stuck with all the shopping or doesn't want their warrior trekking off on a solitary mission late at night. Yet, all too often, the avoidance "choice" is what the warrior makes. This is a big part of the problem, and leads back to the first skill of this chapter: learning to "inoculate" yourself against irritating or anxiety-provoking situations (such as waiting in lines). The bottom line: Avoidance is a trap. If you want a more "normal" life, you'll have to find a way to face these situations.

You Can't Change Other People

Another critical thing to learn in situations involving people is that you can't change people. People will be who they are. When they're doing stupid things there's no point in trying to "educate" them. Warriors can be very effective at "educating" people, but unless they're very creative, more often than not this leads to a mess.

As crazy as all this sounds, the specific skill in dealing with people is to recognize the things you can control and the things you can't control, and to have a sense of humor about the whole thing, because what people consider "normal" is often nuts. You'll constantly encounter people who make mistakes, do stupid things, and interfere with your life in appreciable ways, intentionally and unintentionally. These are things you can't control. You'll also make mistakes yourself, do stupid things, and interfere with other people's lives in appreciable ways, because you're human, too. So what you're left with is that the only thing that you *seem* to have control over is your own actions. You don't even have control over your options, and some situations are catch-22s in which you're caught in a loop, or between two or more undesirable options. Humor is the only way out.

In summary, monitor your need for control by using the Control Scale. If you're high in certain areas, do something to dial down the level (or, if you prefer, and understand the downside, tear it up and tell everyone to fuck off).

For specific situations or encounters with people that have the potential to result in conflict, frustration, or anger, stop and ask yourself:

1. "Do I have any control over this?"
2. "Is there an option that doesn't have a downside?"
3. "How much does this matter?"

Most important, accept that the answers to numbers 1 and 2 are usually "No"; that the answer to 3 is usually "Not much"; that life is an endless series of catch-22-like situations that you have little control over; and that the only thing you can do at times is to simply laugh at the absurdity of it all. This may be hard to accept, but that's the way it is.

(At this point, if you feel like it's time to seek me out in person to let me know, in no uncertain terms, exactly what you think of this "training"— and it's true that I'm skating on thin ice telling anyone, much less a combat vet, to "deal with it"—I'll be happy to make myself available, at least as much as the character named Major Major did in the story *Catch-22*—that is, at convenient and well-advertised times when I'm not in. See you then!)

SKILL 3. DEALING WITH MORE-SERIOUS SITUATIONS INVOLVING PEOPLE

Putting humor aside, the example in skill 2 involving "stupid stuff" people do doesn't address more serious situations where people you encounter act in various irresponsible, disrespectful, malicious, abusive, or cruel ways. These are situations that call for a different approach.

As a warrior who has deployed to a war zone, you likely have a greater appreciation for what's important in life. Even though killing was part of your training, you, more than anyone, know how precious life is, and why it's worth protecting, saving, and fighting for. You know what it means to protect and care for your buddies. You know what it means to risk your life for others and for others to risk theirs for you. You know what it means to live with honor and sacrifice. You may have known buddies who made the ultimate sacrifice. You probably have experienced a wider range of emotions than most people. You carry these experiences with you, which help to define who you are as a warrior.

When warriors encounter people being cruel, malicious, abusive, or grossly irresponsible, it strikes at the heart of who they are. As a warrior, you may be more likely to step up and confront injustice than a person who's not a warrior. This doesn't necessarily mean a physical confrontation. Confrontation can take many forms, including verbal, written, or through the legal system. As a warrior, you'll be more likely to "fight" for what you believe in, using all the ways that word implies.

This exercise is simply to understand how important this is. As a warrior, you have an obligation to respect this quality in yourself, and to act in the most honorable and virtuous ways that you can. It's important to choose your fights carefully and to understand the risks and consequences, whether physical, social, financial, legal, or emotional. A physical confrontation can carry health and legal repercussions. A verbal or written confrontation can easily escalate and risks social repercussions (e.g., isolation or lack of acceptance from others). A legal confrontation risks incarceration or financial repercussions. All can have an emotional toll. Nonetheless, as a warrior, you're likely to be more willing to take risks than other people.

I'm not advocating fighting, but the opposite. A warrior, probably more than anyone else, understands how far it can go, and therefore has an obligation to exhibit restraint and walk away from any situation that doesn't warrant fighting for. A warrior's pride, arrogance, egotism, selfishness, narcissism, desire to "educate" someone else, demonstrate strength, or "prove" superiority over another undermines what it means to be a warrior. A warrior doesn't fight unless it's absolutely necessary. A warrior doesn't fight unless it's the right thing to do, is consistent with their values and beliefs, and the situation calls for nothing less.

A word about disrespect: Warriors, who live based on a culture of respecting authority and each other, will often step up to confront someone if they perceive disrespect. However, disrespect doesn't generally fall into the same category as being cruel, malicious, abusive, or grossly irresponsible. Disrespect can range from a simple slight that is unintentional to severely abusive or threatening behavior; the higher the severity, the more likely it is that the warrior will respond. Most situations fall on the lower end of this scale, and involve a judgment that another person should be acting or behaving in a different manner. Some warriors are so sensitive to feeling disrespected that they overreact with hostility at the slightest evidence of it, and end up abusive themselves. This is a form of being overly controlling and not being able to tolerate mistakes. People have varying levels of tolerance to feeling disrespected, but feeling disrespected isn't in and of itself a reason for confrontation. A feeling of being disrespected is your feeling, and usually doesn't warrant a response.

In summary, accept that being a warrior means you have a responsibility to apply your wisdom and experience and know when a fight is necessary to protect what's valuable and precious, what has meaning, and what's worth fighting for; and when it's best to walk away, knowing that strength and courage require no exhibition—the path of the Samurai.

SKILL 4. DEALING WITH ANGER, RAGE, AND RELATED EMOTIONS

Another vital topic is anger. Anger is an essential survival emotion in combat, driving a warrior's focus, concentration, and intensity toward the sole task of neutralizing the enemy. Anger is a natural response to being threatened and an antidote to sleep deprivation and exhaustion; it helps to get the job done, and serves the vital function of offsetting fear. Warriors often struggle with anger after they return home. Anger and detachment are two of the most common emotional reactions that warriors experience after coming home. On the battlefield, both serve to suppress other emotions that could distract from a warrior's concentration.

Anger is frequently misunderstood, considered to be a "negative" emotion, or a symptom of larger problems. There's a lot of attention given to anger "management" in the military and society, but very little appreciation of how important this emotion is to a warrior in the course of his profession. Anger benefits survival and success in combat.

Anger is not the same thing as rage, fury, hostility, resentment, loathing, or hatred. Anger, like most other emotions, generally comes and goes quickly. I slam my finger in a car door or bang my head on a kitchen cabinet and I immediately get angry at the door, cabinet, or myself. The anger then rapidly dissipates and is replaced by greater attention to the level of pain, frustration, or other feelings. Someone pulls out from a side street, and I have to slam on my brakes to avoid a collision. I immediately get angry at them, but this is quickly replaced with relief at the narrow miss, or going back to whatever thoughts I was having before this happened. For most situations, anger generally comes on, gets expressed, and then is gone, over and done with.

In contrast, emotional conditions like rage, fury, hostility, loathing, or hatred involve behaviors that can persist. Anger can certainly progress to rage, hatred, or these other conditions, but it's these conditions that cause problems. If I tear the kitchen cabinet off the wall or chase down the guy who almost broadsided my car to teach him "a lesson," this has notched the situation up into rage. Anger is an emotion, an immediate internal reaction to a situation. Rage and fury, which involve emotion that has built up, disproportionately forces actions and behaviors.

Confusing Anger with Behaviors

A problem in our society, and in the approach to anger "management," is that anger—the emotion—is often confused with these other responses. It's not the anger that needs managing, but the various behaviors that can rise from it. Yet people often think that simply the expression of anger, by definition, is the root cause of a larger problem. People often mistake assertiveness for aggressiveness, both of these for anger, and anger for rage or hostility. These are not the same.

Anger is a sudden strong feeling of displeasure related to pain or hurt that quickly loses steam. It's usually directed at someone or something specific. Rage, fury, hostility, loathing, and hatred have no boundary, no end, and are often nonspecific in focus. No matter how much steam is let off, there's always more, and letting off any steam only serves to build more up. There is often a feeling of bitterness that has built up as a result of cumulative perceived injustices. Rage and fury are violent, uncontrolled, vehement, extreme. They can fester and become compulsive, along with loathing or hatred. Hostility reflects smoldering rage or hatred, ill will directed at people or groups that can become self-sustaining. If I'm feeling hostile, my hostility will be directed at everyone around me. I push every-one away, and my actions are hurtful to others. Resentment and passive-aggressive behavior are closely related.

Being assertive is confidently or forcefully taking or stating a position or claim. Being aggressive may mean taking an attacking stance or pos-ture, but can also mean showing determination, as in "an aggressive busi-ness position." Neither of these are the same thing as anger. You can be aggressive or assertive with or without feeling angry.

So why is this important? What's crucial here for you (and your family members and friends) to understand is that anger—the sudden emotion when a driver cuts you off, your boss denies your request for leave, an air-line loses your luggage, your spouse tells you out of the blue that they're thinking of divorce, someone breaks into your car, or an enemy combatant or mugger on the street points a weapon at you—isn't the problem. Anger is a natural emotional reaction to any of these situations. The problem only comes when the warrior allows the anger to fester or progress to per-sistent rage, fury, hostility, resentment, or hatred; in other words, when the immediate feeling of anger leads to a persistently angry state and behav-iors and actions that have negative consequences.

A warrior who returns from combat, and who has experienced the extremes of emotions, including anger, often finds him- or herself in an awkward position. Anger has been an important survival emotion, and there may be deep and intense feelings of anger related to things that happened during combat. This anger needs a way to be expressed (and going to the gym isn't going to cut it). However, the warrior's loved ones take any expression of anger as a sign that there's a much bigger problem, a smoldering cauldron of rage waiting to pour forth. The warrior may also fear that if any anger is expressed at all, it may get out of control. As a result, legitimate feelings of anger are withheld.

Unfortunately, when the feeling of anger isn't expressed or acknowledged in some way, it's more likely to fester. Think about a child who grows up in a home where anger isn't permitted for any reason. It would be very unusual in such a circumstance if the child didn't slowly fill up with rage and hostility as he grows older. If the warrior doesn't find a healthy way to acknowledge and express legitimate feelings of anger, then the deep anger that may be present upon return from deployment can rapidly become a permanent condition of rage and hostility. When this happens, situations that might otherwise trigger a brief verbal expression of anger instead end up in extreme hostility, passive-aggressive behavior, confrontations, and actions that cause problems.

Healthy Expression of Anger

The skill is to distinguish between the normal feeling of anger and any behaviors associated with these other emotions. Rage, fury, loathing, etc. are all in some ways similar to depression, a morass that a person can fall into and wallow in. All of these, including depression, can result from unacknowledged and unexpressed anger. If you find yourself wallowing in hostility or the need for revenge, then your LANDNAV skills have faltered, and the goal is to navigate yourself back to a healthy expression of this important emotion.

Consider the traditional image of the samurai warrior. The samurai remains completely relaxed until the split second that he has to respond or attack, at which time he commits himself in the present moment with all of his intention, force, energy, and skill. Then immediately he returns to a relaxed state. He doesn't hold on to the energy that he discharged at his enemy.

A healthy expression of anger generally involves recognizing and expressing it, along with indicating what the source of the anger is, and any other emotions tied to it. It's helpful to think of two types of situations: those in which you would expect anger to dissipate rapidly after being expressed, and those that may involve more-prolonged expressions of the emotion.

There are many situations in which the expression of anger resolves the feeling immediately, while holding on to it leads to bigger problems.

With a healthy expression of anger, many people will have little recollection a short time afterward about what made them angry. If you stub your toe and yell "Ouch!", that expresses the anger. If you stub your toe and add it to a long list of other aggravations in your life, or destroy the piece of furniture you bumped, then you've moved from the angry feeling to the behaviors associated with resentment and rage. If you get stuck in traffic or your boss denies your leave request, and you say to yourself, "That pisses me off!", you express how you feel. However, if you start getting on yourself for taking the wrong turn or adding this to a long list of things you hate about your boss, this can lead to festering resentment. If you're camping and someone starts to shake your tent violently like they want to tear it down, you'll probably come running out of the tent angry as hell. However, when you discover that it's a bear pushing on your tent, your anger will magically evaporate, and turn into fear, surprise, and "Uh-oh." Good luck if you hold on to your anger with the bear.

If a child's misbehavior results in an immediate, short, sharp reprimand, the anger is expressed; if this behavior is instead considered further proof that your child isn't living up to your expectations, then you're holding on to it. Imagine your child crossing a road, and suddenly a car appears out of nowhere. You immediately respond by yelling, throwing yourself at your child, and doing whatever is necessary to avert the disaster, after which, assuming that both you and your child are okay, your initial emotion of anger (mixed with shock and fear) rapidly dissolves. If someone you're supervising makes a serious mistake through their own negligence, you'll immediately do whatever is necessary to correct the situation, discipline them, and ensure that the same thing doesn't happen again. But if instead you hold back your reaction, don't give your subordinate the immediate feedback he or she needs to correct the mistake, and start mistrusting other subordinates, then you're holding on to the anger and letting it smolder.

If someone smashes the windshield of your car, it would be normal to become extremely angry (here it might be appropriate to say "enraged" or "furious"). You may yell or curse, but after a short period of time, it won't do you any good to hold on to it, and you'll focus on cleaning up the glass and getting a new windshield. Expressing a momentary feeling of being furious or enraged isn't the same thing as letting fury or rage build up inside over time. If you hold on to your anger, blame your spouse for where the car was parked, or spend days trying to track down the individual who did this in order to exact revenge, it has turned into behaviors of rage.

These examples illustrate that there are legitimate expressions of anger, and that when the anger is expressed in a short, pointed (and appropriate) manner, it dissipates rapidly and is unlikely to become a problem.

What about more serious situations? For example, you're fired from your job without any warning, you discover your spouse is cheating on you, or you get stop-lossed after two deployments (or mobilized again), just at the point where you've made major life plans or your career is starting to take off. It would be natural to be extremely angry, and this could come and go for quite a while. However, in these situations, anger is only one layer included with other emotions, such as hurt, frustration, worry, fear, sorrow, demoralization, or betrayal. These situations require that you be aware of your feeling of anger, as well as any other emotions that exist with it. You'll feel a strong need to express your feelings by acknowledging them to yourself and those you're closest to, and perhaps rail at the unfairness of the situation. However, the goal is to put space between your feelings and any actions that you might later regret. The goal is to express anger in a healthy and beneficial way, and avoid getting stuck in the morass of rage, or turn venting and railing into a full-time occupation.

Whenever anger is acknowledged and expressed verbally, it dissipates. In some situations it may come back quickly, but it doesn't remain constant because there are other emotions also present. Acknowledging your feelings and being aware of the distinction between feelings and behaviors of rage, resentment, or hatred are important. If you turn the anger onto yourself or another person with thoughts like, "What did I do to deserve this?", "Why did I get into this situation?", "I'm worthless like this", "Why didn't I see this coming?", "Why did she/he lie to me?", "What the fuck is wrong with that person?", then the anger stews, and becomes a much larger problem.

Here are more difficult examples: You lose a close friend in combat, or someone breaks into your home and seriously injures a loved one, or your child gets abducted, or you get violently assaulted or raped. Anyone in this situation will be intensely angry (enraged, furious, murderous thoughts), and this will be mixed with grief, loss, sadness, helplessness, fear, and other emotions. The anger will not dissipate. It will come and go with high levels of intensity over a long time. The anger and other emotions need to be acknowledged. Holding on to feelings in the form of anger at God, hatred, survivor's guilt, self-blame, depression, loathing, or disgust with your life, slowly turns the anger into a solid mass of despair, pent-up rage, hostility, or behaviors that can have serious consequences. It also locks up the grief and makes it harder to express this essential emotion.

"Rageaholism"

When anger turns into blaming, hostility, rage, loathing, or passive-aggressive behavior, it becomes habitual, compulsive, and addictive. Anger, which is associated with an adrenaline high that is helpful to warriors in combat, may turn into a "craving" after returning home, much like a craving for tobacco, alcohol, or drugs. But the adrenaline also increases heart rate, blood pressure, and anxiety; disturbs sleep; and causes various other physical changes in the nervous system and body. Anger isn't something that you, a warrior, can afford to hang on to.

Persistent rage and hostility, labeled "rageaholism," has many telltale signs. These include frequently flying off the handle or repeatedly getting into heated arguments with people, having ongoing trouble at work because of temper outbursts, going over scenarios in your mind for hours, or lying awake at night thinking about what you *should have* said or done to someone, frequently saying things you regret, being verbally abusive to people, thinking of ways to get even, and getting so angry that you throw, smash, or break things or get physically violent.

Blame, "Fault," Responsibility, and Accountability

An important manifestation of rage, hostility, loathing, and resentment is when the anger is displaced or projected onto someone it has no relation to. This happens all too frequently. For example, exploding at a loved one or blaming them for something, when the real issue is pain, feeling hurt, frustration at work, or other worries; picking a fight at work, when the real issue is anxiety concerning financial trouble or marital difficulties.

A common problem is blaming others for one's difficulties; blaming someone for something they weren't responsible or accountable for. This often comes up in arguments in which the hostility is expressed by accusing someone that something they did was their "fault." Blaming in this way is usually a personal attack and implies that there's some "fault," something personally "wrong" with the other individual. This is almost always hurtful.

To understand this in greater depth requires an examination of responsibility, accountability, and "fault." Responsibility is generally used in the same way as accountability; here however, responsibility refers to the ability to respond appropriately to something or someone (e.g., responsible for picking up the groceries); accountability refers to being held to account or answerable for your actions, i.e., the cause of the event (e.g., accountable for drinking and driving). If you're responsible you may also be accountable, but if you're accountable you had to be responsible.

For example, by owning a car you accept responsibility for it—for its road-worthiness, insurance, registration, and how you drive it—but you also have to accept responsibility for driving and knowing that there are all sorts of people with different types of personalities and varying levels of driving skill, including student drivers, new drivers, sick drivers, sleepy drivers, drunk drivers, police/fire/ambulance drivers, truck drivers, unlicensed drivers, etc.; and this means recognizing their possible impact on you and accepting the responsibility for driving among them. So, if you're in a car accident, you'll always be responsible but you might also be accountable, i.e., you may have caused the accident.

If while approaching a stop sign you properly apply the brakes but they fail to function and you hit someone's car, various causes and therefore different possible accountabilities exist. If you had a brand-new car and the brakes failed because of a manufacturing or part's defect, you would not be accountable. If you had owned the car for a long time and kept up routine maintenance and repairs and a part failed, then the part manufacturer and/or the mechanic would be accountable but again, you wouldn't be. If you had owned the car for a long time but didn't keep up routine maintenance and repairs and a part failed, then you would be accountable. If someone sabotaged your brakes, you wouldn't be accountable. If you were looking for a street address while driving and failed to apply the brakes, you're accountable.

However, "fault" is entirely different. If you hit someone they'll probably "blame" you and say it's your "fault." But could the accident have been your "fault"? No! Why? Because it presumes that you *could* have made a different "choice" to do something differently. Since every "choice" you make depends on who you are (your genetics, brain function, knowledge, experiences, perceptions, memories, thoughts, feelings, values, physical characteristics, etc.), then to make a different "choice" would require *you* to be different, to be a different person. What you and I (and everyone else) experience as "choice" is really the *illusion* of choice.

So, it wasn't your "fault," it could never have been your "fault," and it can never be your "fault"; and of course, this also applies to everyone else. But this doesn't mean there aren't any consequences for your actions. If you're accountable (the cause), then you have to face whatever the results may be (paying damages, going to jail, etc.). You're responsible and accountable for your actions, but they're not your "fault."

You can act differently in the future because you (and everyone else) *will* be at least a little different. We learn and therefore can do something else when a similar situation arises. You'll always be in some way responsible and may also be accountable, but your actions are not your "fault." People often get very hurt when they're told, "It's your fault!" It changes the examination of facts into a personal "fault" finding pursuit of accusation and blame, where the intent is to hurt the other person and avoid acknowledging and resolving whatever the real issues are.

To summarize, the bottom line is that acknowledging and expressing your anger is necessary, but you have to swear off the more prolonged or addictive emotional conditions or behaviors having to do with hostility, rage, blaming, or hatred. There are several steps involved in doing this:

Steps to Deal with Anger

- For most day-to-day situations, if anger is necessary, follow First Sergeant Schindler's advice to keep the frequency, intensity, and duration of any verbal expression of it to low, mild, and short, and only to the level that is required. "Ouch, that hurts!" "Damn, I wish that hadn't happened!" A short, quick reprimand to a misbehaving child (not physical). Sharp, direct, and immediate verbal (and/or written) feedback to a subordinate who is negligent. Keep the expression of anger very brief and verbal, and it will immediately dissipate.

- When anger needs to be expressed or acknowledged, follow these three steps: a) express your anger verbally to yourself; b) clearly identify what you're angry about; and c) identify any other emotions that may coexist with the anger. This does not mean yelling at someone or acting on the anger. Here are examples: "I'm angry at the bastard who smashed my windshield, and frustrated at how much time has been wasted trying to fix this problem." "I'm furious at the fuckers who attacked us, and I feel helpless." "I'm angry and torn up over my buddy being injured; it hurts so much." "I'm angry and hurt that my boss denied my leave and I can't go on the trip." "I'm angry that I have this illness, and scared that it could be serious." "I'm angry that I didn't get the promotion, and frustrated that they didn't recognize what I have to offer." "I'm angry at what my spouse said, and worried about losing her." Accept how you feel. Don't deny how you feel. Don't hold on to your anger. Express it verbally by first acknowledging to yourself how you feel and identifying other emotions that are present, such as hurt or worry.

- Talk about what's bothering you with someone you trust. This helps greatly to sort out exactly what you're angry about and what other emotions exist. It helps if the person can empathize with your feelings of anger and not judge you or tell you that you *shouldn't* feel that way.

- If you share your anger with the person you're angry with, only express it verbally by using "I" statements, and find other words to express any underlying feelings. Respect that their views might be very different from yours. Do not direct your anger in the form of a personal attack, such as name calling, or using threatening, berating, mocking, sarcastic, intimidating, or abusive language or behavior. Phrases that start with "You," such as "You're a _____" (fill in the blank), or declarative statements that start with the words "You always . . ." or "You never . . ." are off-limits (e.g., "You always do that" or "You never follow through on anything"). Starting phrases with "I" is essential.

- Pay attention to other emotions underneath the anger, and express them as well. Sometimes recognizing the underlying emotions helps the anger subside. For example, "I'm angry you said that" could be expressed as "I feel hurt that you said that"; or if the anger is still present, "I feel angry and hurt that you said that." Go for the underlying emotion even if anger is still there. "I'm angry you didn't do what you said you would" could be changed to "I'm angry that you didn't do what you said you would, and I'm worried we won't get it done in time." In other words, express your anger with an "I" statement, not a "you" statement, and try to find the words to express any underlying feelings.

- Once you've expressed how you feel, shut up. Don't justify or defend your feeling. Don't criticize, interrupt, or lecture anyone around you who seems not to understand or appreciate what you're feeling.

- Don't play the blame game. Don't blame others for how you feel or for unfortunate things that are happening in your life. Everyone is doing the best they can and the worst they can at any given moment, including you. Yes, they can do better or worse in the future, and may have done better or worse in the past, but at any moment in time we're only doing what we can. It's appropriate to feel angry with someone who smashed your windshield, at your boss for not giving you a promotion, at your spouse for cheating on you, or at the mugger for attacking you. You may have a legitimate reason to hold someone *accountable* for something that they did or didn't do, but blame is a useless part of a warrior's vocabulary. Own your own feelings. If you're constantly blaming, criticizing, or finding "fault" with people around you, then you've arrived at the wrong coordinates and are holding on to resentment and anger in an unhealthy way.

- Put space between your reactions (in this case, your *feeling* of anger) and your actions or behaviors, as noted in chapter 5, skill 3. This is another way to say, "Count to ten." You can do this by not speaking when you feel like you're going to explode at someone; taking a deep breath from the abdomen; telling yourself to keep the frequency, intensity, or duration low, mild, and short; or by removing yourself completely from the situation or environment. For example, if you discover your spouse cheating on you, it probably would be a good idea to leave immediately and let things cool down before you engage in any conversation about what's going on or how you feel about it.

- Do some physical activity that you enjoy and that takes your mind and energy off the angry feelings, like taking a long hike, a run, or a bike ride; throwing yourself into the surf; going camping, fishing, or hunting; playing sports; dancing; or doing anything that works your body outdoors. Anger sits in the mind and muscles of your body, and often it's very helpful to clear your mind and get into your body for a while in a different way.

- If your anger is expressed in a harsh or inappropriate manner, apologize as soon as possible. Make sure your apology is sincere and complete. Never follow an apology with a "but" ("I'm sorry, but . . .").

- If you have any murderous feelings, you're not crazy. Murderous feelings don't just stop the moment you come off the battlefield. It's part of being human. Picturing what can be done to someone can actually be relaxing for some warriors. So what do you do with these feelings? Acknowledge them to yourself or someone you're close to who understands that you're not crazy, and then let them go. Feelings are feelings; they are not the same as actions. If these feelings are more than momentary, and you find yourself researching options for how to accomplish it, or develop intent to actually follow through, then it's time to visit a mental health professional, chaplain, or go to the nearest emergency room.

- If you have a persistent problem with rage behaviors that are interfering with your work or social life, or that include threatening actions, verbal or physical abuse, or homicidal plans, then get help. There are two crisis lines available where you can reach a counselor twenty-four hours a day: the National Suicide Prevention Lifeline at 1-800-273-TALK (8255) and the National Domestic Violence Hotline at 1-800-799-SAFE (7233) or 1-800-787-3224 (TTY). Both of these hotlines are connected with crisis centers where you can get immediate assistance for yourself or a loved one you're concerned about. Traditional anger management programs, or programs that consider persistent rage in the same way as an addiction, do a good job of helping with rage behaviors.

Here are some additional thoughts from First Sergeant Mike Schindler:

I believe that most people have certain expectations about warriors—such as everything is okay now that you're home. As long as people believe that you're "okay," they do not have to think about the horrors of war and what you actually have endured. You, the warrior, will try to live up to these expectations. Like, take it all in stride, keep your mouth shut, don't talk specifics about your combat experiences, keep your cool—no matter the situation.

Basically after someone asks you, "How are you doing?" and you say, "I'm okay," most people want you to shut up, go away, and not talk about combat. However, if you do begin to talk in depth with civilians about how you really feel concerning your combat experiences, they usually stop listening after thirty seconds. Then they respond with, "But you're okay, right?" This response means the end of the "discussion" on their terms about your combat experiences. They just don't want to listen to your "war stories." What civilians want is for you to hear what they have to say about war, combat, and killing the enemy. This way they can go home and stuff cheese-

burgers in their mouths and not have to think about you or war; because you're "okay," combat must not be so bad after all.

I can't count the times that I have personally gone through that scenario, which fed the anger deep inside of me, waiting to explode onto some unsuspecting person or persons when I finally couldn't take it anymore. I have always felt that I was an alien when I came home from war, or that I was on the outside looking in.

This "I'm okay" scenario made me want to scream, punch someone's lights out, and/or run away and hide because I could not deal with the everything is-okay environment. The truth being that everything was not okay with me. So for the next thirty-plus years, I suppressed my anger, guilt, and trauma of combat, which at times came out of me with certain people or situations when I couldn't take life anymore.

The subject of killing is a hard one to talk about and understand. We all know that killing is bad. We learn this from our family, school, our churches, mosques, synagogues, etc. Killing is against the law and morally wrong in society. The thought of going to war to be in combat and kill is at best extremely difficult for most people. For me the process of becoming a combat warrior took all of two seconds to pull the trigger and kill some poor bastard, without remorse. In every firefight—although different situations—my mind-set was always the same: Kill the bastards. The reasons don't matter in a firefight. Your job as a combat warrior is to kill, kill, kill the enemy, save yourselves, and accomplish the mission.

Combat warriors while in a firefight are not killing for the greater good (whatever that is). We are killing to survive and keep each other alive. I killed and would have gladly died for my brother warriors. The only solace we have is each other.

Combat warriors don't have the luxury to always be moral, and we don't make U.S. policy; we just carry it out. The transition from the battlefront to the home front and being "okay" is very challenging; learning to understand that your actions in combat were necessary for survival, for the success of the mission, and a result of your training. By definition, the job is to kill the enemy, as per U.S. policy. That sounds cold-blooded—well, that's what war is about. Combat is the ruthless desire to kill the enemy for many reasons. All I know is that to hesitate when the bullets are flying and bombs are exploding is to die; there is no time to be moral.

Then it seems that in no time at all you find yourself home standing on the corner of Packard and State streets wondering what the f%$# is happening. Whenever you meet an old friend or family member, the same two questions are usually asked: "How are you?" and then, "Did you have to kill anybody?" Your answer usually being what they want to hear: "I'm okay, and no, I did not have to kill anybody."

Eventually having to suppress the truth to the questions of "How are you?" and "Did you have to kill anybody?" becomes a source of anger. I felt that no one understood the answers and did not want the hard truths concerning combat, killing, and war. I had to learn to not feed the monsters of anger, guilt, and despair. My personal way was to find an activity that would get me moving outside and interacting with people; in my case, Hawaiian outrigger canoeing.

Controlling your environment back "home" is as critical for survival as when in combat. One of my most difficult emotions to control was anger. My brother called me a rageaholic. Sometimes I would blow my stack for the dumbest of dumb shit and not care about the people I affected. On the opposite end of rage, I could be way relaxed in the most difficult, dangerous, or scary situations.

This rage behavior or uncaring feelings are the direct result of combat and must be dealt with. Controlling how you feel is controlling your environment. If you can't stand crowds, then understand that you can do anything for a period of time. Just minimize the feelings for the duration of time you have to be in big crowds. But trust that you can deal with crowds.

Airports are my challenge and have been for decades. I used to often go through the airport in combat-ready mode. Ready to argue or bully an airport worker, airline staff member, etc. Nowadays airports are a source of entertainment and humor for me when I travel because I accept the chaos as normal. Patience and tolerance for others have kept me from trouble, sometimes big trouble. Rage is like super high-octane fuel for bad things to happen on many levels. Being cool and positive is the way to a happy soul.

Learning how to be cool and happy takes time and constant practice. Dealing with people, environments, and relationships is a huge package. I learned to deal with life by taking it one moment at a time. "Live for the moment" is my motto, and one of my tools for survival in the great game of life.

CHAPTER 8

NAVIGATE THE MENTAL HEALTH CARE SYSTEM

This chapter covers essential information if you decide to receive assistance from a mental health professional, and will probably be useful if you're already in treatment. Topics covered in this chapter include the reasons to consider getting professional help; why it's hard for warriors to ask for help; the stigma and other barriers to receiving services; differences between professional disciplines; what you can expect from treatment; the range of options available; and the benefits and limitations of treatment. The goal of this chapter is for you to acquire knowledge that will help you navigate the mental health system and advocate for yourself (or your loved one).

LAND<u>N</u>AV LEARNING OBJECTIVE: ACQUIRE KNOWLEDGE TO HELP YOU <u>N</u>AVIGATE THE MEDICAL <u>A</u>ND MENTAL HEALTH CARE SYSTEM

Reasons to Seek Mental Health Treatment

Mental health professionals have a lot to offer a warrior who is struggling with transition issues, most importantly support in alleviating distressing symptoms, and a willing ear to facilitate the narration of the warrior's story and expression of emotions associated with the story. It's truly a privilege, as a helping professional, to listen to the stories that warriors and their family members share and to assist them in their journeys. Assisting in the journey doesn't mean providing advice or answers, but rather helping individuals find the answers for themselves, so they can navigate their own course toward greater meaning, purpose, and joy.

There are a number of reasons to consider seeking professional help. Help is indicated if your transition and readjustment process isn't going smoothly and you're experiencing high distress, or are having a lot of difficulty at work or with relationships involving loved ones or coworkers. If you're experiencing high levels of PTSD symptoms according to the PTSD checklist in chapter 1, or high anxiety levels, a persistently low mood, you've lost interest in activities you used to enjoy, or you're flying off the handle all the time, then these are reasons to seek help. Professional help is indicated if you're experiencing significant problems with drinking or drug use, as discussed in chapter 4, skill 5. If you're seriously contemplating suicide or homicide, then professional help is definitely warranted.

Before we discuss how to get help and the barriers to care, if you're experiencing suicidal or homicidal intentions, or find yourself in an emotional crisis, then call the National Suicide Prevention Lifeline at 1-800-273-TALK (8255), which is available to anyone (veteran or civilian) who is in crisis or is concerned about someone in crisis. Counselors, who are connected with a network of crisis centers, are available 24/7. The number 1-800-SUICIDE (2433) connects to the same line. You can also go to an emergency room and be seen right away.

One question that may seem a bit confusing is why should you seek help for PTSD if these reactions are normal expected responses to deployment-related events? If the reactions are normal, why is it necessary to seek help? The answer has to do with the perspective in our society that problems attributed to mental health are "disorders" or "illnesses," and you can only ask for help when something is "wrong" with you or "broken." This perspective doesn't match reality, and we need to get used to the idea that some normal emotional or physical responses can be devastating and life-changing, and that we always need a way to work through these events. We need to start viewing mental health problems as part of the normal human experience.

PTSD symptoms are normal responses to severe stress and trauma but have a physiological basis, and like other medical illnesses, can clearly interfere in serious ways with a warrior's life after getting home. Seeking professional help may be the only path to integrating these experiences into who you are. In other words, don't get stuck thinking that you can only seek help if you view yourself as having something "wrong" with you. Although mental health professionals speak a different language, their primary goal is to ease the number and severity of the symptoms you experience, and help you improve your ability to relate to people, to function at work, and to enjoy life. This goal is consistent with your desire to feel better and integrate troubling experiences so you can live a healthy and meaningful life.

STIGMA AND OTHER BARRIERS TO CARE

It's normal not to want help even when you need it most. Warriors are independent-minded and used to projecting strength and self-confidence, two attributes that help them function in their jobs on the battlefield. They have learned to "drive on" and deal with some of the most difficult circumstances imaginable. They don't want to be seen as weak, and are concerned about how they will be viewed or treated by others if they admit to having a problem that they can't deal with on their own. They have learned during one or more tough deployments to keep personal problems to themselves and to not allow these issues to interfere with their jobs—even when the problems are overwhelming, like receiving a "Dear John" or "Dear Jane" letter/e-mail, or witnessing the death of a friend. They have learned to put education, career, and family goals on hold, and to function independently from their partners. They have missed countless milestones in the lives of their children and family members. They have missed births or left their children shortly after delivery. They have dealt with difficult transitions before, during, and after deployment. They have coped with and managed all of these situations, and it can be very difficult to admit to anyone that they need help, much less pick up the phone or walk into the office of a mental health professional.

A number of studies during OIF and OEF have shown that less than half of service members and veterans with serious mental health problems receive help. There are several reasons why warriors have a hard time asking for help. First, many warriors are afraid that when they start to talk about their wartime experiences, it will open up a Pandora's box and they'll lose control—they fear that they won't be able to keep it together at work or at home. This fear is justified because wartime memories are connected with very strong emotions, some of the strongest that humans can endure—emotions that have to be acknowledged and expressed as part of the process of integrating and living with these experiences. Treatment isn't easy, even when (or especially when) it's needed the most.

Second, warriors are concerned that the therapist won't be able to understand or relate to what they've experienced, or that they will judge them for things that happened. This fear is also justified because many mental health professionals don't have sufficient understanding of the military experience and have been trained to view problems within a psychological or medical framework, which labels war-related reactions as "disorders" or "illnesses," without differentiating the range of what is normal under these circumstances.

Third, warriors worry that they will be perceived as weak or treated differently by others if they admit to having a problem. If they're still in the military, they also worry that mental health treatment could affect their careers. This is also justified. When in combat, the warrior's life depends on his or her "family" of unit members, where even the perception of weakness can affect morale and cohesion, which in turn can contribute to mission failure. Although the military and VA have been working actively to reduce stigma through educational campaigns, many seasoned line leaders still consider unit members who are receiving mental health treatment, particularly if they are taking medication, as less dependable and more likely to break under fire. This has operational ramifications when they decide whom to assign to the more-difficult missions, which is unfortunate; warriors who are able to admit to needing help may be *more* resilient.

The stigma of mental health treatment is also not unique to the military, and continues as warriors transition out of the military and become civilians. Although views of mental health problems are changing, there are still pervasive beliefs in the larger society that these problems reflect a personal failure or weakness of character. This is particularly true in dangerous professions like law enforcement and security, where receiving mental health treatment is considered a sign of weakness or instability. It's also reflected in the disparity in insurance coverage for mental health vs. physical health problems.

The final reason that warriors hesitate to seek treatment is the many other barriers besides stigma, such as finding the right professional, navigating complex insurance or reimbursement processes, and repeatedly having to miss work to receive a sufficient number of appointments for treatment to be effective.

Table 2 shows results from a survey of soldiers and marines after returning from deployment to Iraq and Afghanistan. These service members were asked to rate the concerns that "might affect your decision to receive mental health counseling or services if you ever had a problem." The table shows the percentage of warriors who agreed with each of the statements. Nearly two-thirds (65 percent) of the warriors who had PTSD or depression reported that they'd be concerned that they would be "seen as weak," and 63 percent reported concerns that "unit leadership might treat me differently" if they received services. Half or more reported concerns that their peers would have less confidence in them or that their careers would be affected. Although percentages were lower among warriors from the same units who did not have mental health problems, many of them had similar concerns, reflecting how pervasive these perceptions are. The survey also identified important barriers to care, such as difficulty getting an appointment or getting time off from work.

This survey, which has been repeated in numerous units before, during, and after deployment, showed that perceived stigma and barriers remained elevated throughout the duration of the wars in Iraq and Afghanistan. Massive education campaigns and an emphasis by military leaders at the highest levels to reduce stigma haven't made a dent in the problem. This doesn't indicate a failure of education campaigns so much as the reality of how pervasive stigma is among warriors and in our society at large. Part of the reason that stigma is so pervasive in the military is the ratio of men to women, and the fact that men are much less willing than women to acknowledge when they have problems or need help.

Another pertinent finding from this survey was that nearly 40 percent of warriors who had serious mental health problems expressed distrust in mental health professionals, and one-quarter indicated agreement with the statement, "Mental health care doesn't work." This relates to the concern that warriors have that they won't be able to find a professional who truly appreciates their problems or knows how to help them.

Table 2. Percentage of Soldiers and Marines Reporting Stigma and Other Barriers to Receiving Care

Perceived Barriers and Stigma	Soldiers and Marines with PTSD or Depression (%)	All Other Soldiers and Marines from the Same Units (%)
I don't trust mental health professionals.	38	17
I don't know where to get help.	22	6
I don't have adequate transportation.	18	6
It is difficult to schedule an appointment.	45	17
There would be difficulty getting time off work for treatment.	55	22
Mental health care costs too much money.	25	10
It would be too embarrassing.	41	18
It would harm my career.	50	24
Members of my unit might have less confidence in me.	59	31
My unit leadership might treat me differently.	63	33
My leaders would blame me for the problems.	51	20
I would be seen as weak.	65	31
Mental health care doesn't work.	25	9

(From Hoge et al., *New England Journal of Medicine* 2004; 351: 13–22)

Given this, how do you overcome these barriers and get help if you need it? How do you find someone to work with? And what can you expect from professional help?

ROAD MAP FOR GETTING HELP

Fear of "Losing Control"

The fear that many warriors express is that talking about combat memories will be like opening Pandora's box. Wartime memories may also stir up difficult experiences from childhood and other losses. Warriors often fear that if they start talking about their problems, the dam will burst and they'll lose complete control, along with their marriages, relationships, and jobs. This fear reflects the intensity of the emotions, not the actual likelihood that bad things will result from talking with a therapist. Like many fears, there's an illogical aspect to this, because it only focuses on the what-if of seeking help, not the what-if of continuing to try to suppress these memories and feelings (not to mention that "What if?" itself is a trap). The reality is that when the warrior begins to contemplate getting help for combat-related reactions or other problems, then the floodgates have already started to crack; their emotions are pushing to the surface, and their defense mechanisms of walling off feelings, avoiding and retreating, and staying perpetually in combat mode are no longer working so well.

Emotions are like water; they will always find a way to seep to the surface through any crack or imperfection in defenses. You can contain them for just so long, even years, but eventually they push themselves to the surface and force you to stare them in the face and accept them.

Is the fear of "losing control" unjustified or irrational? No. Dealing with particularly difficult problems often leads to "losing it" in the form of a flood of tears and other emotional expressions. But what's remarkable is that losing it in this way actually helps to make it less likely to lose it in other ways that could be more disastrous. It turns out that what the warrior is most afraid of (not being able to work, losing relationships) is actually more likely to happen if they continue to suppress or hold back their emotions than if they get help to deal with them.

What also happens after starting to talk about painful memories, emotions, and problems is that it becomes clear there isn't anything in Pandora's box other than fear itself. Talking about painful memories may not make them any less painful, but it somehow makes it possible to live with them, and not have them remain a perpetual source of behavior that contributes to further painful experiences.

The only thing you can do is have faith in the process and drive on through it.

Overcoming Stigma

The two most important things to understand regarding stigma are a) that your own perception of yourself is more important than anyone else's; and b) that seeking help is a sign of strength, not weakness. Yes, mental health treatment carries stigma in the military and in society, but that doesn't mean that you should accept this perspective yourself. Service members and veterans often find that their fears of being seen as weak or being treated differently by colleagues, peers, or family members do not pan out when they actually do get help. People realize that seeking counseling for transition problems after combat is a normal part of the readjustment process. In fact, since 2003, a routine part of the post-deployment process for all returning service members has included health assessments for deployment-related physical and mental health concerns.

In other words, don't buy into the perception that seeking counseling is a sign of weakness, but view it as a necessary part of transition and readjustment—however many days, months, or years it's been since you returned home. Seeking help reflects strength. Everyone needs help from time to time. Everyone faces mental health problems or challenges in one way or another. You know that getting help to address difficult issues in your life is not going to be easy, and it takes courage to do it. But as a warrior, you have that courage.

If you work in a profession that requires a security clearance, as many military or former military personnel do, you may be particularly concerned that seeking professional help could affect your career. However, in 2008, the U.S. Office of Personnel Management Standard Form 86 used to apply for a security clearance was changed to accommodate veterans and to reduce the stigma of war-related mental health problems. Question 21 of this form asks if the applicant has consulted with a health-care professional in the last seven years for an "emotional or mental health condition." The instructions now include two exceptions for which the applicant is requested to mark "no"; first, if they received counseling that was "strictly related to adjustments from service in a military combat environment," and second, for counseling that is "strictly marital, family, grief" (as long as this did not involve violence).

These two exceptions represented a huge step forward in acknowledging that there are life situations, particularly involving combat and relationships, where counseling is expected. Although the definition of "adjustments from service in a military combat environment" is somewhat vague, this exception seems open to wide interpretation encompassing much of what we've been talking about in this book. The other thing to be aware of is that even if "yes" is marked on this form, it doesn't lead to automatic denial of clearance, but simply a delay while another form is sent to the mental health professional, who is asked a yes-no question about whether there is any concern that the individual's behavior could jeopardize security. There's no further information provided by the therapist unless they have such a concern.

Unfortunately, the positive changes in the Federal Form 86 have not trickled down to the many different law enforcement organizations where combat veterans like to work; many of these organizations have their own screening processes, and don't provide an exception for combat-related counseling. There is a widespread perception that this frequently leads to non-selection of qualified combat veterans. This is particularly worrisome in recent years, since mental health screenings have become routine in the post-deployment period, and many warriors have received counseling as part of the normal process. Hopefully, the perspective in this book will become more widespread, and law enforcement agencies will learn that veterans with a history of PTSD or other reactions related to combat are often the best candidates because they are experienced, calm under fire, and have learned how to utilize their experiences (including their PTSD reactions) in a positive way.

Overcoming Other Barriers and Taking the First Steps

Although there are numerous ways to get help and various mental health professionals to choose from, the system is complex and often not very welcoming. Unfortunately, all too often when a warrior finally makes the decision to get help, they're met with various material hurdles, like the unavailability of an appointment for several weeks. There is nothing quite as effective at destroying a newly emerging help-seeking attitude than being told precisely at that moment when you most need help (and are finally ready to receive it) that you have to wait for several weeks. Not to mention that you have no idea if the person you'll eventually see will have the knowledge and ability to help you.

But being told that you have to wait several weeks means you've already successfully navigated figuring out who to call in the first place. That first step alone can present a significant-enough barrier to send warriors back into their foxholes. So how do you navigate this process, or even get started? Here are some routes to consider:

A) *Get Advice from Fellow Warriors, Veterans, Veterans' Organizations*

One of the best sources of information for how to begin finding treatment is from fellow warriors and veterans' organizations. Given the complexity of the medical system in the VA, DoD, and in civilian health-care settings, it's helpful to talk with others who have navigated this. Many have experience with how to get into the system and recommendations of mental health professionals who they found helpful. Also, they're often in the best position to both observe how a fellow warrior is doing and to encourage that warrior to seek help when needed. There are also many outstanding veterans' organizations that can provide information, assistance, and advocacy in the journey. For example, see www1.va.gov/vso/ for a searchable directory of veterans' organizations.

B) *Primary Care Referral*

One of the easiest places to begin is to contact your primary care provider in whatever health-care system you're in and ask for a referral. Many systems require that care is coordinated through the primary care provider, so this is often the first place to start.

Your primary care provider (who's usually a family medicine or internal medicine physician, nurse practitioner, or physician's assistant) will be very willing to assist you with this referral, although they may at times choose to initiate treatment themselves, making a referral only if the treatment doesn't work. This is relatively common for mild to moderate depression, mild to moderate anxiety, or sleep problems. However, treatment options are limited only to medications, since primary care professionals are generally not trained in providing therapy.

If you're experiencing anything more than minor difficulties, insist on being referred to a trained mental health professional, and don't let the buck stop in primary care. One exception to this is if there are mental health professionals working inside the primary care clinic (often referred to as a "collaborative care" program).

C) VA Vet Centers

One of the most unique resources available to U.S. combat veterans is the VA-sponsored Vet Centers. If you're fortunate to live near one of the 230-plus Vet Centers across the nation (and U.S. territories), I highly recommend going for a visit, as they have the most specific post-combat readjustment counseling programs available anywhere. You're eligible for these services at no cost if you have served in any combat zone or you're a family member of a warrior. You don't have to be enrolled in the VA to receive Vet Center services. All Vet Centers are staffed by combat veterans, which means you'll find staff members who understand what you've been through and have been there themselves. Vet Centers offer individual and group counseling, marital and family counseling, bereavement services for family members of warriors killed in action, alcohol/drug assessments, counseling for veterans who have experienced sexual trauma in the military, and other services. You can find out where the nearest facility is by visiting www.vetcenter.va.gov. Don't be discouraged by the sparse information on their Web site, because this program has a tremendous amount to offer and is very welcoming to combat veterans and their family members; it's a great place to start your counseling journey.

D) Mental Health Clinics

Although there are numerous mental health professionals in private practice or associated with clinics and medical facilities, the challenge is navigating your particular health-care system to find the professional who's right for you. Unfortunately, in many civilian systems, people end up paying out of pocket for some of these services due to limitations in mental health insurance coverage, lack of available professionals that accept specific insurance plans, or lack of appointments at convenient hours that don't interfere with work or child-care duties. These are some of the many barriers characteristic of mental health services. The other issue in civilian mental health care settings is that there are often problems finding professionals who have any experience with the military or with treating trauma. There isn't a good answer to these realities, other than to acknowledge them and try to do the best you can to find a professional who you can work with. It's helpful to be armed with the knowledge in this chapter of what different professionals can offer and the types of treatment that are available.

For service members, mental health clinics are widely available at military treatment facilities, and many of the professionals are in the military themselves or have worked with the military for a long time. In most treatment facilities, it's possible to walk into the mental health clinic without an appointment (a "self-referral") and get seen on the same day. Another good resource available to military service members and their families is Military OneSource at www.militaryonesource.com or 1-800-342-9647. Military One-Source has free confidential counseling options available in person, by telephone, and online. This counseling is generally limited to short-term issues involving stress or marital difficulties, and is not the best option for serious problems with PTSD, depression, or alcohol abuse. However, one of the nice things about Military OneSource is that you can speak with someone quickly, and if they feel you need a referral to another professional, they'll facilitate it.

For veterans eligible for VA health-care services, there are medical facilities with outstanding mental health services available nationwide (and in the U.S. territories). You can visit www.va.gov or www1.va.gov/health for more information on eligibility, services, and to find the closest facility. OIF and OEF veterans can benefit from priority in VA services for five years after discharge from the military. Note that VA mental health clinics are not the same as VA Vet Centers. Vet Centers are located in the community and are specifically focused on readjustment counseling for combat veterans, while the mental health clinics are located in VA medical facilities that offer the full range of health-care services for both physical and mental health problems to all eligible veterans, including those without combat campaign badges.

Also, there are many more VA mental health clinics than Vet Centers, so depending on your location, they may be the only option.

Both the military and VA health systems can be complicated and frustrating to deal with, but are staffed with professionals who are dedicated to helping warriors. One source of information that may be helpful in identifying resources in your area or in answering questions is the Outreach Center of the Defense Centers of Excellence for Psychological Health and Traumatic Brain Injury (www.dcoe.health.mil/). Their toll free number, 1-866-966-1020, is staffed twenty-four hours a day. Two other sites with extensive information include the Deployment Health Clinical Center (www.pdhealth.mil) and the VA National Center for PTSD (www.ncptsd.va.gov).

E) Emergency Departments, Crisis Centers

If you're in crisis or experience suicidal or homicidal feelings, the quickest way to get into treatment is to call one of the crisis lines (e.g., 1-800-273-TALK) or to go to the nearest emergency room. Emergency departments generally have mental health professionals available on call who can conduct an evaluation and either make a referral to outpatient treatment or facilitate hospitalization if necessary.

Species of Mental Health Professionals

There are several types of mental health professionals—including psychiatrists, psychologists, and clinical social workers—who as a group are also referred to as "therapists," "psychotherapists," "counselors," or mental health "clinicians." It can be confusing trying to figure out which discipline or clinic offers what you need. In most health-care settings, including DoD and VA, mental health professionals of different disciplines often share the same clinic setting, which may be labeled "Behavioral Health," "Mental Health," etc. Mental health professionals also frequently work in non–mental health settings, such as primary care, occupational health, and rehabilitation medicine.

Mental health professionals generally can be grouped according to the services they provide and their level of training, with psychiatrists, clinical social workers, and psychologists being the most common. All are required to be licensed by the state they are practicing in, or any state if they work for the federal government.

The outpatient treatment services generally fall into two categories: medication treatment and psychotherapy (also called "talk therapy," "therapy," or "counseling"). Professionals will be able to provide one or both of these treatment types. Psychotherapy can be administered on an individual or group basis.

Psychiatrists are medical doctors who completed four years of medical or osteopathic school and at least four additional years in a psychiatry residency. They have the authority to prescribe medications. They may also provide psychotherapy, depending on the setting they practice in, their training, and their own inclinations. However, since they are reimbursed at a higher rate than other mental health professionals, in most medical settings the appointment times for psychiatrists are too short to allow for psychotherapy, and their practice is restricted largely to medication "management." Medication management includes evaluating the need for medications, prescribing medications, and monitoring their effectiveness. Generally the first visit lasts approximately one hour, and subsequent visits are limited to ten to thirty minutes, unless the psychiatrist is also providing psychotherapy.

Clinical psychologists and clinical social workers are both trained to provide psychotherapy services, generally in fifty-minute appointment increments, but this may vary depending on the type of services. Social workers and psychologists have either a master's level or doctoral level of education after college. Some professionals (usually doctoral-level psychologists) also have specific expertise in administering complex and lengthy psychological tests designed to provide additional information that may be helpful in diagnosis and treatment. A few doctoral-level psychologists are also licensed to prescribe medications. However, in terms of your needs, the education level of a social worker or psychologist is not as important as their level of clinical experience, and whether or not they have been supervised for long enough to be permitted by their organization to practice independently without supervision by another licensed professional.

There are several other professional disciplines that work in mental health treatment settings, including psychiatric nurses or nurse practitioners;

occupational therapists; and other types of counselors, such as alcohol and substance abuse counselors, and marital and family therapists.

General types of counseling are also available in nonmedical settings. Most notably, many clergy members are trained in counseling, and can provide emotional, social, and spiritual support to individuals and families for a variety of problems that don't require specific medical treatment or psychotherapy. Within the military, chaplains play a central role in providing counseling services in battalions, and often facilitate in helping warriors get treatment from other mental health professionals. Additionally, there's a rapidly expanding industry called "life coaching," or "personal life coaching," which has emerged from the human resources and positive psychology fields. Coaching involves hiring a person (a coach) to help you achieve life goals through a structured process that includes examining values and beliefs, setting goals, defining a plan to achieve those goals, and monitoring changes and progress. Life coaches go to great lengths to distinguish themselves from therapists or mental health counselors, although many of the same principles underlie coaching and more-traditional forms of counseling, particularly in the use of positive psychology and cognitive behavioral approaches. Coaching is certainly not a treatment for PTSD or any other mental health disorder, but it can offer skills that are useful in achieving measurable goals.

Your First Appointment with a Mental Health Professional

If at all possible, avoid your first and second appointment with the mental health professional and start with the third one. When you show up for your third appointment, act like you've gotten a lot out of the first two. (Okay, just joking.)

The most important thing about starting treatment is to have patience and an open mind. It generally doesn't matter which type of specialist you start with, although it's nice to know who you'll see, so you can assess if their orientation is geared more toward medicines (a psychiatrist) or more toward psychotherapy (e.g., social workers, psychologists, and some psychiatrists). Some clinics have everyone see an intake counselor to gather initial information for the convenience of the psychologist, social worker, or psychiatrist; other clinics will have you start with a social worker or psychologist, and then if they think medication is indicated, they will make a referral to a psychiatrist (or vice versa). In some cases, primary care doctors will work with psychologists or social workers to provide medication prescriptions.

The first session will generally last about an hour and will include discussion of your current problems, medical history, history of any prior mental health treatment, alcohol and substance use, and your personal history (e.g., upbringing, education, occupation, marital/family history, current stressors). There will also be questions related to suicidal or homicidal ideation that are routinely asked. Bear in mind that the first session is generally just for information gathering, although it can provide a great sense of relief if you find a professional who seems genuinely concerned and interested in helping you.

It's not uncommon for warriors to have bad experiences on their initial visit. This can happen for several reasons: First, the mental health clinician may not provide sufficient time or attentiveness for the warrior to feel like their concerns are being adequately addressed. Mental health clinic settings can be very busy places, and sometimes the first appointment feels rushed or the clinician may be too abrupt. This can happen because the number of patients has overwhelmed the clinician's ability to give everyone sufficient time; because the clinician seems more interested in communicating with the computer than with the client (which may reflect cumbersome requirements for electronic documentation); because their personality is abrupt in general; or because the clinician is having a bad day or is suffering from their own mental health problems. Whatever the reason, the warrior rightfully feels brushed off or misunderstood.

Second, the clinician might not adequately understand the military context of the problems, or they might speak in a way that reveals their own assumptions about the nature of the warrior's experience. They could be perceived as judgmental or condescending, and this can get things off to a bad start.

Third, the mental health clinician's recommendations, which they provide near the end of the first session, might not mesh with the warrior's needs or expectations, both in terms of the diagnoses or the recommended treatment. If the initial visit is with a psychiatrist, medications are more likely to be recommended than if the visit is with a social worker, psychologist, or other counselor, although this is not universal. This can sometimes relate to what the clinician is most comfortable with, rather than what's best for the warrior at this moment. Many warriors are indeed ready and willing to try medication, and there are many safe and effective options available, but others are either unwilling to take medicines at all or need time to think about it before making the commitment. The psychiatrist will likely do a good job explaining the risks and benefits of several medication options, but may not do as good a job explaining the wider range of psychotherapy alternatives.

On the flip side, if the initial visit is with a psychologist or social worker, they may promote the specific type(s) of psychotherapy techniques they're most comfortable with and focus less on medications. Again, this can relate to what the clinician is most comfortable with, not necessarily what's best for the warrior. These comments are broad generalizations, and there are a lot of individual differences in the approach that clinicians take.

If your initial experience is positive, you're off to a good start. If not, don't lose hope, and try not to get frustrated; just accept that you'll need more patience to work through this. You can tell the mental health professional how you feel and let them know that the visit didn't live up to your expectations; you can ask additional questions to ensure that you understand the full range of treatments and that the professional is giving you a complete picture of your options (both psychotherapy and medicines); and you can ask the therapist what their experience is in treating veterans with combat-related problems. Their response to these questions and feedback will tell you a lot. You can also ask to see a different professional or you can go somewhere else. Just because your initial visit wasn't a positive experience, don't let that affect your determination to get the help you need and deserve, and to keep asking questions until you get satisfactory answers.

Advice for Mental Health Professionals (and Considerations that Warriors Generally Appreciate)

For any mental health professionals reading this, here is my advice for building a therapeutic relationship with a warrior: Be honest, direct, genuine, accessible, and empathetic. Honesty means stating what you know from your professional expertise and admitting when you don't have the answers (as is likely, since treatment of mental health problems is never straightforward). Being direct means maintaining eye contact with your client, not the computer screen (which also means that you'll probably have to write incredibly brief notes to survive your busy schedule). If asked a direct question that you don't have an adequate answer to, say that you don't know but will track the answer down. Don't do what many of your colleagues do, which is to shift to the highly effective (for them) defense mechanism of unintelligible jargon when asked a question that they don't have an adequate answer to. Don't make assumptions about military culture or the warrior's experience; ask for clarification from the warrior if there's something that you don't understand, even seemingly minor things (which aren't minor to warriors), like rank structure or occupational roles. Being genuine means being a good listener and not beating around the bush; warriors can be very attuned to the perception of being brushed off or to indirect forms of communication. Treat everyone with the utmost respect and honor their service, whatever rank or duty they had during deployment (private, general, government worker, contractor, etc.). They are professionals who did highly skilled jobs under very difficult circumstances. Being accessible means making it clear how to get in touch with you and making yourself available with minimal barriers when the warrior needs something.

The foundation for therapy is built through empathy and normalizing the warrior's experience. This means helping the warrior to understand that they're not crazy; that their reactions make sense in the context of their experiences; that their reactions are part of the body's normal protective responses; that it's very hard for anyone to imagine what it would be like to go through what they went through; that no one is in any position to judge or second-guess what happened, except perhaps their own buddies who were actually there (and even then, that might not be correct); that reactions to current stresses make sense in the context of everything that has happened in their life; and that you'll help them to the best of your ability to successfully navigate their difficulties and serve as their ally and advocate. It's helpful to point out to the warrior any of their strengths you observe that will help them be successful and to provide them with a summary of what to expect in future sessions.

The other component of an empathetic response, in addition to normalizing the warrior's experience, is the ability to be aware of your own feelings and reactions, whether there's sadness, horror, disgust, appreciation, laughter, etc. That doesn't mean that you have to express all of these emotions openly (although that can be good, depending on the situation), but you have to at least be aware of them as they're occurring and not filter them. The warrior needs to feel that you're "online." Since warriors often do a very good job of compartmentalizing their wide range of experiences, thoughts, and feelings, as well as dissociating each from the other, modeling the opposite can be most beneficial.

Minimize the use of psychological concepts and jargon; provide clear and straightforward handouts. For example, warriors don't need a detailed education on the topics of "assimilation" or "accommodation," given that the psychological definitions of these terms don't have much to do with the English-language definitions, and the fact that "accommodation" in the English language doesn't mean the same thing as "integration," which is the preferred concept to talk about with warriors.

They also don't need handouts with extensive "if" statements. (For example, "If you had prior positive experiences in your relationships with others and in relation to powerful others, you may have come to believe that you could influence others" or "If you previously believed that 'I can control what happens to me and can protect myself from any harm,' you will need to resolve the conflict between prior beliefs and the victimization experience," two actual quotes from commonly used patient handouts on control and safety from the 2007 Veteran and Military version of Cognitive Processing Therapy.)

Avoid starting sentences with the words, "You need to _____" or "You will need to _____" or "It is necessary to _____ (consider this

or that, do this or that) or "It is important to understand (or realize) that
_____", because these types of statements presume that you know
what's best for them, and that you're there to deliver answers to them
rather than to help them to learn or discover the answers for themselves.

Be very careful with the diagnostic labels that you apply. Avoid personality disorder (Axis II) labels, even "traits," as this often conveys more about
what the health-care professional thinks of the client than what is beneficial for the client's treatment. If you have to write something in the Axis
II diagnosis section, write "No Axis II Diagnosis" rather than "Deferred."
All medical labels, particularly those in the Axis II category, can affect how
the warrior views him- or herself, as well as how all health-care professionals view and treat the warrior. Axis II labels undoubtedly cause much more
harm than good in overall health care.

It's important to appreciate that many behaviors considered "negative" or "maladaptive" are beneficial. They may not be beneficial to others
or society, but serve a useful purpose for the individual. For instance, probably the surest way to reinforce survivor's guilt is by labeling it a "cognitive
distortion" or "negative affect."

In contrast, encouraging the behavior in the right way resolves it by
helping the warrior to discover exactly why they "punish" themselves, why
they believe they deserve punishment, what they're punishing themselves
for, and what they get out of it (they *do* get something positive). See chapter 9 for more on this topic.

TYPES OF TREATMENT OFFERED: THE COLD, HARD FACTS

This section will cover the range of commonly used treatment options and
their effectiveness and limitations, including psychotherapy, medications,
and other emerging therapies. The treatment of PTSD, depression, and
anxiety often utilize very similar or identical techniques and medications.
Consequently, this section will stay focused on PTSD, but bear in mind
that these same treatments are applied to the other conditions as well.
(The treatment of symptoms related to concussion/mTBI was discussed
in chapter 2.)

Treatment Effectiveness

Often just going to see a mental health professional can be of benefit even if the professional doesn't prescribe a specific "evidence-based" treatment (a treatment that has been shown in scientific studies to be effective). This is because there are effects just from making the effort to talk to someone about your problems. Because of this, any scientific study of treatment effectiveness has to include a comparison (control) group of people who receive no treatment or another type of treatment. A treatment is only considered to be "evidence-based" when it has been proven to be effective through such a comparison, preferably repeated in several studies.

So how effective are PTSD treatments for combat veterans?

The answer is not so effective—at least, not what we would like to see. Often the difference in improvement between people who receive treatment and people in comparison groups is small. Because of this, it's necessary to try different strategies, combine them, and modify treatment to find the right approach that will work for each individual.

Medications

A prominent review of the effectiveness of medications for PTSD concluded that overall, 59 percent of people with PTSD who received medications recovered, compared with 39 percent of people with PTSD who were given pills that looked exactly the same but didn't contain any medicine (placebo pills). This means that just going to see the doctor and receiving a placebo pill resulted in a benefit for nearly 40 percent of individuals with PTSD; the medicine was effective in increasing the number of people who recovered by only 20 percent, and there were still 40 percent of people who did not recover among the treated group. The review was based on studies in which both the patients and the doctors evaluating them did not know which pill the patients received (a "double-blind" scientific design). This ensured that the conclusions were free of biases, such as the expectations of patients or doctors that the medicines would be beneficial. The results of this review didn't take into account that some people may have experienced partial improvement in PTSD symptoms or improvement in depression symptoms, which often coexist, so there may have been some benefits that weren't measured.

On the other hand, the review's conclusions were based almost entirely on studies in civilians, and there is good evidence that combat-related PTSD is more difficult to treat and less amenable to cure with medications. One of the only studies involving combat veterans was published more than ten years after it was conducted, and showed no benefit of treatment using one of the medications most commonly prescribed for PTSD, sertraline (Zoloft).

Psychotherapy

Studies of various psychotherapy treatments have also shown less than optimal results. It's generally believed by experts in the field that certain types of psychotherapy, particularly therapies involving cognitive or exposure techniques, are more effective for PTSD than medications. However, there have been very few head-to-head comparisons, especially in combat veterans. Studies of the effectiveness of psychotherapy are often influenced by biases because there isn't a way to keep the patient and doctor "blind" to the group the patient is assigned to. For example, imagine that you agree to participate in a research study of a promising new psychotherapy, but are told that you have to wait ten weeks to get treatment; this indicates that you've been assigned to the no-treatment control group (conveniently termed the "wait-list" group). You (and the other members of this group) may get pissed off, and probably won't get any better in the next ten weeks (and in fact, may get worse), while those assigned to the treatment group get to experience the benefits of treatment immediately. The vast majority of research studies on psychotherapy have been done this way, and this obviously stacks the deck in favor of demonstrating that the treatment (whatever it is) is effective. In one widely cited study of veterans with PTSD conducted by the U.S. National Center for PTSD, 40 percent who received a therapy called "Cognitive Processing Therapy" recovered, compared with 3 percent of those from the wait-list control group. Notice that despite the large difference in recovery between the two groups, the 40 percent recovery rate of the treated group was similar to the overall rate of recovery in medication studies.

The best psychotherapy-effectiveness studies provide a sham "treatment" to the control group that includes regular visits with a therapist, who gives support but doesn't apply any of the specific treatment techniques. These types of studies eliminate biases inherent in the studies that use wait-lists, and result in smaller differences between groups. For example, in a large 2007 study of women veterans with PTSD, 41 percent recovered from exposure therapy compared with 29 percent who received the sham "treatment."

Overall, in various psychotherapy studies for PTSD, it's common for no more than 50 percent of treated individuals to show greater improvements than would be expected naturally (by chance) in the individuals who did not receive treatment. This is referred to as "effect size," and is a complicated way of saying that results in treated and non-treated groups overlap a lot, that many people recover with no treatment, and that the effectiveness of treatment is not as high as we would like to see.

While the rates of *full* recovery from PTSD in research studies are somewhat discouraging, the good news is that most studies show that a larger percentage of people experience *partial* recovery. Overall, most people can expect at least moderate improvement from treatment if they stick with it. One of the key factors in the effectiveness of psychotherapy is a willingness and ability to remain in treatment for long enough to benefit; this generally takes at least ten to twelve visits, and sometimes much longer. Many people drop out of therapy; the reasons are poorly understood, but likely have as much to do with the personality and skills of the therapist as with the client's own circumstances.

Among psychotherapy techniques, there has been a lot of debate as to whether exposure therapy or cognitive techniques are more effective. In 2008, the U.S. Institute of Medicine published an extensive review of the medical literature on treatment of PTSD focused on military and veteran populations. This respected organization concluded that exposure therapy (elements of which are described in detail in chapters 6 and 7) had the highest evidence for effectiveness. One study by National Center for PTSD investigators showed that simply writing about one's trauma for up to an hour each week, combined with reading this to the therapist and briefly discussing it, had nearly the same effectiveness as the complete cognitive processing therapy program. What the overall data appear to mean is that we really don't know what works in therapy and that narrating your story is probably better than any other type of therapy technique or medications.

Harm from Treatment

One thing to consider is that professional treatment has the potential to cause harm. For example, if you're struggling with issues of grief, loss, or survivor's guilt that the mental health professional thinks is depression or PTSD, or you have concentration and memory problems due to PTSD that the professional believes is caused by an mTBI, or your post-war reactions are misdiagnosed as a personality disorder, then this could lead to negative self-perceptions, ineffective treatment, or harmful side effects. Everything that clinicians do in medicine carries risks, including the diagnostic labels they apply.

In a 2007 study, we found that soldiers referred for PTSD from the DoD post-deployment health assessment who failed to show up for their mental health appointments actually did better than soldiers who attended their appointments. Although it's likely that soldiers who followed through with their appointments had more severe PTSD symptoms (and therefore were in greater need of treatment), the study highlighted that many soldiers got better on their own, and that referral from the post-deployment health assessment didn't necessarily result in the desired outcome.

In summary, there have been very few studies of the effectiveness of combining different psychotherapies or psychotherapy plus medications, particularly in combat veterans, but the presumption is that we can improve outcomes by combining treatments. Everyone responds differently to treatment, and there is no one-size-fits-all approach. The best advice is to find someone you're comfortable working with and try whatever method they suggest; if that doesn't work as well as you would like, then inquire into other options. Explore your options until you find the formula that works for you.

Psychotherapy

The most common forms of psychotherapy for PTSD that are evidence-based are *cognitive behavioral therapy*, which includes exposure therapy and cognitive restructuring (also called "cognitive reframing" or "cognitive processing"); *Eye Movement Desensitization and Reprocessing* (EMDR); and *stress inoculation training*. All of the cognitive behavioral therapies and EMDR involve a combination of exposure therapy (either talking about or writing your story), analysis of thinking patterns (cognitions), and body relaxation exercises, along with a supportive connection with the therapist.

Many of the LANDNAV skills in this book are drawn from the techniques used in psychotherapy, which I converted into self-help learning skills. For instance, the resiliency inoculation training and narration skills in chapters 6 and 7 contain the key elements of imaginal and *invivo* exposure therapy. Examples of cognitive restructuring have been woven throughout the book, such as the exercises to reduce "shoulds," the exercises related to control and intolerance of mistakes, the discussion of catch-22s, and the emphasis on viewing yourself in a positive manner. Techniques drawn from stress inoculation training include muscle relaxation, breathing exercises, and mindfulness meditation, as detailed in chapter 5, as well as some of the training related to anger in chapter 7. The material on loss, guilt, complex emotions, and acceptance coming up in the next chapter also include elements of cognitive restructuring.

Below is a brief description of the most common forms of psychotherapy. Most of these therapies require at least ten to twelve sessions to be effective (and often many more). They are usually administered individually, although they are sometimes incorporated into group therapy.

A) *Exposure Therapy*

The elements of exposure therapy have already been extensively discussed in chapters 6 and 7. The essential elements include talking about your experiences with the therapist in a structured manner, or writing about them and going over the writing in the therapy session. It also includes various exercises to reduce the tendency to avoid situations that trigger strong reactions. This form of therapy has the strongest scientific evidence for effectiveness.

B) *Cognitive Restructuring / Cognitive Reframing / Cognitive Processing*

This therapy involves analyzing your thoughts and reactions to situations and combating negative ways of thinking, such as negative beliefs about yourself. Trauma, combined with other experiences you may have had before and after service, can lead to ways of thinking that can negatively affect your mood and perception of yourself. Examples include "should" statements, taking things too personally, all or nothing, leaping to conclusions, focusing only on the negative, oversimplifying things or overgeneralizing, making a mountain out of a molehill, beating up on yourself, altered perception of safety (viewing relatively safe situations as unsafe), and excessive guilt. This type of therapy involves analyzing your thought processes, identifying when you're using some of these negative patterns, and then identifying new ways of thinking. It's a way of changing programs in your brain that keep you stuck and are affecting your mood and functioning. The term *cognitive processing therapy* refers to a therapy that combines cognitive reframing (processing) with written exposure and relaxation exercises.

C) Eye Movement Desensitization and Reprocessing (EMDR)

EMDR combines body awareness and relaxation exercises, exposure therapy, and cognitive restructuring. The exposure component involves talking about and/or visualizing traumatic experiences while the therapist guides you to move your eyes back and forth horizontally in a rhythmic manner, combined with processing of beliefs or thoughts associated with the experiences. The eye movements are thought to stimulate both sides of the brain to help integrate traumatic memories. However, there is evidence that the eye movements themselves are not necessary, and the essential element is probably similar to other forms of exposure therapy— telling your story to someone who cares, and who can provide feedback in a supportive way.

D) Stress Inoculation Training

This includes a variety of exercises to reduce anxiety, such as muscle relaxation, diaphragmatic breathing, and "stopping" certain thought patterns. Again, many of these principles have been incorporated into the training in this book.

E) Group Therapy

Group therapy doesn't appeal to a lot of warriors who may be uncomfortable speaking about their problems in a group. Group therapy also has the least amount of research to support its effectiveness. However, this type of therapy can be a wonderful experience if the group has the right composition of members and a good facilitator, because it puts you in contact with other warriors who are going through similar difficulties and can appreciate your experiences. Many war-related reactions have similarities or common elements, despite vast differences in the actual events. It can be a tremendous relief to meet other warriors who have gone through similar difficulties as you. Sharing your experiences in a group or listening to others can reduce the burden that each individual carries. It can help to feel less alone and more connected with others.

Most group therapy sessions last sixty to ninety minutes, and the ideal size is around eight to twelve people. If you're considering group therapy, find out whether it only includes combat veterans and whether it's a closed group (one that doesn't change membership over the course of treatment) or an open group (one that allows new members in because the group is ongoing). If you can find a group that's geared specifically for warriors, this may be worth pursuing. Closed groups offer advantages, but some open groups can work well if there's good facilitation and a willingness on the part of existing members to allow in new members.

F) Other Elements of Therapy

There are many other supportive interventions that happen during psychotherapy sessions, either as part of the above treatments or separately. These can include grief counseling; marital counseling; counseling related to job or financial stressors; alcohol and drug counseling; or counseling focused on coping with medical problems, pain, or injuries. Depending on the circumstances and the particular stressors going on at the moment, these aspects of therapy can take a higher priority than the other approaches listed above.

Medications

Of all of the available categories of psychiatric medicines, only one, the Selective Serotonin Reuptake Inhibitors (SSRIs) have an acceptable level of evidence to consider them effective for PTSD. There are several other types of medications that psychiatrists prescribe to alleviate PTSD symptoms, but their effectiveness is much less certain and less well studied than the SSRIs.

A couple of disclaimers are needed for this section: First, in this brief overview of medicines I will only touch on relevant information to help you in your decisions. There's a lot of additional information, particularly on side effects and risks, which you'll need to consider if your doctor prescribes one of these. Make sure that you get comprehensive information from your doctor and read the package insert(s) so you're fully informed on the risks and side effects, as this chapter doesn't provide complete information. An easy way to do this for most medications is to simply type www.[name of medication].com (e.g. www.zoloft.com). Use the brand name (e.g. Zoloft) rather than the generic name (e.g. "sertraline"). Second, although the FDA has approved all of these medicines for specific purposes (such as depression), most have not received approval for the treatment of PTSD. This doesn't mean that they are ineffective, but it does mean that they haven't gone through as careful a scientific process to weigh the benefits against the risks. Additional information can be found at the National Institute of Mental Health (www.nimh.nih.gov) or at www.fda.gov/medwatch.

A) Selective Serotonin Reuptake Inhibitors (SSRIs)

SSRIs revolutionized the treatment of depression and anxiety disorders, starting with the introduction of fluoxetine (Prozac) in 1986. Prozac provided a remarkably safe alternative to the tricyclic antidepressants used since the 1950s that had numerous side effects. Since Prozac was introduced, a number of other SSRIs have followed, including fluvoxamine (Luvox), sertraline (Zoloft), paroxetine (Paxil), citalopram (Celexa), and escitalopram (Lexapro). SSRIs are the only class of medicine shown to have consistent and reasonable evidence for effectiveness in PTSD. All of the SSRIs are approved either for depression, one or more anxiety disorders, or both; sertraline (Zoloft) and paroxetine (Paxil) are currently approved by the FDA for PTSD. However, there is no reason to believe that these two are better than the other SSRIs for PTSD, because they all work in the same way on serotonin nerve transmission in the brain.

It is commonly stated that depression, anxiety, and PTSD reflect "chemical imbalances" in the brain involving the neurotransmitter serotonin, and that SSRIs are designed to correct this. The reality is that scientists have very little understanding of exactly why SSRIs help in these conditions, and what "chemical imbalance" they are ostensibly treating. However, don't let that dissuade you from trying out this class of medicine if needed. (The next time your doctor tells you that you have a "chemical imbalance" in your brain, tell him what a tremendous relief it is to finally confirm this, because you've always known you were "imbalanced," that you can't wait to pick up the magic pill that will correct all this, and that thanks to such a thorough explanation, you will at last be able to live happily ever after. You'll likely be rewarded with a perplexed look on your doctor's face.)

Although there are questions of how effective SSRIs are for combat-related PTSD, SSRIs are almost always the first medicine that a doctor will select for this condition. One of the advantages of SSRIs is that they are the leading medicine used to treat depression, and they also may have some benefit in reducing anger, even if they are relatively less effective for PTSD. Many warriors benefit from their effect on depression and/or anger. SSRIs are used routinely in the deployed environment. One recent survey indicated that 5 percent of service members deployed to Iraq and Afghanistan were taking a psychiatric medicine, with SSRIs being at the top of the list. Most preparations of SSRIs are taken once a day, and it generally doesn't matter if it's in the morning or evening.

It's a common misconception that all psychiatric medicines, including SSRIs, "mess with your mind," are addictive, or can impair a person's judgment or ability to think clearly either from their use or from stopping them abruptly. There have been concerns among operational leaders that the widespread use of these medicines in deployed troops could affect their ability to function in the combat environment, putting lives at risk. There has also been the concern raised that SSRIs may increase the risk of suicide because of a "black box" warning issued recently by the FDA. All of these concerns appear to be unfounded. SSRIs do not affect cognitive functioning, judgment, or the ability to think clearly. They are not addictive. Abrupt discontinuation can lead to feeling like you have the flu for several days, but it's not dangerous. There is no evidence that SSRIs increase the risk of suicide among adults, although there has been some theoretical concern about SSRIs increasing suicidal thinking in children and adolescents/young adults. Most important, many warriors have benefited from taking SSRIs, either individually or in combination with psychotherapy. Sometimes the SSRI can take the "edge" off of debilitating symptoms and make it easier to start the necessary work of talking about your experiences.

SSRIs do have some risks and side effects. One common side effect is restlessness, jitteriness, or increased anxiety when first started. For this reason, it's wise to take half of the lowest recommended dose for the first week (by cutting the pills in half) and then increasing it slowly thereafter. Because there are serotonin nerves in the gastrointestinal track, nausea or diarrhea may occur. Headaches can also occur. Generally, the nausea, diarrhea, and headaches will subside after you've taken the medicine for a few days.

The most bothersome side effect, which occurs quite frequently, is sexual difficulties, most commonly in reaching orgasm. This occurs in both men and women. For men, SSRIs generally don't affect the ability to get an erection, and some men find the side effect of delayed orgasm beneficial. However, when it affects the ability to reach orgasm, this can make sexual experiences frustrating for both partners. If this occurs, don't be embarrassed to speak with your doctor about it. This is one of the most common reasons for discontinuing this medicine or switching to another medication.

The most important risk associated with SSRIs has to do with their interactions with other medications. Some of the SSRIs can delay the speed with which the liver metabolizes and clears other medicines from the body, sometimes resulting in medicines reaching dangerous levels in the body. This is more of a problem for fluoxetine (Prozac), fluvoxamine (Luvox), and paroxetine (Paxil), and less so for sertraline (Zoloft), citalopram (Celexa), and escitalopram (Lexapro). As always, make sure you speak with your doctor about any other medicines you're taking (including herbals or supplements) and read the package insert so that you are informed of the risks and side effects. This has only been a partial discussion of side effects and risks.

B) Other Antidepressants

Several newer antidepressants are likely to be useful in PTSD, and studies are now being conducted to confirm their effectiveness. These include venlafaxine (Effexor), duloxetine (Cymbalta), desvenlafaxine (Pristiq), and mirtazapine (Remeron). All of these affect nerve transmission of norepinephrine (related to adrenaline) in addition to serotonin, although mirtazapine works by a different mechanism than the other three. They are likely to be useful in part because of their effect on serotonin (similar to the SSRIs), and they appear to be less likely to cause sexual side effects. However, they do have some additional side effects, which usually make them a second choice after trying an SSRI. Venlafaxine (Effexor), duloxetine (Cymbalta), and desvenlafazine (Pristiq) have a modest effect on elevating blood pressure and heart rate, and it's necessary to monitor these while taking them. Like SSRIs, they can cause increased anxiety when first started. Mirtazapine (Remeron) can cause drowsiness, constipation, and weight gain.

Again, it's wise to talk with your doctor and review the package insert so you're fully informed of the risks, side effects, and precautions. In addition to these medications, there are a number of older antidepressants in the "tricyclic" class that can be tried if there hasn't been response from the newer agents; however, these have more side effects and risks.

C) Blood Pressure Medicine Prazosin (Minipress) for Nightmares

For warriors, nightmares are often associated with increased blood pressure, pounding heart rate, and feeling revved up. Prazosin helps to reduce these physiological reactions, which in turn can help with the nightmares. See chapter 4 (skill 4) for a more complete discussion of this medicine.

D) Atypical Antipsychotics and Mood Stabilizers

There are several new medicines approved by the FDA for treatment of schizophrenia and bipolar (manic depressive) disorder that are now being combined with an SSRI or other antidepressant to try to improve results in

PTSD treatment (particularly sleep problems and nightmares). The most common medication that is being used in this way is quetiapine (Seroquel). Other medicines in the same category as quetiapine (called "atypical antipsychotics") include risperidone (Risperdal), olanzapine (Zyprexa), ziprasidone (Geodon), and aripiprazole (Abilify). Mood stabilizers (anticonvulsants) are a class of medicine used in bipolar (manic depressive) illness, and include lithium, valproic acid/divalproex sodium (Depakote), carbamazepine (Tegretol), oxcarbazepine (Trileptal), and lamotrigine (Lamictal). All of these medicines have significant side effects and risks, which are beyond the scope of this chapter to review. They should be considered only after exhausting other options, and should be prescribed in consultation with a psychiatrist (i.e., a primary care doctor should not be initiating these medicines without input from a psychiatrist).

Quetiapine (Seroquel), in particular, has gained popularity in recent years because of its apparent safety, its antidepressant effects, and its usefulness in improving sleep and reducing nightmares. However, there are emerging concerns about this medicine contributing to diabetes, heart problems, and weight gain, as well as other risks. There needs to be very careful assessment to ensure that the potential benefits outweigh the risks for this medicine, and it should be used cautiously, only after exhausting other options. Monitoring weight, glucose, and lipids before and during treatment are required.

E) Benzodiazepine Antianxiety Medicines

Benzodiazepines include alprazolam (Xanax), clonazepam (Klonopin), lorazepam (Ativan), and diazepam (Valium). These medicines are marketed to alleviate anxiety, and unfortunately are prescribed all too frequently to warriors with PTSD to help reduce anxiety and improve sleep. However, benzodiazepines have not been shown to be effective in alleviating PTSD symptoms, and have very detrimental side effects; most important, they carry a high risk of becoming addictive. Benzodiazepines are sometimes a warrior's favorite medicine because they act like taking a drink of alcohol. They are positively my least favorite medication to prescribe, because they almost always make things worse. Please see the sleep section in chapter 4 for a much more detailed description of this class of medicine.

F) Medicines to Help with Sleep

This topic is covered in chapter 4, skill 4.

Complementary and Alternative Medicines (CAM) and other Potential Treatments

There are numerous new modalities of treatment being promoted for PTSD (and mTBI), and treatments *du jour* seem to be constantly springing up as the latest "answer" to the PTSD (or mTBI) problem for returning combat veterans. A lot of interest has been generated by increased government funding for research for both of these conditions since the start of the wars in Iraq and Afghanistan, particularly in complementary and alternative medicines (CAM). CAM is a fancy term used to describe the large amount of nontraditional approaches that are widely available. Some of these have been promoted in news stories, and many veterans have questioned why the DoD and VA have not adopted them for regular use. The reason is that these modalities have not been proven to be effective in rigorous research studies.

This is only a sample of some of the approaches being promoted as effective for PTSD: virtual reality therapy, herbal supplements, megavitamins, acupuncture, yoga, biofeedback, tai chi, *qigong*, Reiki, massage, heart rate variability monitoring, low-voltage electrical stimulation (e.g., Alpha-Stim), bio-energy work, hyperbaric oxygen, experiential Outward Bound programs, dance therapy, art therapy, Emotional Freedom Techniques (EFT), neurofeedback/EEG feedback, pet therapy, blue light therapy, transcranial magnetic stimulation, and MDMA (the party drug Ecstasy).

Given this lengthy (and incomplete) list, how do you make sense of all this? One simple way is to first group all of the modalities that involve any sort of bodywork or physiological feedback (e.g., acupuncture, yoga, biofeedback, tai chi, *qigong*, Reiki, massage, heart rate variability monitoring, neurofeedback/EEG feedback, bio-energy, and maybe EFT). These may be of benefit for some PTSD symptoms because they likely have a biological basis in reducing the physiological stress response. In essence, they are likely to be complementary with standard stress inoculation and stress reduction techniques that have been studied scientifically, such as diaphragmatic breathing, meditation, and relaxation exercises that reduce anxiety and the physiological processes involved in being revved up. It's doubtful that they are any better than the standard stress reduction techniques, but they do offer alternatives that might appeal to some people. Whatever approaches you find most helpful to relax and reduce your own physiological reactions are definitely going to be useful. Outward Bound, dance therapy, and maybe pet therapy similarly mobilizes the body and mind. It's not likely that any of these modalities can be sufficient for alleviating PTSD without the narration and cognitive components found in other therapies, or the close connection to someone you're sharing your story with.

While herbal supplements and megavitamins are readily available, they haven't been proven to be effective in PTSD, and they carry risks, including negative interactions with prescription medicines. Low-voltage electrical stimulation (e.g., Alpha-Stim), blue light therapy, transcranial magnetic stimulation, and hyperbaric oxygen are experimental, and have a limited theoretical basis to think that they will be particularly useful for the full spectrum of PTSD symptoms. The idea of using MDMA (Ecstasy) is particularly worrisome because this drug can cause irreversible changes in serotonin nerve transmission, as distinct from SSRIs, which have effects on neurons that wear off quickly. We just don't know enough about how any of this works in the brain to take that kind of risk.

Virtual reality simulation for treating PTSD has received high public attention in news stories. Virtual reality is a method designed to expose warriors to traumatic wartime images similar to those from their own experiences in an effort to desensitize or habituate them to these experiences, thereby reducing their level of anxiety. Essentially, virtual reality is another way to deliver exposure therapy, and involves an interactive process between the warrior and the therapist related to the combat experiences. To date, there has been no definitive head-to-head comparison between virtual reality and standard exposure therapy. My assessment of the current evidence is that there is nothing that beats talking with someone face-to-face without any other distractions, and it's unlikely that virtual reality will play a prominent role in PTSD treatment after thorough evaluation.

Where virtual reality will probably be most useful is in helping to prepare warriors before deployment through combat simulation. Tough realistic training can improve preparation and may offer the possibility of improving resilience and preventing PTSD in the future.

The discussion of CAM and other modalities highlights the critical need for high-quality research of all new PTSD treatments. Many of these are being actively promoted to veterans and health professionals as cures for PTSD, without adequate research data to support these claims. Initial reports of effectiveness, even for many conventional treatments, often do not meet expectations when rigorous research is conducted, and sometimes treatments that show high promise initially are ultimately found to be harmful. The bottom line is that there is no "magic bullet" for PTSD, and claims to the contrary should be taken with more than a grain of salt.

How do you evaluate if a new treatment has adequate evidence for effectiveness? Although there is no simple answer to this question, the most direct answer is that the treatment has been shown to be effective (evidence-based) in one or more controlled scientific studies in which the proposed/experimental treatment is directly compared with a standard treatment or no treatment, as described above under the "treatment effectiveness" section. To do these types of research studies, patients with PTSD are invited to participate and provided with a detailed explanation of potential risks and benefits (informed consent). They are then randomly assigned to either the treatment group or the control group, and both groups are followed for an equal duration of time. The evidence is stronger if the control group includes a standard treatment (or at least a sham treatment); if there are several studies that show the same results; and if studies involve "blinded" methods, where the researchers evaluating the outcomes don't know which groups study participants are assigned to. These types of studies are difficult to do, expensive, and require a high level of ethical and scientific oversight. Obviously, it's a lot easier to just claim that a treatment is effective without doing the research, which is why there's a glut of snake oil salesmen in this business now. For this reason, it's critical that both medical professionals and veterans advocate strongly for evaluation through rigorous scientific methods, and not accept claims at face value.

DISABILITY AND TREATMENT

One final topic that I hesitate to bring up, but needs to be discussed, is the relationship between treatment effectiveness and receiving disability compensation for the condition that is being treated—in this case, PTSD. This is a particularly important topic if you have gone through (or are going through) the disability evaluation processes in the DoD, VA, or both. (The topic of mTBI disability was covered in chapter 2.)

PTSD can be a severely disabling condition, and it's appropriate and necessary for warriors who have severe PTSD symptoms to receive compensation up to the level that matches their functional impairment, which may be as high as 100 percent. If they can no longer function in an operational setting, hold a job, or have a meaningful relationship as a result of wartime traumatic events incurred while serving their country, then they need all the assistance and support that this country can offer. Unfortunately, however, when warriors embark on the journey of seeking disability compensation for their wartime experiences, they find themselves in the most peculiar of catch-22s, more insane even than some battlefield scenarios that they may have encountered, and akin to the situation that the main character in *Catch-22*, Yossarian, found himself in (see chapter 7, skill 2).

This peculiar situation, generated by the ponderous and almost incomprehensible DoD and VA disability regulations (contained in the Code of Federal Regulations) is as follows: A warrior who is in legitimate need of assistance with wartime trauma must be sufficiently ill with the disorder for a long-enough period of time to qualify for PTSD disability. However, in order to accomplish this, he has to be well enough to navigate the slow, cumbersome, frustrating, and bureaucratic disability application process, which if successful likely means that: 1) He wasn't able to find an impossible-to-get job that would have permitted him to spend innumerable hours away from work dealing with the application and treatment process, thereby making it more likely that he is jobless; 2) His interpersonal skills were severely tested on a daily basis by the situation, thereby making it more likely that he was deemed to have "interpersonal problems"; 3) He was able to show up for all of his therapy appointments, as required, but the time in these many sessions was only sufficient to focus on improving his ability to cope with his "occupational" and "interpersonal problems" and not kill anyone; and 4) There wasn't sufficient time in the many therapy sessions to focus on the real issues of treating his PTSD, which turns out to be a "blessing in disguise," because if there had been time to really address his PTSD symptoms, this may have resulted in his disability application being denied or his disability rating lowered. Welcome home, warrior!

Let's hope that my somewhat cavalier summation turns out to be a gross exaggeration for you, but nonetheless, be prepared to be caught in some variation of the above catch-22 if you embark on this process. The effort may be worth it to you in the long run, but don't automatically assume that this will be the case. The process itself can take a toll. Although the disability and compensation system is there to help you, it can trigger a lot of frustration and anger, negatively affect your transition experience, or become a way of life. If you know the expression "a dog being wagged by its tail," this is how it can feel. All of this is okay, as long as you understand the risks. It also helps to remember that you're not the one who is nuts here.

SUMMARY

In summary, this chapter attempts to cover the very broad topic of how to navigate the medical system, advocate for yourself, get help, and find the best formula that works for you. It provides information on what treatments are available, what to expect from treatment, and how the various treatments work. The subject of navigating the medical system could fill a complete volume, so please take my advice only at its face value. There was a lot left out, such as many of the side effects and risks associated with medications. It's strongly recommended that you get additional advice as needed from fellow warriors, veterans, veterans' organizations (of which there are many excellent ones), and your health-care providers. The most important goal is good health, and the health care system is there to help you. Also, this chapter illustrates the importance of keeping your sense of humor and objectivity in dealing with very complex health-care issues.

Enjoy First Sergeant Mike Schindler's personal story of his mental health treatment:

After many years of outrageous adventures and behavior, I finally stopped running away from myself. In July of 2002, I mentally, physically, spiritually, and soulfully crashed and burned, thirty years after returning from Vietnam and four years after retiring from the Army. My second marriage was in its final months, my son and daughter had moved away from our home in Maui to escape my insanity, and my brother had decided that I was a complete asshole—as in whole ass.

Luckily for me, my other "brother," a close friend and fellow Vietnam veteran, noticed my mood swings, depression, anger, hopelessness, lack of social skills, and general piss-poor attitude toward life. He had suggested many times in the past that I seek help for PTSD and I always blew him off, thinking to myself that I did not have PTSD; I'm a combat warrior and I am a strong man.

Wrong. Not only was I a "carrier," I was also an active transmitter of the disease, as in contagious, infecting loved ones around me. Somehow my friend finally managed to convince me, at last, to get some help. On that fateful day in July of 2002, my brother warrior called the local VA clinic and spoke with his psychiatrist, Dr. K, about me. After a few moments he handed me the phone and ordered me to speak.

My face went blank. I felt scared and confused. I knew that it was now or never and that I could no longer run away from myself. I managed to say aloha (hello in Hawaiian). Dr. K then asked why I wanted to talk with her. My answer surprised me. I said that I was burnt out, worn out, and tired of feeling alone, angry, hopeless, and a failure. My first of twice-a-month therapy sessions for the next five years was scheduled for August 6, 2002.

Thus began my painful personal commitment to regain my true self. The hardest part was admitting that I needed the "system's" help. By "system," I mean the VA or green machine that had ground me up and spit me out—the system I distrusted and hated, or so I thought, for many years while running away from myself.

The next most difficult thing was actually showing up for my first scheduled therapy appointment. I changed my mind hundreds of times in the few weeks prior. I had a hard time admitting to myself that I had some serious issues to deal with, such as anger, distrust, hopelessness, life, relationships, social behavior, substance abuse, and inability to live as a happy, productive person with joy in my heart.

I was ready to bolt and run. During the two to three weeks prior to my first therapy session, I analyzed myself constantly. I finally decided that if I could survive combat in "Nam," I could at least show up for therapy "once." At last the day arrived: August 6, 2002, my first session with a "shrink."

I drove down the mountain to the VA clinic in Kahului, Maui, thinking of at least a hundred reasons not to go. Then all of a sudden I was there in the parking lot. I parked, turned off the engine, got out of my car, walked to the door, and hesitated. I was one second from bolting and running. I took a deep breath, opened the door, and walked in, pushed the elevator button, took another long deep breath, got in, pushed the button for the third floor, and broke out in a cold sweat.

Thinking to myself what a chicken shit I am to feel this way; after all, I am "just" going to see this shrink "once." I can do this. I'm a combat warrior, piece of cake, easy stuff. I envisioned my therapist looking like a female doctor Franken-Mean—someone who would not be of any help to me. After all, she was part of the "system" that I distrusted and hated. You know, "the green machine," the one that chewed me up and spit me out like a piece of meat. But I could see her "once."

The elevator stopped. I got off and walked into the waiting room, signed in, took a seat, and went through my usual threat-assessment-escape-route-weapons-check routine that I had been doing since the "Nam." Decided that no threat was active, checked out the two visible exits, looked around to see what could be used as a weapon—saw several objects: large glass vase, water-cooler glass bottle, two-inch wooden dowel curtain rods. Feeling relieved, I settled in for the inevitable long VA/military hurry-up-and-wait.

As I watched everyone coming and going, I noticed a nice-looking woman enter the room from behind the check-in counter, look at the sign-in sheet, turn around, and to my surprise call my name. I was shocked. First off, the wait was short; second, she was nice-looking (definitely not a doctor Franken-Mean), and third, she smiled. The nice-looking lady introduced herself to me as Dr. K and invited me to follow her to her office.

I found her office to be bright, cheerful, and inviting—not a dark, old, stuffy, dungeon-like room with two goons in white jackets waiting outside. Dr. K invited me to sit in a comfortable chair facing her. I sat down, looked at her, and waited. She sensed my confusion as to what to do next and encouraged me to talk about whatever I wanted to. That was all the opening I needed. I unloaded, spilled the beans, let the white tiger inside of me loose.

I initially spoke of my reasons for seeking therapy: that "things" were not right and I was tired of faking it; that I had become discontented with life and family; my multiple job losses and disdain for authority. The session included my feelings of how Vietnam combat veterans who served in the "Nam" before 1970 minimized my service because they believed combat actions had stopped by then. My point here is that I talked about whatever I wanted to that day—my service record, family, war experiences, multiple job losses, authority issues, failures, and fellow veterans.

In a future session I spoke of my anger concerning the singular treatment of returning Vietnam combat veterans and how we were vilified and thought of in less than a heroic manner by the American public and previous generations of veterans from the Korean War and World War II—like we Vietnam veterans didn't matter, and neither did our war.

This kind of treatment toward Vietnam combat veterans angered me and still causes some residual bad feelings toward the American public and older veterans from previous wars; also, a little bit of jealousy toward recent generations of returning veterans, who have been welcomed home as heroes—which they are. It's a wound that has not healed for many Vietnam vets.

While talking, I observed Dr. K sitting in her chair and looking at me in such a way that I knew for the first time that I was going to be all right—that I was not alone. I felt such relief that I could have talked for hours. I began to shed tears of relief—which felt good; a burden of such magnitude was lifted from me that the tears just poured out. I apologized many times for crying. Dr. K said it was okay and I knew it was.

I also spoke about my feelings of anger, distrust, hopelessness, life, relationships, social behavior, substance abuse, and what in later sessions I labeled as my inner white tiger that can be ferocious, uncontrollable, angry, and unpredictable. After a long emotional hour she said the time was up.

Before I left, Dr. K informed me of the therapy process and the personal commitment to therapy. She also explained that my behavior patterns and feelings are "normal," that fight-or-flight is a skill that I used in combat that is hard to stop when you are trying to transition and readjust to civilian life. She also gave me the first of some tools to use, like a "blueprint." She asked me to remember the words "frequency," "intensity," and "duration." She explained that whenever I feel anger, distrust, hopelessness, or the inner white tiger wanting to get loose and cause some damage to me, family, friends, or anybody, to practice keeping the frequency low, the intensity mild, and the duration short. This practice became and still is my mantra and way of life.

I walked out of her office after one session feeling so damn happy that I was smiling from ear to ear. My inner white tiger had been put in the sun for now and was purring. I felt that there was hope for me, and maybe, just maybe, joy would return to my heart.

My therapy sessions lasted for five years. Therapy helped me to understand why I was behaving in negative and destructive ways; why I was feeling angry, disconnected, helpless, hopeless, lost, scared, and just wanting to go away and hide from the civilian world. Therapy helped me realize my desire to live, love, and laugh. Before I chose therapy, substance abuse and dangerous jobs were my "blueprint." Bad choices on my part. The results were devastating to me, my family, and my friends.

During the years after starting therapy I would also talk with other Vietnam combat veterans. This type of "therapy" has many benefits, such as venting, a sense of camaraderie, and a feeling of safeness and connection talking about common experiences. Warrior discussions are fun, and rewarding. After all, these are your brothers and sisters in arms, so embrace them; the camaraderie is good. However, these warrior discussions at times also fueled the fires of anger, distrust, and substance abuse. So I would say that warrior discussions are necessary, but be careful to accentuate the positive whenever possible.

Therapy gave me the tools to process and deal with my traumas of combat and war. We are all different and will develop our own working blueprint. A psychiatrist or therapist can help you to find your way "home," and there are many options for getting help. My psychiatrist, Dr. K, became a valuable "tool" for me as I created my blueprint, by enabling me to use my own strength as a warrior to find joy, happiness, love, and purpose of life.

Transition and readjustment may sound scary. Well, to do nothing and not get help is even scarier. Trust me—been there, done that. As one combat veteran to another, it's okay to feel alone, angry, confused, helpless, hopeless, and lost, and to have a sense of not belonging to the "real world." Well, guess what? You are "normal." These feelings are skills that you learned and used to survive the horrors and absurdity of combat.

There are many ways to get help. Getting help from the VA worked for me, and they offer several different ways to get help, through clinics or Vet Centers. This book provides useful information, but is not a substitute for talking with a "shrink" if you need to. Commit to yourself, and find the right blueprint that works for you, even if this means talking to a therapist. I know firsthand that this is a daunting and unpleasant task. The VA system is over-bloated with bean counters, bureaucrats, fools, idiots, and politicians. So are military treatment facilities.

No matter; you must use and work the system and not let the system use and abuse you. There are many good people who care within the walls of VA and military offices, medical centers, and Vet Centers. Seek them out and talk with other veterans. Never give up. Somehow navigate your way through and within the system. In the end you will be glad that you did. The results are joy, happiness, and living a positive life.

My therapy sessions became a source of normalcy. What helped the most was being able to have regularly scheduled therapy sessions with the same psychiatrist. Because of this routine, my doctor and I gained trust *and respect for each other. This helped me feel safe and secure that what was being said was between us and only us, warrior to doctor. Trust was important to me. I had to feel and know that I was safe from betrayal by the system that I felt had ignored me.*

I feel that having a psychiatrist who understands the culture and language of the military is important, because once I began to narrate my story, I didn't have to stop the flow to explain terms. In a short time I began to open up and narrate my story because I felt safe in the fact that I would be talking to the same person every time I went to my appointments. Just like hoisting up the flag each morning; with every session I opened up and narrated more of my story, without feeling judged, criticized, or analyzed.

My psychiatrist assured me many times that no matter what, the subject was okay, and that it was normal for me to have feelings of anger, depression, guilt, and loneliness. The more I went to treatment, the more I appreciated it. Bottom line: I knew that I needed help, and therapy provided a safe atmosphere to be able to tell my story to someone I trusted. The more I talked, the better I felt. Being able to ask questions and get answers (both from my doctor and from myself) let the light shine in.

Trust me, you will survive. Hell, you survived combat, right? Remember, you are not alone, my brothers and sisters. You are "normal," and with commitment to yourself and the therapy process, the light of joy, happiness, and life will shine. We combat veterans are an exclusive group. Learn to put that inner white tiger in the corner, face your demons, run up the white flag, and lay down your saber. So live, love, forgive, be good to yourself and others, and stay safe.

CHAPTER 9

ACCEPTANCE: LIVING AND COPING WITH MAJOR LOSSES

This chapter was placed near the end of the LANDNAV section because it addresses a difficult subject concerning living with and accepting painful losses resulting from deployment, including things that may seem impossible to "accept." The goal of this chapter—to reach a place of being able to live with major losses through acceptance—is simple to state, but can be an enormous challenge.

LANDNAV LEARNING OBJECTIVE: ACCEPTANCE— LEARNING TO LIVE WITH MAJOR LOSSES AND GRIEF; LEARNING TO COPE WITH SURVIVOR'S GUILT, DEPRESSION, AND OTHER EMOTIONS

The word *acceptance* (and *accept*) is used frequently in psychotherapy, and consequently has an overused and "touchy-feely" quality to it. Also, its definition means agreement, concurrence, or assent, which doesn't have anything to do with its meaning here. However, there is no better word to describe the intent and subject of this chapter.

Life frequently involves coming to terms with and accepting losses that we would rather not have to come to terms with or accept. This can include injury, illness, accidents, loss of a buddy or loved one, loss of a relationship, loss of time (something that is often not appreciated), loss of identity, loss of financial stability, and various other significant losses that can happen over the course of a lifetime.

Difficult life experiences involving loss are connected with painful emotions of loss. These include hurt, sadness, grief, fear, anger, depression, hopelessness, worthlessness, despondency, despair, demoralization, guilt, shame, rage, hate, and others. Often these emotions are so intertwined with each other that they become difficult to distinguish. Emotions of hurt, fear, sadness, or grief can get turned inward in feelings of despair, worthlessness, hopelessness, guilt, shame, or the desire to die. Hopelessness and guilt can become substitutes for sadness and grief. Hate can become a substitute for anger or fear. This chapter acknowledges how powerful these emotions are, and provides considerations for learning how to navigate them.

Note that "acceptance" of significant losses is not the same thing as "making peace with," "finding meaning in," or believing that your life is guided by the will of God, karma, or an angel of destiny. Your spiritual beliefs and values are certainly important in the process of acceptance, but they do not define it. Fundamentally, acceptance is the act that allows us to come to terms with or live with major losses; acceptance requires us to acknowledge all of the feelings that relate to a loss, while at the same time believing in ourselves and our value. This can be a very difficult thing to achieve.

Life is rarely fair. No one knows this more than a combat veteran. Bad things happen to good people; random and unexpected things happen that we have very little or no control over, and are in no position to criticize or judge ourselves for. Yet it's natural when we learn of tragedy to make judgments by asking in various ways, "Why?" For example, "What did I do to deserve this terrible diagnosis?" "What could I have done differently to prevent this tragedy from happening?" "Why did this happen to my buddy and not me?" "How can my spouse be unfaithful and say she still loves me?" "Why is God punishing me?"

All of these questions we ask ourselves relate to the inherent belief that we are capable of controlling our destiny. Although the ability to ask questions like these helps to define who we are as humans, it is also our downfall, because implicit in each of these questions is the assumption that our value is measured not by what we do in the face of adversity, but by the adversity itself that strikes us. If I ask, "Why me?" upon learning that I have cancer, or "Why him and not me?" after an IED attack, or "Why is God punishing me?", I am placing a value on myself based on the adversity that has occurred. Implicit in these questions is, "What did *I* do wrong to get cancer?", "It *should* have been *me* instead," or "God must be punishing *me* because *I* have sinned."

Our human minds search for cause and effect, for a reason that a tragedy has occurred, for meaning. Often this is useful. Figuring out why something happened can prevent a future tragedy of a similar nature, and can also keep our minds occupied so that we don't dwell so long on painful feelings. However, we frequently get stuck in the process, trying to figure out the answer to questions that we are convinced *should* have an answer, but have no answer at all—at least, not one that is available to us.

Virtually everyone who has deployed to a war zone is affected, some much more than others; their loved ones are also affected. Deployment can be life-changing in positive ways. However, there are also experiences that happen during combat, or as a result of deployment, which involve significant loss that no one, not even a highly trained warrior, can sufficiently prepare for.

The skills in this chapter have to do with learning to live with major losses or tragedy through reaching a place of acceptance. The two principal skills are: 1) doing whatever you need to do to acknowledge and express your feelings related to a loss, and 2) believing in yourself and your value. Another key skill is not getting trapped in unanswerable questions that turn painful emotions, such as grief, against you in the form of self-blame, shame, worthlessness, or the desire to be dead.

SKILL 1: UNDERSTANDING THE EMOTIONS OF LOSS

Warriors often struggle with themselves (and with their loved ones) when they don't fully realize or accept how many things in their life have changed as a result of deployment. They want things to go back to "normal." They want to take off their body armor and let go of some of their memories and emotions. If a warrior experienced a serious injury, they want to heal and move on with life to the best of their ability with as few limitations as possible. Warriors and their loved ones often look forward to being able to continue with education, pursue relationships, start a family, continue with careers, or catch up on life goals that they may have put on hold. The recent wars in Iraq and Afghanistan have resulted in some warriors and families putting life goals and aspirations on hold for years.

This forward-looking perspective is very healthy. It provides energy and motivation for accomplishing goals. However, warriors sometimes plunge into their goals without fully appreciating where they're plunging from, and this can result in frustrating situations. For instance, they might pursue an educational goal that they had before deployment but find that the subject doesn't hold their interest in the same way, that their ability to concentrate on classroom studies isn't what it used to be, or that new family or work responsibilities make it difficult to achieve this goal. They might want to return to a previous job they had before mobilization but find that it's unavailable or has been "restructured." They might try to reunite with their partner or spouse but find that the relationship has weakened under the strain of the months (or years) of separation or other stressors, like infidelity. The warrior might discover that neither they nor their partner is the same person after deployment. The warrior might find it hard to enjoy things or connect with loved ones because of war-zone memories or grief. The warrior might feel like a completely different person, like a foreigner to their previous self. Having a realistic understanding of how these many changes and losses are affecting you is essential.

The first skill in this chapter concerns understanding the emotions of loss by recognizing the things that have changed as a result of deployment, and any feelings associated with these changes. To begin this exercise, start by answering the questions on the following worksheet. Indicate positive and negative changes that have resulted directly or indirectly from deployment. Focus on how things have changed in your life compared to before deployment (this could be before your first deployment or before your most significant deployment). Positive changes could include increased self-confidence; greater connection with your partner, children, or friends; improved career opportunities related to deployment; increased educational opportunities related to the GI Bill; improved financial stability from combat pay or promotion; spiritual growth; greater appreciation for what's important in life; stronger friendships and bonds with peers.

Personal Changes Resulting from Deployment

	Positive Changes/ Benefits	Negative Changes/ Losses
How have I changed?		
How has my partner changed, and how have things changed between us?		
How have my relationships changed with my children, other family members, or friends?		
How have my career opportunities or goals changed?		
What have I gained most or missed out on most as a result of deployment?		
What other major changes or losses resulted from deployment?		

Examples that might be written down in the negative changes/losses column include physical impairment from being wounded or from an injury; the breakup of an intimate relationship; divorce; loss of custody or separation from children; feeling distant and cut off from family and friends; your child not recognizing or connecting with you in the same way; difficulty relating to people you used to enjoy being with; losing a job or promotion opportunity; loss of interests that used to be enjoyable; not being able to complete major educational goals; financial problems; loss of years and feeling old; not being able to attend important events, such as the marriage of a sibling or the funeral of a close relative; missing time with children as they grow up; and difficulty coping with experiences that occurred downrange. All of these represent losses of one kind or another, and are accompanied by substantial feelings.

If you experienced a major loss, like losing a buddy in combat or your marriage, it may be hard to focus on other losses that also occurred. However, try to write down all the major ways things have changed in your life since before deployment.

The next step in this exercise is to select the most difficult or painful loss from the list you made and write it down in the left column of the next worksheet, under the heading, "Most Difficult Change/Loss Resulting from Deployment." This could include the breakup of an important relationship, separation from children, physical injury, the loss of a buddy in combat, or something else.

Identify which emotions are connected with the loss and circle them. Add any other emotions that you're experiencing if they aren't on the list. Also, are you blaming yourself in some way by asking "why" questions or using "should" statements (per chapter 5, skill 4)? For now, just write "yes" or "no" if you are, and then later on in this chapter (skill 3), we'll look at this in more detail. If you experienced more than one major loss, photocopy or scan this worksheet and repeat it as necessary.

The key to this exercise is to fully acknowledge the feelings/emotions associated with the most difficult losses. Experiencing loss hurts, and it's supposed to hurt; however, acknowledging and expressing how you feel

Loss Worksheet

Most Difficult Change/ Loss Resulting from Deployment	Emotions of Loss	Am I blaming, using "shoulds," or asking, "Why?"
	When I think about the loss, do I have any of these feelings? (Circle each one)	Yes No
	Primary:	If yes, list:
	Hurt, fear, anger, sadness/sorrow, grief, helpless, powerless	
	Complex:	
	Depressed, despondent, demoralized, despair, hopeless, worthless, guilt, shame, rage, hate	

helps the feelings to shift and change (see also chapter 5, skill 2). The key skill is to acknowledge any important losses, notice and accept all of your feelings, and understand the nature of your feelings.

Primary Emotions

There are two categories of emotions of loss: primary and complex. Primary emotions are relatively pure, single feelings that are right here, right now, as a direct result of the loss. They may be high- or low-intensity, but don't have any specific direction. When we hurt, we hurt; when we're sad, we're sad; when we're afraid, we feel fear; when we're grieving, we're bereaved and mourning; when we're angry, we're angry. When we're helpless or power-less, we feel that we're unable to respond in any way. These emotions are not made up of other emotions. They are directly related to the particular loss, are immediately present to us, and are untainted by thought processes.

Primary emotions are also raw and more primitive, less connected with thoughts, processed more in the limbic system, and extremely unpleasant; you want them to stop, they exist outside of time (which is why they can be so unbearable and feel like they'll go on forever), and you can feel them in your gut (for example, you feel nauseous or you feel discomfort in the pit of your stomach). Emotional pain can hurt just as much and be just as physical as physical pain.

Complex Emotions

Complex emotions are very different. They reflect mixtures of several emotions, involve detailed thought processes that extend in time, are often directed at others or ourselves in self-deprecating or judgmental ways, and are there to protect us or motivate actions. These emotions are often closely linked, although each has its own unique quality. Being despondent is a state of being extremely disheartened or dejected over a specific loss. Demoralization carries more of a feeling of powerlessness, injustice, or lack of fairness also related to a specific situation or loss. An example would be a severely hostile work environment (e.g., abusive or sexually inappropriate behavior by a supervisor) but not being able to leave the position or get anyone in higher authority to believe that this is happening. Being in despair—which carries a sense of futility, defeat, and utter hopelessness—spreads the hurt over various emotions that may include elements of sadness, helplessness, hopelessness, powerlessness, grief, despondency, demoralization, and sometimes the desire to die. Depression, which is a medical diagnosis, a physiological process, and an emotional state, has various definitions and manifestations involving different mixtures of primary and complex emotions, often including fear.

Complex emotions involve ruminative thought processes where the person goes over and over events and situations in their mind in an effort to figure out, make sense of, or assign some meaning or reason to what happened. Often these processes include "should" statements and "why" questions (e.g., "Why is this happening to me?", "Why am I being punished?", "What did I do wrong to deserve this?"). Complex emotions may involve feelings of betrayal, anger at self or others for failing to respond in some way, repeatedly going over scenarios or conversations in the mind, hopelessness that anything can ever change, feeling morose, and isolating oneself from others. Complex emotions often involve thoughts of blame or judgment as to the value of oneself or another. Examples include feeling worthless or being racked with guilt or shame. In keeping with the discussion in chapter 7 (skill 4), anger is considered a primary emotion, and rage and hate are complex emotions; hate moves in the direction of judgment. We can get stuck in complex emotions for extended periods of time. Complex emotions are private caves where we can reside and remain indefinitely.

One state that can be associated with both primary and complex loss emotions is dissociation—feeling as if things are unreal, or feeling separate from one's body. Dissociation is essentially what people do when they freeze in a situation where they can't fight or flee. If we are hurt to such an extent that we can't bear the pain, there are chemicals in our nervous system that cause us to feel dissociated from our body and numb to the primary pain. After the trauma or loss has passed, dissociation can become a defense that helps to numb us to the emotional pain and is closely associated with complex emotions.

How Complex Emotions Protect Us

How do complex emotions protect us or motivate actions? Here's an example to help address this. Severe neglect or abuse of a child by a parent who the child depends on for safety, security, and love is probably one of the greatest and longest-lasting hurts that a person can ever endure. There are several reasons why it can have such a lasting effect, including the direct physical or emotional pain and hurt caused by the parent (which may induce dissociation); fear associated with the shock and confusion of the irrational nature of what is happening; sadness and grief resulting from the difference between when the parent is loving and when they are cruel; powerlessness and helplessness resulting from the inability to escape or change the situation, and an inability to express emotions; and the lack of understanding of what is happening or what is being felt to buffer the impact and help the child to understand that it's not their "fault" they're being abused, despite what the parent wants them to believe.

Perhaps most important, the child is not in any position to understand their primary emotions. They might not have the vocabulary to understand what they're feeling, and because they don't feel safe, are unlikely to verbally express their primary emotions. They certainly *feel* hurt, fear, sadness, grief, anger, helplessness, or powerlessness, but they may not consciously understand what they're feeling and may not be allowed to fully express their feelings.

What happens to a child in this situation, particularly if the abuse continues, is that they can't remain or live with the primary emotions of hurt, fear, sadness, grief, anger, helplessness, or powerlessness forever. These emotions can't be endured forever without being understood or expressed. If the child continued to live with the intensity and weight of these primary emotions, powerless and helpless to express them or understand them, the child would become unable to move, function, or cope, and might stay dissociated or become psychotic.

The complex emotions are key coping mechanisms involving various thought processes that help the child separate from or suppress the primary emotions. The complex emotions are part of the brain's attempt to "figure out" something that is totally irrational and incomprehensible. These emotions provide a way for primary emotions, which are not permitted to be expressed openly, to be processed and felt in solitude. Depression, demoralization, despondency, hopelessness, worthlessness, despair, guilt, and shame all provide a way to privately *feel* and try to make sense of what's happening. They allow the child to cope with deep feelings involving the primary emotions that they can't otherwise express, understand, and endure. All of this happens automatically, and subconsciously.

One feature of these complex emotions is the feeling that no one else in the world can possibly understand or relate to them; these emotions feel unique. Everyone can relate to primary emotions. Complex emotions provide a unique identity that fosters a feeling of self-preservation for the individual separate from others. These emotions offer a way to cope through engaging the mind in figuring out why something is happening, creating distance from the environment, and minimizing the hurt through shutting down and altering certain physiological functions (e.g., energy level, sleep, appetite, interest in activities, personal hygiene); they allow the child to remove and protect him- or herself in an act of self-preservation. Feeling worthless, guilty, ashamed, or filled with self-blame provides meaning for what's happening and reduces the fear, confusion, and hurt associated with something that's utterly irrational and incomprehensible. There's a repetitive and ruminative quality to the expression of these emotions, and no one can do anything to change them.

One of the benefits of complex emotions to the individual is that they can actually motivate others around them to step in and intervene in an attempt to alleviate the suffering or take over the duties and responsibilities of the individual. Underlying feelings of helplessness may be transferred to family members and friends, and become a shared experience. The emotion of rage, when it gets expressed, can drive the individual toward action. Although it may seem counterproductive and detrimental to live with depression, rage, guilt, shame, low self-worth, despair, etc., these are far preferable for the individual than remaining in a powerless state, unable to express (or comprehend) the underlying primary emotions.

It's important to know that some children who grow up in circumstances involving severe neglect or abuse are able to demonstrate extraordinary resilience and not end up with lifelong depression, rage, shame, or other complex emotions. Often the children who are able to rise above their situation and escape the "ghetto" (literally or figuratively) are ones who had someone in their life who loved them and provided a buffer to protect them, or at least to let them know that they were not the ones who were crazy—that they actually had *value* in the meaningless and nonsensical universe into which they were born.

This is a very important concept that many mental health professionals don't understand. When a person like this requests help later in life for their depression, rage, shame, despair, and other symptoms, what they need most is someone who is kind, compassionate, and who will love them. They need someone to ask, "What's *bothering* you?" rather than "What's *wrong* with you?" They need someone who has the ability to tell them that they're not crazy for wanting to kill their mother or father, not crazy for feeling rage and anguish on a daily basis, not crazy for being perpetually depressed and suicidal, not broken for feeling worthless and filled with shame, not wrong for being hostile and self-destructive; someone who is willing to spend the time necessary for them to fully express their emotions, whatever it takes and however long it takes, and who won't judge them or make them feel like they're a living example of every major mental disorder in the psychiatric *Diagnostic and Statistical Manual of Mental Disorders* (DSM). This is hard to find during most fifty-minute psychotherapy sessions.

One other thing that might not be recognized is that sometimes the most painful thing for someone who has gone through severe trauma is experiencing the *difference* between the world they have lived in and a caring, loving, nurturing, and just world. In other words, an act of kindness, compassion, and caring can unravel a person who has lived the opposite for so long, particularly if at the end of the fifty-minute session, they have to bottle it all up and go right back to what they knew before. It's hard under these circumstances to feel any security going to therapy, even though it's necessary.

Experiencing Major Loss as an Adult

Major losses occurring as an adult (e.g., losing a battle buddy, losing a close relationship, losing a parent or family member, losing custody of kids, serious injury or illness, being raped or assaulted) can be just as emotionally devastating as the above example of child abuse, and can include all of the same emotions. The initial emotions with these types of events usually are the primary emotions of hurt, fear, sadness, grief, anger, helplessness, and powerlessness. These are often mixed with shock, confusion, and sometimes dissociation; the pain can be felt on a physical level (e.g., nausea, pain in the heart, chest, or pit of the stomach).

They are then followed by complex emotions, for many of the same reasons as in the example of child abuse. Although adults have more awareness of what's happening, the shift from primary to complex emotions can happen rapidly; there's an automatic subconscious shift that might be instinctual, a wall that goes up to protect the person.

The difference between the example of child abuse and major losses as an adult is that the adult has more knowledge to draw upon and is in a better position to find ways to cope with or respond to the loss. They're in a better position to understand and put words to what they're feeling, to express their emotions—both primary and complex—and to act on those emotions. It's very difficult (or impossible) for a child to be resilient under the circumstances of abuse because they lack the knowledge and understanding of what's happening.

Contrast this, for example, with U.S. prisoners of war in Vietnam, who endured extraordinary suffering but who often proved themselves to be the most resilient and remarkable men, capable of transcending and growing from their experiences. The human capacity for resilience is remarkable. Although all of the primary and complex emotions occur in adults as well as children, adults have a much better chance at saving themselves through greater awareness and understanding of what's happening.

Keys to Resilience

Given this information, what are the tools that you can use to navigate your own losses? I'm convinced that there are three important keys to resilience, defined here as the ability to bounce back after adversity and the capacity to live with major losses: 1) the capacity to feel, express, and accept all emotions connected with loss, particularly the primary emotions; 2) the belief in yourself and your value; and 3) a connection to any loving person (or people) who can provide feedback and help in facilitating the expression of all of the emotions connected with loss without judging you or labeling you "crazy."

It's true that genetics, upbringing, environment, and all the nature vs. nurture theories that occupy entire libraries are also important in resilience. However, I believe these three keys to resilience are the most useful for each of us as individuals. The remainder of this chapter will focus on the first two of these keys. The third, connection to a loving person, is inherent in everything we do, and is addressed in various ways throughout this book.

SKILL 2: EXPLORING THE CONNECTIONS BETWEEN COMPLEX AND PRIMARY EMOTIONS

The loss worksheet you filled out in this chapter's skill 1 is intended to help in the process of acknowledging your emotions. That might be as far as you want to go depending on the intensity of the loss you've experienced, how recently it occurred, whether you feel like you're stuck in complex emotions, and whether you're ready to move on. If you're experiencing mostly primary emotions, which are expected after a major loss, the only thing you might want or be able to do is acknowledge and express them and allow them to exist until they've shifted, however long that takes. If this is where you are with your loss, you might want to skip to the next section titled "An Example of Coping with Primary and Complex Emotions." (You could also read through this without spending time on it, and if you feel it might be valuable, go back and complete it.)

If you've gotten stuck in complex emotional processes, and they're making you miserable, then this skill is designed to help. To start, look back at the previous loss worksheet in skill 1. If you circled complex emotions and you feel like they're interfering with your life significantly now, then continue with this exercise by circling them again on the worksheet on the next page. The next step is to explore how they are connected to the primary emotions. Every complex emotion is made up in part by primary emotions. For each complex emotion that you circled, feel what primary emotions they are connected with, and draw lines to connect them. It might be helpful to use a different colored pencil or marker for each complex emotion.

For example, if you circled "depressed," consider which primary emotions are part of this feeling. You can only do this through feeling it. Your depression could be made up of a combination of all of the primary emotions. Use one color to connect depression with the primary emotions you feel contribute to it. For instance, you might become aware of "sadness" or fear" underlying the depression. If the next complex emotion you circled was "hopeless," feel which primary emotions are included in this; there might be sadness, helplessness, powerlessness, grief, or others. Use a different colored pencil or marker to draw lines from your feeling of "hopeless" to the primary emotions connected to this.

Change/Loss _____

Complex Emotions	Primary Emotions
Depressed	Hurt
Despondent	Fear
Demoralized	Anger
Despair	Sadness/Sorrow
Hopeless	Grief
Worthless	Helpless
Guilt	Powerless
Shame	
Rage	
Hate	

Continue this exercise until you've identified which primary emotions underlie the complex emotions you experienced as a result of your loss. You will find in doing this that you can *feel* each of the primary emotions that play some role in the complex emotions. There might be other factors that contribute to the complex emotions, but the primary emotions likely play a large role. What you're doing in this exercise is identifying which primary emotions are *causing* the complex emotions. You are also identifying how your mind is working to protect you by involving you in the more complex emotional processes. You might want to repeat this exercise for any other loss you've experienced.

Some losses are very painful, and the primary emotions connected with them can be next to impossible to live with, which is part of the reason why the mind creates complex emotional processes. Consequently, you might ask why I want you to connect with these primary emotions if they're so painful. The reason is that in order to come to a place of acceptance of major losses, it's necessary to acknowledge and express the primary emotions. That doesn't mean that you have to live there or stay with those emotions indefinitely, but it is necessary to recognize them, understand how they're present deep within you, and be able to experience and express them.

An Example of Coping with Primary and Complex Emotions

Here's an example to help solidify these concepts: After returning from a combat deployment, a soldier flies into a rage at something his wife does and shoves her. She's not hurt, and this is the first time that this has ever happened. The soldier feels shocked, scared, and angry with himself. His wife had a very difficult time with their two young kids during the deployment, and she's been feeling dissatisfied with the marriage for a long time. She responds by saying that she wants a divorce, and tells him that she plans to move herself and the kids back with her parents.

The soldier now might feel helplessness, grief, and a strong fear of being alone along with the other primary emotions he's experiencing. Although the couple had some marital difficulties before deployment, the soldier loves his wife deeply, missed her throughout the deployment, and is overwhelmed by the pain of facing separation from her and their kids. This situation makes him well up with tears and have difficulty concentrating. He loses his appetite and starts to experience sleep difficulties. He asks her to go to counseling with him to try to save the marriage, but she refuses. He feels longing for his wife and is filled with sadness and fear.

It would be understandable in this situation for the soldier to then start to experience more complex emotions in the form of despondency, guilt, shame, feelings of worthlessness (believing that the entire marriage is a failure because of him alone), and depression. He might go over and over in his mind what happened that caused him to shove his wife, as well as all the different things that he could say or do to get her back. He might blame himself in multiple ways through "shoulds," "what-ifs," and "why" questions (e.g., "How *could I* have done that?", "*Why* did this happen", "What was I thinking?", "What *should* I do to fix this?", "How will she respond *if* I say that?"). He might feel desperate to reconnect with his wife. He might not acknowledge feeling angry with her for her refusal to attend counseling because he feels like the whole reason that she's leaving is his "fault." Ultimately, all of these feelings could progress to despair and feeling that life isn't worth living without his wife and children at his side.

At this point the soldier has turned all of the primary emotions, particularly his grief at losing his wife and kids and the fear of being alone, toward himself. He's incapable of staying for long with the primary emotions of grief and fear, and slides into depression and self-deprecating thoughts of worthlessness, self-blame, or feeling that life isn't worth living. He's unable to see value in himself, and blames himself for the entire situation, ultimately becoming filled with despair. Self-destructive behaviors might emerge, such as drinking excessively.

Clearly this soldier needs some resiliency to get through this situation. He may need to see a therapist or his pastor. He certainly needs to talk with a close friend or family member who cares about him. If he were to do the exercise in this section, then he might draw lines from "depressed," "guilt," "shame," "worthless," and "despair" to "hurt," "sadness/sorrow," "grief," "fear" (of being alone), "helpless," and maybe also "anger."

For this soldier, connecting the complex emotions that he's stuck in to the original primary emotions will help him free himself. Experiencing the primary emotions brings him back to a place where he feels the loss directly without judging himself as the cause of it. He fears being alone, but he won't be able to live alone unless he faces his fear. Once he does that (and only when he does that) can he move on to his new life. He feels grief at losing his wife and kids, and grief hurts terribly, but he can only learn to live with the loss by acknowledging how much the grief really hurts, not by trying to change it. Grief has to be allowed to run its course.

Yes, he has reason to be angry with himself, but he won't be able to resolve that until he realizes that he's also angry with his wife for refusing counseling, and for using this situation as her reason to leave. He feels helpless, but he won't be able to stop feeling helpless and create the possibility of a new life for himself until he acknowledges how helpless he really feels.

Basically, primary emotions need to be allowed to run their course and not get bottled up or locked up behind complex emotions and thought processes. The complex emotions are ingrained processes of the mind that help cope with the pain of primary emotions. However, they have a huge downside that can only be addressed through awareness.

The next thing that this soldier would probably benefit from doing is examining how his mind is trapping him in an endless cycle of self-blame, "should" statements, and "why" questions, which strongly connect with the complex emotions of worthlessness, guilt, and shame. Perhaps a friend can help him see that the marriage had difficulties for a long time, and that the one episode of shoving his wife was not the main problem, but rather the excuse (or catalyst) for his wife to make a decision she had already been contemplating. Perhaps he can come to accept that he really did the best he could to save the marriage, and that his wife was just as accountable for its failure as he was. Hopefully, he can let go of the repetitive mind games and realize that ultimately, he can't figure it all out.

His wife will do what she does for whatever reasons, and he has very little if any control over her decisions. Hopefully he can appreciate how precious his children are in his life, and will continue to build a strong connection and relationship with them through shared custody. The key for this soldier is to reach the point of believing in himself and his ability to independently move on in life while living with this loss, as painful as it is, and to recognize and accept that he has *value*—not only to himself, but also to his children and everyone else in his life who matter to him.

Looking at his wife's perspective is also helpful to put this soldier's experience in context. His wife had also experienced many of the same primary and complex emotions leading up to the above incident. For her, the marriage had been strained since well before the deployment, and the long separation only added to this. In addition, her husband seemed more distant, withdrawn, and angry since his return. She was tired of being blamed and yelled at for little things. Although she still loved her husband and wanted him to be part of the lives of their children, she knew that she didn't want to remain married to him. She felt like she had put her life on hold for years, and wanted to move on with educational and career goals. She felt like she would be able to get more support for her plans from her extended family. She also didn't think it would be helpful going to counseling, wanted to move in time for the kids to start school, and was somewhat angry with her husband for not accepting or supporting her decision.

Coming to this decision was difficult for her, filled with sadness (both over the loss of the connection with her husband and the loss of time in her life); fear of being alone and making it on her own; fear of how her plans would affect the kids; and some bitterness over how her husband had changed as a result of wartime service, and how much she sacrificed to support him. She experienced feelings of guilt, hopelessness, and depression. She blamed the military and herself for the marriage not working out, and asked herself a lot of questions about why she was feeling the way she was. Ultimately, she came to accept how she felt, and realized this was what she needed to do. For her, what will likely help most in continuing to feel secure as she moves forward in her life include acknowledging and expressing her feelings (including her fear and sadness), valuing herself, reaching out for support from her family, and letting go of any lingering guilt, self-blame, or "why" questions.

SKILL 3. LETTING GO OF UNANSWERABLE QUESTIONS

The above description of the couple dealing with a serious marital problem is also a good example of the skill of letting go of unanswerable questions that fuel complex emotions and make us feel worse, particularly starting with "Why?". Go back to the original "Loss Worksheet" to the question of whether you're blaming, using "should" statements, or asking "why" questions. Are you blaming yourself (or someone else) in some way for the losses that have occurred in your life by asking various "Why?" questions? "Why me?" "Why is this happening?" "What could I have done differently to prevent this?" "How could he/she have done that?" "Was it my fault?" Are you using a lot of "should" statements (e.g., "I *should* have done that instead.")? If you are, list them out on the same worksheet. Once you've identified them, it's time to let go of them, because they're traps that can demoralize you and bring you a world of hurt tied up with complex emotions.

Letting go of persistent and repetitive unanswerable questions can be very difficult. The brain has remarkably tenacious programming that's built to not let go of any nagging question until it's answered. Strangely, the parts of the brain having to do with trying to solve nagging questions (even if they're unsolvable) seem to be much more developed than the parts of the brain having to do with formulating the questions in the first place. Nagging questions are plentiful, and we instinctively and immediately engage in trying to solve them without even considering why we're asking them or if they're answerable (or worth answering).

We're particularly prone to being caught up in unanswerable dilemmas; we do it all the time. "If I break up with this person to be with that person, will I be happier?" "Which of these two jobs will be more satisfying?" "Is this a good decision to join the military or not?" "Which road will have the least traffic?" "Which university will be the best?" These *seem* like they have a "right" answer (often the one we come up with), but in fact are unanswerable at the time that they are posed. You might leave your current partner to be with someone else, only to discover a year later after the passion starts to wear off that you feel you would have been much better off staying with your original partner; or it might be the best thing that you ever did. Joining the military could have ended up being the best decision you ever made (or not), but you couldn't know this at the time that you made the decision, no matter how much research, consideration, or contemplation you put into it. Your GPS might tell you that if you take a detour you'll avoid all the traffic, but an accident might happen the moment you take the turn and you end up getting stuck in a bigger traffic jam. The point is that we love to ponder dilemmas, but we can't know what will happen or how we'll feel; we just have to make a decision to the best of our ability now, go for it, and not look back.

We're raised to believe that all questions are reasonable and that there is no such thing as a stupid question. We are also raised to believe that merely the act of asking the question is sufficient to assume that there is a reasonable answer waiting to be discovered. However, it's pretty easy to come up with stupid questions. Many of the "why" questions we propose to ourselves are no less stupid than asking, "What's the difference between a duck?" or "Is it colder in Montana or in January?"

Zen Koans

In Zen Buddhism there is a long-standing tradition of contemplating Zen koans as one route to enlightenment. Zen koans are questions that are posed by the teacher to the disciple, who is told that they must be solved in order to progress to the next level of their training. The disciple may be put through tremendous ordeals or asked to report back to the teacher on their progress in arriving at the correct answer to these questions. However, the "correct" answer is always elusive because koans are questions that are either unanswerable or have an infinite number of answers. Famous Zen koans include questions like, "What is the sound of one hand clapping?", "What is the color of wind?", or "Who hears?" Another asks, "If not even a thought has arisen, is there still sin?" Two koans that seem to be particularly popular these days are, "Who am I?" and "What's the meaning of life?"

The Zen Buddhist practice of pondering unanswerable questions is a clever way to reprogram the brain. By directly asking such questions, and forcing the disciple to get stuck in them, this paradoxically kicks the brain circuitry out of its propensity to get stuck in these types of questions. It can be a very confusing moment, but when this happens, the result is often an outburst of laughter, letting go, and reaching a place of wonder or presence in the moment where there is no longer any necessity to "figure" everything out. If you've found this section somewhat humorous, you may have already arrived at this state of being.

I hope no one thinks that I'm making light of difficult matters; quite the contrary. Many changes and losses related to deployment are particularly painful, and it's necessary to go through the sadness, grief, and anguish associated with them. What is not beneficial in the long run is turning these feelings against yourself in the form of chronic hopelessness, guilt, shame, self-blame, depression, or other complex emotions, where you get stuck for an indefinite period of time. There is a strong connection between these emotions and the brain's propensity to ponder unanswerable questions. If you ask yourself "why" questions that have a self-blaming quality to them, they connect directly to these complex emotions, making you feel worse about yourself. It's a cycle that feeds on itself.

Resilience of the Wounded Warrior

When a warrior is seriously injured, it's common for them to ask, "Why me?" and to be self-critical of what happened or their progress in recovery. They may blame themselves for joining the military in the first place, for not being able to do something at the time to change what happened, or for how much their injury is affecting their loved ones or family. There's often guilt that they're not able to remain with their unit. Coping with the physical injury, the pain, the multiple medications, medical appointments, and the transition to a life living with the effects of the injury can be extremely challenging for the warrior and family members.

However, the capacity for resilience is enormous, and the same principles apply as to other losses: not getting stuck in the cycle of self-blame, "why" and "what-if" questions, or the trap of complex emotions. Indeed, the injury affects everyone greatly, but the only thing the warrior has any control over is his or her own responses to it. The adversity itself is not what defines the wounded warrior, but rather, how the warrior rises to face the adversity. The thing that makes humans great is the ability to rise to challenges and bounce back after tremendous adversity. There is no other group of individuals who embody this more than wounded warriors.

Letting Go of Self-Criticism

I don't know how many times I've counseled soldiers who are blaming themselves for not accomplishing their goals (e.g., education, promotion, career, etc.) when the reason is obvious: a recent divorce, a new baby (or two), multiple deployments, family illness, etc. In these situations, the soldier is often stuck in a "should" ("I *should* have accomplished that goal"), and believes that they're to blame for the failure, and that the situation provides proof that they're "worthless." This is all a trick of the mind.

The reality is that these soldiers were dealing with things outside of their control that made it next to impossible to have the time to accomplish their goal; they could not be held accountable for achieving the goal under the circumstances. Nevertheless, even though I point out this fact, very often the soldiers return to their original thoughts and repeat them like a broken record.

I've also frequently counseled people who are blaming themselves for their spouse being unfaithful or for leaving when it was clear that they did what they could, and their spouse had major issues they were powerless to influence. In these situations the underlying feeling the person is often experiencing (but not acknowledging) is the fear of being alone. Instead of identifying the fear and acknowledging it, they cast blame on themselves for the failure of the relationship.

Self-blame takes on many colors and forms. We tend to judge ourselves in thousands of ways on a daily basis: the tint of our hair, our weight, how many pounds we can lift, success in achieving certain goals, how we think others view us, how we think of ourselves, what we should have said or not said, how we perform in bed, what we should have eaten or not eaten, what thoughts or desires are acceptable to express, what we think should have happened instead of what actually happened for every conceivable situation we can think of, asking why this is happening, etc. We judge ourselves constantly.

In summary, this skill is to practice reducing the amount of energy and time you spend judging yourself by eliminating self-blame, letting go of unanswerable "why" questions and "should" statements, and noticing every time you criticize yourself in subtle or not-so-subtle ways. Basically, become more aware of how often you judge yourself in some critical or negative way, and practice reducing this behavior.

SKILL 4: COPING WITH GRIEF AND SURVIVOR'S GUILT

Now we shift to a very painful topic: coping with grief and survivor's guilt stemming from the loss of buddies or unit members you have known who were killed or seriously injured. Although this discussion focuses on combat, this could also relate to loss or serious illness involving a loved one, family member, or friend outside of the military.

Losing a buddy on the battlefield is like losing a member of your family. The personal bonds in combat are some of the strongest anyone can experience, and warriors won't hesitate to die for their buddies, just as any of us would not hesitate to die protecting our loved ones. Their love for one another and commitment to each other on the battlefield is absolute, and their main "mission," in addition to neutralizing the enemy, is to protect each other and get everyone home safely.

No amount of training can prepare a warrior for losing a close buddy. Intellectually, they know that this can happen, but when it happens it's as devastating as losing any other member of their family. It's normal to immediately feel dazed, shocked, in pain, angry, helpless, empty, hollow—like there's a gaping hole inside; it's normal to feel physically sick, to be unable to function, and to cry and well up at the slightest reminders of the person who was injured or killed. Grief (also called bereavement and mourning) is one of the strongest of human emotions, and one that connects all of us together because we all experience it at some point in our lives. Grief is not a sickness or a disorder, though it can feel like one.

The Mystery of Grief

One of the problems with grief in the war zone is that there isn't any time to express it. Grief doesn't respect time and can't be conveniently locked away so that we can get on with our next mission. Grief doesn't just resolve itself and allow you to "move on." There are many myths about grief. Contrary to what people believe, grief doesn't gradually diminish over time, and time doesn't necessarily heal all wounds. The loss remains; waves of grief come and go with an intensity that rises and falls like the tides. However, over time the waves of grief generally come less frequently, and it becomes possible to live life with the loss and memory of the loved one who has passed on. How this happens is a bit of a mystery, but it does.

Unfortunately, warriors are expected to lock up their grief immediately after a tragedy on the battlefield because they have to remain focused on the mission. This is necessary for their own survival and the protection of other team members. However, what this does is delay the full expression of grief, not resolve it. Trying not to think of a buddy who died or was injured doesn't help in the long run with learning to live with the loss and memory of this precious individual. The grief process is put on hold until eventually the warrior is forced to face it. Grief has to run its course. This is part of its mystery.

Sometimes when grief is put on hold or "locked up," as warriors have to do in combat, it starts to get expressed in indirect and unhealthy ways, such as alcohol or drug use, aggression, rage, hostility, avoidance, risky behaviors, withdrawal from close friends and family, and all of the complex emotions. Unexpressed grief can lead to depression, despondency, despair, feeling that life has no purpose, and thoughts of wanting to die. Suicidal intentions may not be conscious. Sometimes warriors become so self-destructive from alcohol, drug use, rage, or driving recklessly that they end up killing themselves accidentally.

Grief is often intimately connected with guilt and the feeling that there *should have* been something that *could have* been done to prevent this tragedy. It's normal for warriors to feel survivor's guilt, and to feel that it was they who *should have* died or been injured. One warrior told me, "I don't know why he was killed. It would have been better if it was me. I'm single and don't have any kids. He had a wife and three kids waiting for him." Another warrior tore himself up with guilt over not spotting a trip wire to a roadside bomb that blew up his vehicle, killing the driver and seriously injuring two other soldiers. Here's how my dialogue with this soldier went:

Soldier: I keep going over what happened in my mind, looking at every little detail, trying to figure out what could have been done differently. I should have been able to see the wire and yell to the driver to stop.

Dr. Hoge: What was your position in the vehicle at the time that this happened?

Soldier: The gunner.

Dr. Hoge: Which vehicle was yours in the convoy?

Soldier: The third.

Dr. Hoge: How many vehicles were in the convoy?

Soldier: Three.

Dr. Hoge: What time of day did this occur?

Soldier: Probably around midnight. We were returning to our COP [combat outpost].

Dr. Hoge: Why do you think that the two front vehicles didn't trip the IED?

Soldier: I don't know. They ran right over it and for some reason didn't trip it.

Dr. Hoge: As the gunner of the rear vehicle, weren't you covering the rear?

Soldier: Yes.

Dr. Hoge: Let me get this straight: It was nighttime, the vehicles in front ran over the trip wire without triggering it, and you were in the last vehicle facing toward the rear of the convoy. How on earth could you have seen the trip wire before your vehicle hit it?

Soldier: Sometimes when I'm the gunner I turn around and look toward the front.

Dr. Hoge: How often do you do this when you're covering the rear?

Soldier: Not very often.

Dr. Hoge: Like 1 percent of the time, 10 percent of the time?

Soldier: Maybe 1 percent.

Dr. Hoge: So how would you have known to turn around at that instant?

Soldier: Sometimes I just sense things. I get feelings. One time I ducked the moment a round went over my head. Sometimes I have a feeling and it makes me turn around.

Dr. Hoge: And you blame yourself for what happened because at that moment, you didn't get that feeling and turn around to look toward the front?

Soldier: Yes.

Despite the fact that this soldier wasn't facing in the direction where he could have seen the trip wire, despite the fact that it was nighttime, and despite the fact that two other vehicles in front had cleared the way, this soldier was convinced that he should have been able to do something at that moment to prevent the tragedy. He blamed himself for what happened, even though he had no accountability for it and his responsibility was to cover the rear. He blamed himself for the tragedy because he failed to have a premonition in that instant and turn around. And his mind was able to construct this belief and rationalize why he *should have* been able to turn around in that moment. His self-blame for the death and injuries of his buddies contributed to depression and PTSD symptoms.

You may ask why this type of illogical thinking occurs. The interesting thing when we talked about this tragedy is that this soldier could clearly see that his thinking was illogical. Yet, he was not able to accept this or let go of this way of thinking. He said, "I know it's crazy to think this way, but I can't stop it."

Distinguishing Between Grief and Survivor's Guilt

It's important to distinguish grief from survivor's guilt. Although they can be closely connected, with grief being a primary emotion beneath survivor's guilt, they aren't the same thing, and can occur independently. Survivor's guilt, a complex emotion, is tied to illogical thought processes involving self-blame, self-punishment, second-guessing, and a belief that I *should have* died also (or instead). The fact that I'm alive means that I made the "mistake" of saving myself, that I "chose" to live while my buddy died.

Frequently, when a serious illness or injury brings someone near death, people around them will comment on how they're "choosing" to keep fighting, or alternatively have reached a point where they've "chosen" to let go and pass on. This reflects the pervasive believe in our culture that we're in control of our destiny and can "choose" our path, even when lying in a coma.

If we're able to control our destiny—as our culture and our own minds lead us to believe—then it's inconceivable why my buddy died and not me, and the reality that I'm alive is unforgivable. Guilt and self-blame is how I punish myself.

The reason that survivor's guilt can hold so much power over us has to do with how painful and confusing it is to come to terms with a tragic loss of this magnitude on an emotional and rational level. The loss confronts our confidence in our value and ability to determine our lives, and to protect those we cherish and love.

The soldier could understand intellectually that he wasn't responsible or accountable for what happened, but on an emotional and rational level, he couldn't stop blaming himself. Being stuck in the process of trying to figure out what he *should have* been able to do differently was actually less painful and more reasonable to deal with than the irrational, arbitrary unfairness of the loss itself. The degree to which the belief was illogical was related to the strength and intensity of the unjust loss, and the inability of the mind to reconcile what happened.

In a strange sort of way, illogical thought processes also help to keep us connected in our minds to the loved ones we've lost. It can be tremendously difficult to reach the point of acceptance—to be able to let go of the one we loved. If we keep the person present in our thoughts through re-creating the event over and over in our mind, as if to undo it, we don't have to say good-bye or accept the reality of our lives, and can manage to some degree the waves of grief and other emotions that wash over us.

Considerations for Coping with Grief and Survivor's Guilt

Given this, how does a warrior who has lost one or more buddies in combat (or anyone who has lost someone close to them) cope with grief and/ or survivor's guilt? Is there anything that they can do to ease the burden and be able to live life with the loss and memories?

The answer is to go back to the primary emotions and allow them to run their course, believe in yourself, and try not to get stuck in the complex emotions and thought processes. However, *not* having a clear navigation strategy in this case is what this process is also about. You can't figure something like this out. You can only ride the waves of emotion, with the support of loved ones, and eventually they will settle down in you; instead of constantly thinking about the events surrounding the tragedy, you'll be able to live with the loss and keep the memory of your buddy alive in other ways. It's a mystery how this happens, but it's a universal experience that we face as part of the human condition.

Here are some considerations that you may find helpful:

A) Do whatever you need to do to express your grief. Don't lock it up or allow it to cause you to engage in risky or self-destructive behaviors. Don't isolate yourself. Talk to people you're close to. Write about how you feel. Share your memories. Accept the tides and waves of whatever emotions are present. Don't let others tell you how you *should* feel. Don't tell yourself how you *should* feel.

B) If you experience survivor's guilt or blame yourself in any way, look beneath the blame at what other emotions are present, and understand how blame and fault are traps of your mind. Try to figure out any illogical thinking and let go of unanswerable questions.

If you blame yourself, imagine a conversation with your deceased buddy and ask them if they blame you for staying alive. They don't, and would be very upset with you if they could express it. For their sake, stop blaming yourself. For your sake, stop blaming yourself. For the sake of everyone you love, and for everyone who loves you, stop blaming yourself. Stop punishing yourself. Let yourself off the hook. *Forgive yourself.*

Forgive yourself for not spotting a trip wire. Forgive yourself for holding on to a capsized boat while others perished. Forgive yourself for getting out of a burning vehicle that others were trapped in. Forgive yourself for something that you had no accountability for and could never have done anything differently about. Forgive yourself for whatever you did or didn't do that no one, including you, could ever imagine needing forgiveness for. *Forgive yourself for staying alive.*

C) Don't try to find "meaning" in what happened beyond what is. Every life is precious and that's the meaning of it. Whether or not you believe in God (and most of us do), or believe in the greater good of a country, everything in God's miraculous creation of nature, including human creativity and the workings of government, has randomness in it (at least from our perspective).

We live in a world of haphazard events that somehow work together for us as a species, although not always for the individual, whether it's random mutations that result in some people getting cancer, the random sperm that carries the genetic material for Down syndrome, the random thought arising in the mind of a scientist that an atom can be split, the random accident or hurricane that destroys a life or home, the random electrical failure that causes the traffic light to fail, or the random sniper round that kills a warrior as he's handing a gift to a child.

A war zone is about as chaotic as anything we humans can create, and a warrior's death on the battlefield isn't something we can understand or find a greater meaning or purpose in, other than to honor how precious this warrior's life was, and how great the loss and sacrifice is.

D) For any buddies who were seriously injured, go visit them. Keep in touch. Reach out and make yourself available to them.

E) For any close buddy who was killed, find a way to honor and remember them. This is very personal, and can involve visiting the grave site; setting up a small place to honor the memories with photos or stories; building a memorial Web site or contributing to one that the family has established; making a list of all the things that you appreciate or remember most fondly about your buddy; asking yourself what your buddy would want to be remembered for; doing something you know your buddy would have enjoyed doing with you; and finding a way to say good-bye through a ritual of some sort. If you're going over events that happened or blaming yourself in some way, find another way to keep your buddy alive in your mind through the memories of the relationship that you cherish, and what you appreciated and loved most about this person. Honor the memories and the love for your buddy that continues.

F) Don't be afraid to make contact with close family members and friends of your buddy if you're inclined to do this. Warriors often hesitate to do this, mostly out of fear that it will be too painful to handle—either for themselves or the family—or that the family will want information about what happened that contradicts the more sanitized official versions that they may have received. However, making contact can be enormously healing for the warrior, as well as the family, because it provides a way for everyone to share memories of someone they all cared deeply for. It can also help in the process of saying good-bye, because warriors are often not able to make it to funeral or memorial services. Saying good-bye is a way of honoring the memories of their buddy.

Although making contact with a spouse or family members might help in the grief process, it's important to be very attentive to their needs and to not provide information that isn't desired or asked for. It's best to keep things general by letting the family know that you were a good friend from the same unit, and by expressing your love for your buddy, the fact that you miss them, and that you're sorry for the family's loss. If there's something that you would like to know, like where you can visit the grave, ask; this provides a good way to make an initial contact, and the family will appreciate that you're interested in honoring your buddy in some way.

You can also gently let the family know that if they have questions or if there's something that you can assist them with, you're available, but don't volunteer information about what happened in the combat zone without being directly asked, and don't make contact if this is your main intention. If the family expresses a desire to know exactly what happened, warn them before you provide information that it may not be easy for them (or you) to talk about. Ask them how much detail or information they want, and let them make the decision. It may be helpful for you to have another buddy with you, or for the family member to also have a trusted friend with them. There aren't any good rules on how to handle this type of communication. Many families want honest and complete answers; others are content with the information that has been provided, and are appreciative simply that a close friend from the unit has reached out to share in their grief. This is a very personal and individual experience.

G) Finally, seek solace and comfort in whatever way works best for you, whether it's through your religious faith, the support of loved ones and close friends, or taking a walk in the mountains. Life is a journey, and part of this journey is to honor the memories of those who have gone before us, and in turn, to give the gift of memories to those who will remain after we are gone.

SKILL 5: ACCEPTING OTHER DIFFICULT EVENTS THAT HAPPENED IN COMBAT

The final skill in this chapter is accepting all the things that happened in combat that you would rather forget or not talk about. This can include witnessing collateral casualties involving women and children, seeing the results of brutality or torture, witnessing ethical misconduct by fellow warriors, treating combatants or noncombatants inhumanely, and killing. War is hell. It is a totally insane human undertaking in which life, death, and suffering are intertwined and inescapable. Collateral casualties occur. Warriors often feel helpless to protect civilians, although this is one of their responsibilities, and sometimes the enemy uses women or children as shields or weapons themselves. Rage may get out of control, particularly when there are casualties in a warrior's unit. Rage and fear, in combination with exhaustion and sleep deprivation, can sometimes result in warriors taking out their aggression in inappropriate ways.

In two surveys conducted in Iraq in 2006 and 2007, approximately 10 percent of soldiers and marines reported that they had unnecessarily damaged Iraqi property, and 5 percent reported that they had kicked or hit a noncombatant unnecessarily. Units that had experienced high levels of combat intensity or high levels of PTSD symptoms reported higher rates of ethical misconduct.

Upon returning home, warriors frequently report feelings of remorse, regret, guilt, and shame related to things they witnessed or participated in. Some of the things can't be discussed for fear of prosecution. Some are too gruesome to discuss with a civilian therapist or loved one. Some are associated with so much shame that the warrior is too embarrassed. In all these instances, the warrior is left holding the bag and trying to find a way to bury these images and memories. Warriors sometimes ask me if they are "a killer" because they killed on the battlefield. They sometimes express the belief that they are unworthy of love because they acted inhumanely or did not stop inhumane treatment from occurring. Living with these experiences can be very difficult, and a warrior may come to believe that how they acted on the battlefield reflects their true identity.

One thing that is misunderstood is the topic of killing during combat. Contrary to what some people believe, killing the enemy isn't difficult. That's what war is about, and success in combat means neutralizing the enemy by whatever means possible before they neutralize you. As one warrior said, "It takes about a second." Killing isn't something that's just drummed into you through training. The capacity to kill is in all of us. When threatened, we fight or flee depending on the situation. If the lives of our loved ones are threatened, we'll kill to defend them. If the lives of our buddies are threatened in combat, we'll kill. If our own life is threatened, we'll kill.

In all of these situations, it's understandable that there isn't remorse, and anyone who thinks that there should be is passing judgment. Warriors sometimes report increased stress, including PTSD symptoms, in situations where they're constrained from killing; for example, they witness severe ethnic violence but are prohibited by the rules of engagement (ROE) from intervening.

The situations that may bring about remorse (as well as regret, guilt, shame, and second-guessing) are those that involve collateral or friendly-fire casualties, those in which you somehow connect with the person who was killed, or feel like you failed in your responsibility to protect someone. One battalion commander told me what caused him to question his actions on a mission was when he saw photos of an enemy combatant's wife and children that were on him when he was killed. Suddenly, the enemy had a human face—not any different than his own—and this officer started to wonder if there were things that could have been done to capture this combatant rather than kill him.

A soldier on guard duty at a checkpoint near Taji, Iraq, tore himself up with guilt after opening fire on a vehicle that he thought was a suicide bomber (because it was moving too fast and erratically) but actually turned out to be an Iraqi family driving that way because they were scared. Friendly-fire and collateral casualties involving women and children can

245

be particularly painful and difficult. Part of a warrior's job is to protect innocent people, and they can experience remorse or guilt when they believe they've failed in that responsibility.

Not infrequently, a group of warriors (e.g., a squad or platoon) will act in ways that are not consistent with the values of all individuals in the group. Rage may erupt in mistreatment of civilian noncombatants or detainees, and fellow unit members will later feel guilty that they didn't intervene. What is often not appreciated is how powerful group processes are. Since your life and those of all of your team members depend completely on one another, you'll hesitate to step into a situation that involves confronting a fellow unit member. Unit cohesion is one of the strongest protective mechanisms for a combat unit, and going against another unit member in your group can mean putting yourself at risk, tantamount to suicide in some combat environments. You would be crazy to intervene in some circumstances, even if the situation that is occurring is morally wrong. However, this fact is often ignored, and when warriors later start to go over what happened in their minds, it's not uncommon for them to believe that they *should have* had the ability or courage to do something differently.

In combat, where there is high threat, high ambiguity, extreme physical stress, sleep deprivation, and rapidly changing requirements, mistakes happen, and situations like all of the examples above can be over before anyone has time to think about them. Then, when time catches up, the thoughts, guilt, second-guessing, remorse, shame, and other reactions set in.

All of the previous learning material concerning grief, guilt, "why" questions, blame, catch-22s, the nature of choice, and primary and complex emotions apply to these situations as well. As in previous skills, the first thing to consider in addressing your reactions to situations such as these is to acknowledge their existence.

These situations can encompass complicated forms of loss and emotions (e.g., loss of innocence, loss of certainty in a just world, loss of one's sense of identity, living with the horror or disgust associated with the memories, or feeling like one has failed). Next, it's important to connect with the *primary* emotions and, to the best of your ability, let go of complex emotions and unanswerable questions that leave you condemning and beating up on yourself. There are so many factors that influence what happens in the war zone; there's no point going back over a situation to try and find ways to "undo" it or to resolve it in your mind. Accept that you did what you could do at the time in a completely insane situation, and that perceiving different "choices" in hindsight is an illusion.

Here are some considerations that you may find helpful in accepting other difficult things that happened in combat:

A) What happened on the battlefield is not who you are.

B) Accept that no one, not even you, is in any position to be the judge of what happened on the battlefield. It's easy to look back at a situation (pretending that time on the battlefield was logical and linear) and think of things that *could have* been done differently; however, it's impossible for the warrior to act differently than the way they did at that moment. That's a hard pill to swallow. We all like to think of ourselves as always capable of taking the high road in every situation by doing the "right," "moral," and "just" act. However, the reality on the battlefield is that we are imperfect animals operating in an insane situation, where our lives (and those of our brothers) are seriously threatened; where things happen in mere seconds; where we're influenced by extreme physical stress, sleep deprivation, group processes, and a million other things; where mistakes happen (like they always do); and in which "right," "moral," and "just" can end up being very unclear constructs.

You truly did the very best that you could downrange—the only thing that you could have done under the circumstances you were in—and there's no point second-guessing things based on your current ability to look back in time, and your ability to believe now that somehow you *could have* done something differently *then* that *would have* resulted in a better outcome. This is very important to accept. (Also see chapter 7, skills 2 and 4.)

C) Try to find a way to talk about what happened with a therapist, a clergy member, or close confidant, for all the reasons that were discussed in chapter 6. Whatever the images or memories, whatever situations that occurred, none are too horrific or embarrassing to talk about. If there were situations that have legal ramifications (e.g., murder, misconduct, etc), ask your therapist about any limits of confidentiality, and get their advice on how to talk about these situations without fear that they will be put in records that could be subpoenaed. There are ways to talk about how experiences affected you without sharing specific details about what happened. One way or another, talk about your experiences and try to work through any feelings that they evoke so you can come to understand that your experiences downrange are not who you are—that you are much greater than the individual experiences you've had.

D) It's your right to consult a lawyer before speaking with or confessing anything to police or investigators about what happened downrange. Even if the investigators treat you with the utmost respect afforded any war hero (or lock you in a room with a one-way mirror and a single bag of Doritos), it's your right to consult a lawyer. Warriors have been convicted and imprisoned for murder related to battlefield scenarios that occurred months or years earlier when there was absolutely no material evidence available (no body, no weapon, only their testimony) and virtually no risk that they would commit a similar crime in any other circumstance.

E) Find a way to make amends with yourself by giving back to the world in positive ways, through charity, gifts, and compassionate acts in whatever way feels right for you. As a warrior with war-zone experience, you have a unique perspective and an appreciation for the value and dignity of human life and what it means to be compassionate. No matter what happened downrange, you're a warrior, and you always have the responsibility to live to the fullest of your capability, doing good and righteous acts of kindness and compassion that only a person with a warrior's experience, knowledge, and wisdom can achieve.

To conclude, First Sergeant Michael Schindler offers his thoughts on the topic of acceptance:

The first rule of combat is that there are no rules, so to try and accept what happens in combat is impossible. The process of navigating my way through PTSD gave me the tools and a blueprint to free myself of guilt and lingering negative behavior patterns which blocked my life from moving forward, and from inner joy and happiness. For me, moving forward meant doing the impossible: accepting what occurred in my past.

Like many mornings, on this resupply day in July of 1971, my platoon had to hump 7 to 10 clicks through mountain terrain and elephant-grass jungle to find a suitable landing zone (LZ) for the choppers to drop off ammo, supplies, C-Rations, mail, and hot food. Spirits were high as usual on this resupply day. Squads from 2nd Platoon linked up with each other to begin the hike to find an LZ. As I remember, we found a suitable LZ late in the morning.

We halted and spread out on a trail near the hilltop. The LT checked his map and told Sergeant S to take a few men to patrol the LZ. I took the point in front of Sergeant S, followed by Doc and a PFC. While walking slowly I noticed the wind blowing hard and saw that the hilltop was thick with razor-sharp elephant grass. Clearing this LZ would be a pain in the ass. We came up the slope cautiously, looking for signs of VC. All of our combat senses were engaged now, listening for metallic sounds, scanning for quick movement, the smell of death, detecting booby traps. We stopped a couple of times, crouching, looking, and listening for any threats.

The next event changed my life for thirty-six years. I stood up and slowly walked about twenty-five steps when Sergeant S stood up and took three or four steps in the same spots that I did and hit a booby trap. Sergeant S hit the ground, screaming, "My fucking leg!" as I hit the ground just ahead of him and looked back and saw him grabbing his leg while writhing and squirming in massive pain. I crawled back to him while firing into the elephant grass. Doc came from behind and administered first aid on Sergeant S's leg.

The rest of the patrol blindly opened fire into the elephant-grass hilltop. After a frightening few minutes, a cease-fire order was given by the LT. Frantically we determined there was no VC in the elephant-grass hilltop, and that the booby trap was old. Attention shifted to Sergeant S's condi-

tion while securing the LZ for a medevac chopper to land and pick him up. Sergeant S's foot had been blown off cleanly at the ankle just above the boot. Within twenty-five to forty minutes, the medevac chopper set down. Doc and I put Sergeant S on the stretcher, then loaded him onto the chopper. I picked up his foot, still in the boot, placed it on the stretcher next to him, and signaled the chopper pilot to take off.

During the next thirty-six years I blamed myself because I hadn't seen the booby trap that exploded and ruined Sergeant S's life. Shortly after my mental crash and burn, during the beginning of my therapy sessions, while narrating my story, I was told by my psychiatrist that because combat events can happen so fast, warriors only remember fragments of an event. In my case, I for sure thought that I was responsible for what happened because of my negligence as point man.

My closure for "causing" this came while attending my Vietnam platoon's first reunion in July of 2007 in St. Joe, Missouri. Fifteen members from 2nd Platoon, Bravo Company, 1st Battalion, 501st Geronimo Brigade, 101st Airborne Infantry Division (Screaming Eagles) attended. We spent four days reconnecting, laughing, crying, and talking story together. The experience was truly outstanding and long overdue. During this reunion I talked with Doc, now a lieutenant colonel, and asked him what he remembered about that day. Doc told me, "Not much, except a lot of chaos, yelling, blood, putting Sergeant S onto the stretcher, and putting his foot next to him before the medevac chopper took off." During my retelling of the story, I told Doc that I had put Sergeant S's foot on the stretcher, not him.

On the last day of the reunion, I finally worked up enough courage to talk story with Sergeant S, who was also there. By then, we were the only ones who remained at the hotel. So I finally asked him what he remembered about that day. He said that he did not remember anything after he stepped on the booby trap. That's when I told Sergeant S of my guilt—that I blamed myself and accepted responsibility for him losing his foot because it was my job to clear the way as point man.

Sergeant S's response completely surprised me. He looked at me for a few moments, gave me his Georgia chuckle, and said, "That's silly, Mike, what happened was nobody's fault except the son of a bitch who put the booby trap there in the first place." He also added, "Besides, I was the one in front when we walked up to the LZ." I said that I remembered turning to look back toward him after the explosion, but after we talked about it, I realized that Sergeant S had actually been off to my left as well as behind me, and was probably not directly in my footsteps as I had been remembering it through the years. Somehow talking this through lifted a great weight off my heart. My reaction was to laugh and feel real stupid for having accepted the guilt and blame all that time.

My point here is that although the three of us—Doc, Sergeant S, and I—were involved in the same incident, we all remember that day differently. Each of us will swear that we "remember" correctly. The truth, of course, is that we are all correct, and to accept this as a fact.

Instead of dwelling, analyzing, and feeling guilty about combat experiences that make no sense in the real world, accept that combat is completely surreal. Trying to understand the sense of combat is impossible. Instead, understand your combat warrior experiences and loss of combat buddies as something that you can't make sense of. Accept the random insanity, and turn the negative feelings into positive actions that will set you free from guilt and inner turmoil.

Combat warriors often ask themselves, "Why me?" Why did I survive that battle and my buddy got killed? The randomness of combat is a real pisser, and the hardest thing to accept. We frequently feel that we should have died, and that our buddy is dead because of something that we did to cause this. The pisser here is that there is no way to understand the randomness of death in combat. Moving on and accepting the "why" of combat loss takes a full measure of faith in yourself and blind acceptance of combat as unexplainable. Acknowledge your feelings, honor your combat brothers, and accept the loss. Free yourself from the guilt and stay strong; life is good.

Extinguishing the flames of combat, killing, death, loss, and despair was perhaps the most difficult task that I have ever done. Sometimes during the narrative and acceptance stages, I wanted to scream, and did, plenty of times. The sense of having no control over my emotions was more than I could bear at times, but it was better than when my emotions mani-

fested in anger, beer drinking, and dangerous living, among a long list of negative behaviors. Acceptance for me was to not think of myself as a killer, but to think of myself as a combat infantry warrior doing his job, just as many generations had done before me (and after).

The first time that I heard the concept that I could possibly be remembering my combat experiences differently than others involved in the same incidents was during my first therapy session. My reaction was total confusion. My shrink had to explain it several times.

My experience is that we all feel, remember, and see things differently even though we all are part of the same events, occurring at the same split second. I truly believe that this is a way that we process the event as individuals. In general, all combat memories are the "correct" memories. Fiction is fiction, but should not be confused with remembering differently from another who was with you in battle.

Funny how in a firefight, time seems to slow down so that you can react to the combat actions taking place around you. I felt that I was having an out-of-body experience, like being on the outside looking in. This outside looking-in feeling stayed with me for thirty-plus years. Acceptance of my combat warrior actions of death, killing, loss, grief, confusion, and pain began when I realized that I could not and should not try to make sense from chaos. Chaos is what it is—random confusion. Accept your combat experiences as part of your life, not what defines your life.

CHAPTER 10

NAVIGATION STRATEGIES FOR SPOUSES, PARTNERS, AND FAMILY MEMBERS

This is a huge issue. We have lived six months, twelve months, or however long in Hell. We just want to come home, relax, and do what we haven't been able to do for the past time frame of the deployment. At the same time, our family members have been in Hell for the same amount of time. They have taken care of finances, children, and everything else. Time didn't stop for them, but for us, "reality of home" did stop. Both sides have sacrificed, but all too often that's forgotten. Neither side of the coin is the same. Both have experienced significant change and adaptability. Both want a break upon redeployment home.

ARMY COMBAT MEDIC, POST-IRAQ

This chapter is intended primarily for spouses or partners of warriors, but also acknowledges the tremendous impact that deployment can have on children, other family members, and friends. It's also a very important chapter for warriors. Just as it's beneficial for spouses, partners, and family members to gain a better understanding of warriors' experiences by reading the earlier chapters, the warrior can benefit by gaining perspective on the experience of their loved ones by reading this. If you have children, there's material for helping them. This chapter is about shared resilience through supporting each other.

DEPLOYMENT AFFECTS EVERYONE

Wartime service can have lasting effects (both positive and negative) on spouses or partners, no matter the length of the relationship or how much time has passed since the warrior returned from deployment. As a spouse or partner, you might have known your warrior throughout the deployment cycle, or you might have come into each others' lives well after their return. This chapter can be useful either way.

If you were with your warrior while they were deployed, you know that deployment to combat can be just as hard on spouses, partners, children, and other family members as it is on the warriors, although in a different way. In many ways the war zone is "simpler." The warrior's responsibility is to stay focused on the mission together with their team members. At home, everything gets more complicated for loved ones during the warrior's absence.

When I was thinking of the quote to use above, I wanted one from a spouse, but ended up selecting this warrior's words because of its reference to the sense of time. Warriors put the home front "on hold," stopped in time. They look forward to the moment they can break from the hell of deployment and return home, and the passage of time can be agonizing (particularly demoralizing if the tour length is extended). But they are singularly occupied on their mission and don't feel the passage of time in the same way as those left behind. They know the connection with their loved ones exists, and may depend on it and long for it, but they also tuck it away somewhere, like all of their other emotions, so they can get on with the mission at hand. One day runs into the next.

Spouses, partners, children, and close family members *feel* the passage of time as they wait to hear from their warrior; as they wait for the safe return of their warrior; as they witness the devastation of the war on other families in their unit or through the news; as they go through each day filled with ordinary activities that make up life. It isn't only the burden of having to juggle all of the responsibilities when the warrior deploys (finances, child care, work, education, etc.). It's also the burden of waiting, of having to hold fear somewhere deep inside (just as the warrior does) to get through each day. The connection with their warrior is an active living experience within the passage of time, which can be accompanied by intense loneliness and isolation.

For modern warriors and their families, the availability of rapid communication between the war zone and home by e-mail, phone, and webcam has helped tremendously to keep relationships strong, to maintain the commitment, and to provide ongoing reassurance that the warrior is safe and their loved ones at home are doing okay. This reassurance is vital for everyone. However, the advances in communication don't reach all areas of the operational theater, and many warriors experience sporadic or no contact with home for long periods of time, just as in past wars. If there are extended operations or casualties, communication ceases, and loved ones may panic at the sudden gap in contact. In addition, even during communication "blackouts," some information trickles through, and loved ones may learn of casualties before official notification, or hear rumors that increase their worries and fears.

Although rapid communication provides mutual support and may be beneficial in solving problems at home, neither the warrior nor their spouse/partner want to burden each other in the time they have to communicate. The warrior doesn't want to share the details of their combat experiences for fear that it will unnerve their partner; their partner doesn't want to burden the warrior even if there are severe stresses at home, because they don't want the warrior to be distracted by these issues and lose focus in the war zone. What this means is that neither person can rely on each other for support on a day-to-day basis and have to grow as individuals. Warriors get most of their support from unit peers, which is essential in the operational environment; spouses get support from other spouses, friends, and family. This may create distance and lead to challenges upon reunion. Partners/significant others who are not married to the warrior can have a particularly difficult time finding support because they aren't able to easily tap into the military community.

The other by-product of easy communication is that strains in the relationship can rapidly become evident. Warriors might hear rumors of their spouse or significant other hanging out with other people and become suspicious or jealous (rightly or wrongly). The relationship could unravel and end during deployment, leaving the warrior feeling bereft, angry, helpless to do anything, and unable to concentrate or focus on the mission. The anger can be compounded by financial strain if the warrior's bank accounts with hard-earned combat pay are drained or credit cards maxed out during a breakup. Unit leaders are often not very receptive to a warrior's request to take unscheduled leave to go home and try to resolve a relationship crisis in the middle of deployment.

Everyone grows, matures, and changes during the absence. Spouses and partners become much more independent. Children may reach major milestones (e.g., walking, talking). Young children may not remember the warrior, or may have difficulty adjusting to new routines, shared custody, or a move when the warrior returns. Role changes in the household can be challenging. Warriors may have a hard time transferring responsibilities to their spouse/partner, and then on return unrealistically expect that the roles should go back to the way they were before deployment.

Family structure has changed considerably over the years, and the current wars bring unique challenges. In particular, the large number of single parents and dual military families with children has led to significant child-care burdens falling for extended periods on grandparents and other relatives or friends. This expands the impact of the current wars to many people outside of the immediate military family. Child custody issues can be particularly challenging due to military and deployment stresses.

Women have for the first time been involved in direct combat operations in large numbers. Nearly 40 percent of military women serving during the Iraq and Afghanistan wars have children. Women have faced deployments within a year after delivery. The first four years of an infant's life, and, in particular, the first year, are critical in the child's development. Separation during this period can result in the infant forming bonds with another caregiver—perhaps a grandparent—which can lead to difficulties when the mother attempts to reunite after deployment. There are concerns that this could increase the risk of long-term developmental or interpersonal problems for the child. All of this adds to the complexity of readjustment on the return home.

One of the greatest challenges in the current wars in Iraq and Afghanistan has been multiple deployments. Warriors who remain in service (and their families) are expected to "reset" rapidly after return and be ready for another deployment. Even the time at home is interrupted by extended absences for military training, and it can be challenging to nurture a strong relationship or resolve issues related to the previous deployment. Both the warrior and their loved ones may immediately start bracing for the next deployment, and as a result, keep buried their reactions from the previous deployment.

Lingering Postwar Effects

No matter how long ago the warrior returned from deployment, spouses, partners, and family members can be impacted by how the warrior was affected by their experiences. Sometimes there is a sense that the warrior is a different person. Family members often feel that they have to "walk on eggshells" due to the level of rage. Household sleep patterns can get disrupted when the warrior repeatedly leaves the bed in the middle of the night. There might be arguments and conflict over roles and responsibilities, the amount of time the warrior wants to spend with unit peers, the amount the warrior is drinking, or the spouse moving something that belongs to the warrior. In extreme cases family members can experience "secondary traumatization" and start to exhibit PTSD symptoms related to the warrior's behavior. One of the most difficult things to cope with is the emotional detachment and withdrawal.

Loved ones may recognize that the warrior needs help for war-related problems, but be frustrated in attempts to convince the warrior to follow through. They may also need help themselves but not have an opportunity to receive it, because they feel like they have to remain "strong" or because they find themselves still managing the household by themselves even after the warrior returns.

Both the warrior and their spouse/partner want a break when the warrior returns home, but the reality is that they might have a difficult time adjusting and finding an equilibrium that's mutually supportive. This can be influenced by how much each individual has changed, where they got support from during the deployment, and the various life stresses related to employment, finances, moves, family strain, or transitions to civilian life. Life back home is very complicated, and warriors sometimes yearn to return to the "simplicity" of the operational environment.

When there are serious war-related reactions, such as PTSD, depression, rage, alcohol abuse, or effects of traumatic brain injury, one of the most common emotions that spouses, partners, and close family members experience is a sense of helplessness. They feel powerless to be able to do anything to help their warrior, and fearful of the warrior's response should they try. They might also continue to fill roles that the warrior usually assumes rather than confronting the behavior and attempting to work out an equitable solution. Hopefully, the knowledge gained from reading this book puts some of this in perspective and offers hope that there are things both the warrior and their loved ones can do during the transition period.

The following considerations are directed primarily to spouses, partners, or significant others of warriors. Ask your warrior to read any sections that you think would benefit both of you.

YOUR STRENGTH AND INDEPENDENCE

Your most important strength is your individuality and ability to live a fulfilling and meaningful life independently from your warrior. The more comfortable you are with your independence, the happier you'll be, and the more there will be for you to share with your warrior. Your independence allows you to effectively take over roles and responsibilities when your warrior is deployed, and there's no reason to stop doing this when your warrior returns. Independence doesn't mean being on your own. You can be intimately connected with each other and independent at the same time. In fact, that's ideal. There is great joy in two people sharing with each other and appreciating the many qualities that make each other unique individuals. If you have your own interests, dreams, and friends that motivate and inspire you, then you have things that give meaning to your life when your warrior is away, as well as when you're together. They add to your sense of confidence, self-worth, accomplishment, and connection to others. When warriors encourage and value their spouse's independence, this adds to the health of the relationship.

TAPPING INTO YOUR RESOURCES

In addition to your own strength and independence, as a spouse or significant other of a warrior, you likely have a great many resources available to you, particularly support from family and friends. Although the exercises in this book are geared for warriors, they can be just as useful to you. Being aware of your feelings and reactions, ensuring good sleep, physical exercise, noticing your breathing, meditation, eliminating "shoulds," acceptance, letting go, coping with the emotions of loss or grief, dealing with anger, and many of the other skills presented in this book are worth learning. There is also tremendous value in narrating and sharing your story with whomever you're comfortable with.

You may need support from a mental health professional yourself at some point. In one survey of Army spouses, nearly 20 percent had significant symptoms of depression or anxiety, and 8 percent reported that mental health symptoms were seriously affecting their relationships or ability to function at work. If you're experiencing depression, isolation, difficulty sleeping, rage, increased alcohol use, loss of interest in things you used to enjoy, or severe worry or anxiety on an ongoing basis, then you should consider getting help. Suicidal or homicidal thinking are definitely reasons to seek help.

One of the challenges for you, which may be less of an issue for service members or veterans, is navigating the civilian health-care system, such as TRICARE. This can be difficult and frustrating at times, and requires a lot of patience. One of the easiest ways to get started is to see your primary care provider and ask for a referral, or contact Military OneSource at www .militaryonesource.com or 1-800-342-9647. If there is suicidal thinking, homicidal thinking, or verbal or physical abuse going on in your household, then contact one of the crisis lines, where there are counselors available twenty-four hours a day: the National Suicide Prevention Lifeline at 1-800-273-TALK (8255) and the National Domestic Violence Hotline at 1-800-799-SAFE (7233) or 1-800-787-3224 (TTY). Both of these hotlines are connected with crisis centers where you can get immediate assistance. See chapter 8 on navigating the mental health care system for more information on how to get help.

STRENGTHENING YOUR RELATIONSHIP AND CONSIDERATIONS FOR COPING WITH POSTWAR REACTIONS OF YOUR WARRIOR

From the material contained in this book you're likely to gain a good understanding of the reasons why your warrior reacts the way they do after serving in a combat zone. Many of these reactions are normal and a result of the body's physiological survival defenses. There is much information on what the warrior can do to modulate their reactions, as well as how to get help if necessary. In general, your responsibility lies in finding a way to provide clear, honest, direct, authentic feedback to your warrior, as objectively as possible, all while taking care of yourself and being able to get your own needs met. People need feedback to grow, mature, and develop; healthy relationships depend on this. The challenge is how to provide this in such a way that it's appreciated and not rejected as nagging, meddling, or interfering. It's also important to not become codependent by enabling your warrior in some way to continue detrimental behaviors.

Suggestions for Strengthening the Relationship
Start sentences with "I" rather than "you."
For example, "I'm worried about how your anger is affecting our kids" is better than "You're hurting our kids with your anger." "I'm scared of your anger" is better than "You're scaring me." "I'm sad that we're arguing so much" is better than "You always argue with me." "I'm angry at what you said" is better than "You make me angry." "I feel hurt that you seem so distant" is better than "You're so distant from me." "I'm concerned about how much you're avoiding going out or being with people" is better than "You're avoiding everything and everybody."

The first statements starting with "I" express how you feel directly in relation to your warrior's behavior. Each of the second statements starting with "you" implies that there's something wrong with your warrior. Basically, stick with how *you* feel, rather than turning it into an attack on your warrior. The same advice is useful for your warrior as well. Ask them to start sentences with "I." Both of you may want to read the learning skills on anger in chapter 7 (skill 4) for more information on this approach.

Communicate with your warrior.

If there's something that you want or need from your warrior, directly ask for it. Don't be afraid to ask for what you need. "Honey, I need a hug." "Honey, I need you to get off your ass and take the garbage out now." "Is it possible for you to pick up the kids tomorrow, so I can have a break?" "Can you stop by the store on your way home?" "It's important to me that you control your anger." "Honey, I want to make love tonight." "I want you to go shopping with me." This is normal behavior for couples, and just because your warrior has returned from a war zone where they lived with ever-present danger doesn't mean that they're a VIP, exempt from the normal things that all couples do. Life goes on.

If there are important things that you want to communicate, let your warrior know that you'd like to talk, give them a heads-up on what the topic is (so their imagination doesn't run amok), and then work out a time to sit down to do this. Don't launch into your concern without allowing them at least a little time for preparation. They don't always do well with sudden changes or what they might perceive as an attack. Speak directly from your feelings and perceptions. Tell them how you are affected personally and what concerns you want to see addressed. One piece of advice for warriors is to listen to your spouse or partner. Try to figure out what they're saying and be responsive to it. Accept their feedback, suggestions, and assistance. Even if you don't agree with it or get annoyed by it, there's always something deeper to pay attention to. Be grateful that you have each other in your lives.

It's really true that men and women have completely different ways of communicating. Women tend to *express* how they feel in direct, indirect, and apparently illogical ways. This drives men crazy. Men think that expressing themselves means talking things out in a logical, rational manner. This drives women crazy. Each feels that the other is wrong and isn't listening or appreciating them. There isn't really any way to fix this, other than to recognize it and find a way to laugh about it (although you might want to be careful when you laugh).

Men, when you can't make sense of what your woman is saying, the general advice is to listen attentively, don't make any excuses or argue with her (certainly don't point out how you think she's being illogical), tell her that you love her, and take her in your arms at the earliest opportunity that she allows (and not a moment before). Women, when your man is going off into rational, logical, fix-it la-la land (we men should hear our-selves sometimes), the general advice is to listen attentively, don't make any excuses or argue, tell him that you love him, and find a way to take him in your arms at the earliest opportunity, which generally will be quite a bit longer because he has to finish his lengthy logical diatribe. (You also have the added skill of being able to turn on your seductive magic to facilitate his brain turning to mush.) If you get really frustrated or bored listening to your man "express" himself, call up a friend and get out of the house for a while.

It's not your job to change your warrior.

They need to do this for themselves. (Warriors, the same thing applies to you; you can't change your spouse or partner.) You can love them, make them laugh, tease or cajole them, praise them, get angry with them, get frustrated with them, expect them to act differently, demand they act dif-ferently, request that they go see a counselor, etc. But in the end, they'll do what they do, and what they do is not up to you and not about you. This gets into the next point on codependency.

Don't become codependent by enabling your warrior to continue detrimental behaviors.

Codependency is defined as acting in a way that inadvertently facilitates (enables) the negative behaviors that your warrior is exhibiting. For exam-ple, if you walk on eggshells all the time around your warrior, they will come to expect a very quiet and organized household and won't ever learn how to live with noise, unpredictability, or chaos. Oddly, warriors are often much more capable of dealing with extreme chaos on the battlefield than with the more mundane chaos at home. Nevertheless, that doesn't mean that it has to stay that way if it doesn't work for you. If you always go to the store because your warrior gets bad reactions when they go, then you may be enabling them to continue this pattern of behavior. If you make excuses for their rage or their avoidance, then this implicitly permits them to continue to behave this way. If you always place your warrior's needs or wants above yours, then they'll come to expect this on an ongoing basis, and you'll eventually end up feeling resentful, dissatisfied, or unfulfilled. The bottom line is not to compromise the way you want to live because of how your warrior behaves.

All relationships involve some level of mutual dependency. The trick is not to let the dependency become an ingrained, ongoing pattern of behavior that compromises who you are. To do this, you want to ensure that you maintain your own independence and self-confidence, not make excuses for your warrior's behaviors, and be clear about your own values, beliefs, and needs. Stay true to yourself and who you are at all times. You too have a warrior spirit inside you.

Values have to do with our sense of self-identity—who we are, what's true for us as individuals—and they are almost always reflected in the little things we do. If you like a very quiet household and like doing all of the grocery shopping, then there's no issue; but if you want to blast your music sometimes or you want your warrior to do some of the shopping, then don't compromise your values by always agreeing to their preferences. If you need a break from your work or your children and you want your warrior to step in and assist you, or you want your warrior to come with you to some activity or function, then say so clearly, directly, and without anger (expressing that this is important for you); don't compromise by making an excuse (to yourself or others) about why your warrior is somehow unable to participate in the activity. As long as you feel that you're doing what's right for you, then you're okay, but once you start compromising your own sense of self, or sense of what feels right to you, then there's a problem.

Getting help for domestic violence.

If your warrior is raging to the point of making you afraid or becoming abusive to you or your children, get help immediately. Contact the National Domestic Violence Hotline at 1-800-799-SAFE (7233) or 1-800-787-3224 (TTY). If your warrior is in the military, contact the social work or family advocacy services on post. Your warrior may be concerned that this will affect their career, but these services are necessary and there to help and support relationships and families.

Improve intimacy and sexual functioning.

If there are difficulties with intimacy or sexual functioning involving either or both of you, the first thing to know is that it's probably not due to anything physically wrong. Sexual problems are very common, reported in up to half of couples. Sexual functioning—including the ability to get aroused, maintain an erection, and reach orgasm—is highly affected by stress, including work stress, relationship stress, the stress of caring for children, emotional detachment or other reactions from war-zone experiences, worries about things that need to be done, anxiety, depression, sleep disturbance, alcohol intake, recreational drug use, medications, and numerous other factors. A problem with sexual functioning more than likely reflects whatever else is going on in your life.

Things that help most include making time to enjoy each other's company, learning to express gratitude for each other, exploring intimacy in various ways without specific sexual goals, and reducing anxiety by understanding that sexual intimacy has a "mind of its own" and isn't something that necessarily responds whenever you want it to or think it should. Honesty is essential; if you are hiding things from each other, this can have a big effect on intimacy. Take time to talk about what's going on in your lives. Go on dates with each other. If you have kids, it's particularly important to schedule time for just the two of you.

Explore physical intimacy through touching, holding hands, hugging, cuddling, and making out, initially without the goal of intercourse or orgasm. Talk with each other about what turns you on. Self-stimulation during sexual activity with your partner is also natural. When together, you and/or your partner may feel like touching yourself or masturbating to get aroused or reach orgasm; it's natural. The more relaxed and comfortable you become with each other, and the more open you are about what turns you on, the more comfortable things will be in the expression of intimacy. If these types of things don't help, then see your doctor to get an evaluation and perhaps a prescription for one of the medicines that can help.

Finally, for both of you, directly express gratitude and appreciation for each other. Compliment and praise each other. Even if your partner annoys or irritates you at times (and any healthy relationship will have some of this), honor and give thanks for their presence in your life.

CONSIDERATIONS FOR COPING WITH INFIDELITY

Infidelity occurs all too often in committed relationships because of separation, loneliness, emotional detachment, desire for connection, fear, escape, and for other reasons. Infidelity is experienced as a devastating loss, and a blow to trust, innocence, and self-worth that can affect relationships forever. When there is a strained relationship associated with infidelity, it's important to believe in yourself, understand that you're doing the best you can, not turn your feelings against yourself through judgments or complex emotions of loss, not try to figure everything out, and learn from your experience.

If you were the one who cheated, then it's likely that you lack empathy, concern, and respect for your partner. If you want your relationship to continue, accept that you'll have to make substantial, ongoing, lasting reparations. Your partner will likely never trust you in the same way again, and you better do whatever it takes to honestly and sincerely apologize, without any "buts" or even a hint of excuse or justification. You're accountable for the consequences that ensue, including what you feel and your partner's responses. Be completely honest in your answers to questions. Don't tell partial truths or hide what really happened, which is an attempt to control an uncontrollable situation. Also, don't make any excuses or rationalize why you did what you did. You did it because you wanted to. You didn't think or care about the consequences. It didn't matter how much it could hurt your partner. Try to imagine and appreciate what your partner is going through. There's rarely any justification for a purely selfish act that ends up hurting someone else. Not believing or feeling this indicates a lack of empathy and compassion. Pay attention and don't detach from the jumble of thoughts and emotions going on inside (shame, guilt, avoidance, denial, fear, trying to figure out what to say or do, etc.). Remember what you've put your partner and yourself through so you'll be aware (and maybe get sick to your stomach) the next time you even get a flicker of a thought about doing something like that again.

If your partner cheated on you, this is *not* about you. It could have been because they were lonely, scared, depressed, overwhelmed, wanting escape, under the influence of alcohol or drugs, under the influence of pheromones (natural chemicals in the body that act like perfumes to attract people to each other), drawn by the sirens' song, taking their aggression out on you (or themselves), or a narcissistic asshole. Who knows? Does the reason for their behavior make any difference?

Your partner may try to convince you that it was a stupid and insensitive act that "meant nothing" because they were overwhelmed by whatever; or give you any of a thousand other rationalizations, denials, excuses, or reasons why they did what they did, and why they'll never, ever do it again. None of these statements mean crap, no matter how much your partner believes them or how much you want to believe them. Why? Because, it's impossible to absolutely know why humans do what they do. Your partner broke their commitment to you, and it's hurtful, unloving, disrespectful, unkind, cruel, risky, disgusting, etc. (it was certainly more than "stupid" and "insensitive"); but why it happened isn't clear-cut. They were only doing what they were capable of at that time—no better and no worse. One thing is for sure—it's not about you.

Infidelity, or the potential for infidelity (thinking about it, wondering about it, looking into it, fantasizing about it, etc.), happens in many, if not most, committed relationships at one time or another. Human behavior is not governed very well by societal and religious sanctions designed to hold families and communities together (generally for the well-being of society, the stability of families, and the interests of propriety and reasonableness). Love, commitment, marriage, and human relations are enormously complex processes that aren't fully understood even after thousands of years of experiential "research."

How you handle the situation, what actions you wish to take, whether you still want to be with your partner, and whether or not you can (or want to) continue to love your partner despite what happened, are all things you can deal with when you're ready. And when you're ready, completely acknowledge how you feel—particularly those primary emotions of loss (e.g., hurt, anger, sadness, grief, helplessness), and all of the other feelings and values that are important in your experience of this relationship (e.g., love, commitment, loyalty, faith, ambivalence, pleasure, displeasure, disappointment, caring, empathy, passion, comfort, safety, etc.). Then as you face this challenge, base your response(s) on what feels right to you and reflects who you are now. Don't base your response(s) on self-blame, despondency, depression, hopelessness, fear of being alone, rage, feelings of worthlessness (e.g., "I'll never find anyone better" or "I'm not attractive anymore"), judgmental thought processes, "shoulds," "what-ifs," or what your friends, society, your pastor, your rabbi, or your mother thinks you should do.

Many people assume there's always a right or a wrong option in a situation like this (e.g., "You must leave immediately" or "You must remain for the sake of your kids"). However, there's no absolute right or wrong option, other than the one that feels right for you. It may feel right to end the relationship, or it may feel right to try to work things out and stay in it. Furthermore, there's no requirement that once you make a "choice" that you have to stick with it. You can change your mind depending on what's true for you then (the "then" of the time you change your mind).

The bottom line in a situation like this is to recognize that you have value; that your partner's behavior is about them and not you; that it does hurt; that it happens very often (far too often in relationships); that there's no right or wrong answer; and that you're free to respond in a manner most consistent with your values, beliefs, feelings, and being. Follow your truth. Whether or not your relationship survives, you'll recover. Relationships are complex, frustrating, wonderful, precious, meaningful, and crazy. They can't be and don't need to be figured out.

It's possible for relationships to continue to grow even after the blows of infidelity. When trust is broken, you can have faith in the ability to recover. Recovery is not necessarily smooth; it can take a convoluted course over a long period of time. It's possible to reconcile early on and feel a greater sense of closeness accompanied by forgiveness and compassion, then falter later as a new sense of vulnerability shows up in the relationship. This sense of vulnerability can evoke memories of the hurt, lead to doubt about reconciling in the first place, or a tendency to distance yourself from your spouse or partner. It's important to remember that the vulnerability was always there, part and parcel of any intimate relationship, but has been exposed through the unfaithfulness. Feeling exposed in this way is uncomfortable, and it's normal to want to avoid it. Stay connected to your vulnerability; it's precious and powerful. It's a testament to how much you feel, care, and love.

HELPING YOUR CHILDREN COPE WITH THE STRESSES OF DEPLOYMENT AND TRANSITION

Children and adolescents are impacted in numerous ways by deployment and the transition home. They experience many of the same feelings and fears as adults, but are less able to express them verbally. Children and adolescents need a sense of security, a consistent routine without too many disruptions, and a loving parent or guardian who is consistently present in their lives. When they experience stress, they often act out, behave aggressively, develop academic problems, skip school, or have other behavioral problems. Things that point to a potential mental health problem include irritability; aggression; getting in fights; withdrawing from friends; acting unhappy, sad, or depressed; academic problems; or, if you get calls from teachers expressing concern.

The most important things you can provide your children are your love, time, attention, reassurance, and encouragement, as well as a consistent, secure, stable, and safe environment for them to grow and develop. Give them honest and direct answers to their questions suitable to their age, be available to them, make time to do things they enjoy, and set clear boundaries and rules that you're comfortable with and will be able to enforce. Children and adolescents will always see how far they can push the limits or how much they can get away with before you say "no" or need to discipline them. That's their "job." It's important that you make it clear what you expect, where the line is, and what will happen if they cross that line. When they do cross the line, it's important that you follow through on what you indicated would happen. This is how children learn what is right and appropriate.

Codependency and Your Children

The discussion on codependency concerns your children as well. If you make excuses for your warrior or facilitate negative behaviors in some way, your kids will also learn to do this. It's important for their growth and development that they experience your sense of self-confidence and ability to stand up for what you believe and what is true for you. Life is complicated and difficult, but if they see that you're clear about who you are and what you value, their self-confidence will grow. For example, if your warrior is frequently in a rage or avoiding things they should be doing, and you're walking on eggshells and afraid to confront or address the situation, then your kids will also start walking on eggshells and experience the same fears and uncertainties. If you address the situation directly and from your own sense of what's right for you, you'll help your children to understand the importance of having a sense of their own value. For example, if you're considering separation or divorce, but are filled with guilt, anxiety, and self-doubt, then your kids may also become anxious, fearful, and depressed. If, on the other hand, you're clear about what you're doing, and know what's true for you, it'll help to reassure your kids that they'll be taken care of and continue to have the love and support they need.

Children and Counseling

There are times when children may need professional help. It can be very difficult to find a mental health professional with training in counseling children because of their limited availability. The best place to start is to ask for a referral from your child's pediatrician. You'll probably have to be persistent and assertive to get the support you need through your health-care plan. Sometimes the only professionals who are available are ones who don't accept insurance, which puts you in a difficult position of having to decide if you will pay out of pocket. If there's a crisis situation, you can take your child to an emergency room or call one of the crisis numbers listed earlier.

To close this chapter, my wife, Charise Hoge, also an author *(A Portable Identity)*, has the following story to share from her experience:

> Soon after I got the news that my husband, Charlie, would be deployed to Iraq, I got a raging sore throat and felt like someone had whacked me on the back of my head. I also started to look at Charlie as if he were a ghost— a fleeting presence—especially if he was acting normal, talking and laughing. Looking back, I must have been terrified of what was about to happen, and it made no sense to me that life was going on as usual.
>
> Then Charlie decided to gather the family together for a going-away speech, which was akin to speaking from beyond the grave, as he thanked each of us for being in his life and told us he wanted us to know how much he loved us in case anything happened to him during deployment. Our teenage daughter and I fell into tears, and our youngest daughter just sat there, probably too young to process all the "what-ifs" in the conversation.
>
> Seeing how he seemed to have a handle on what was happening, I began to feel a divide in our experience of the same event. He was moving forward, preparing for his first-ever war experience, and I was staying behind, unsure how to cope with our separation. We had already been married for twenty-two years.
>
> So let me entertain you with some of my internal gyrations that surfaced as thoughts or feelings pre-deployment. I felt that I was being left behind, abandoned, and that nobody cared. I felt that the Army was stealing my husband away from me like some evil sorcerer who I was powerless to reach. I felt that the whole situation was unfair to me, my marriage, and my family.
>
> I didn't know anyone else who was in the same situation as myself. I was not living on a military post, and I had never imagined that my husband would be sent to do research in a war zone. I was dismayed when I received two identical packets in the mail (a week apart) with information on support for spouses during deployment. Didn't anyone know I'd already gotten the first one? Was the system of support that disorganized and impersonal?

I wondered how the war experience would change our relationship. Our lives had been intertwined for so long, going back to college days. He was usually the first person I would want to share anything with, and anytime we were apart for travels (conferences and such), I missed having him around to talk to. I also wondered if I'd go nuts without physical contact. How would I deal with missing him?

We didn't talk about any of this. It was like he was already gone; his focus was on doing whatever it took to ready himself for being in Iraq. He had all this equipment spread out in the sunroom—I dubbed it the "deployment room"—as he was going through lists of supplies to bring.

When the day came for him to leave, I hugged him and started to fall apart, and he didn't want any part of this; he said something like "Come on," and had such composure that I felt even more of an idiot for being so emotional. He left and I was alone, sitting on the stairs beside the living room, falling into a funk of sadness. I felt that a piece of me had walked out the door and that without this piece, I wasn't sure how to hold myself together.

So began a journey of finding my strength without him, and also my ability to build a community of support. I turned to my friends, to other parents at my younger daughter's school, and to e-mail contacts to ask for their positive thoughts, prayers, blessings, and wishes for Charlie's safety and for the well-being of our family. I specifically asked others to visualize his return home and did this myself.

I was already engaging in movement expression as a yoga teacher and dancer, and I utilized these practices to stay grounded and to have a nonverbal way to give some form to my feelings. It just so happened that the choreographer of my dance company decided to create a dance called "Always Near," and this became my place to put my desire to connect with Charlie on an emotional level.

The way we actually did connect during his deployment was very matter-of-fact—just brief check-in calls, where he would update me on his whereabouts, or just to say he was okay. The life of our relationship was kind of on hold, and I learned to accept that this was just the way it was.

Of course, when Charlie did return safely, I was ready to resume where we left off—but he wasn't. Our whole family was excited to have him home, and he could see this, but it seemed more like he wanted to go curl up in a ball somewhere. There was something out of reach about him, and I wasn't sure how to be with this. I tended to give him space, and so I felt I was still missing him—still missing him while he was right here.

I found I had to wait; I had to gather great patience, had to allow him to "unroll" himself bit by bit, as he was tightly coiled. He especially seemed far away while he was sleeping next to me. It was like he was in a cocoon, or wanted to be in a cocoon, gathered into himself, and I missed finding his arm draped around me. The space between us turned into a gap. I had to hear it from a wise friend of mine to change my approach to this gap. "Move in," she said. "Bring yourself closer."

It was up to me to bridge the gap, which Charlie probably wasn't even aware of. It was as simple as bringing my posture more forward, toward him, during a conversation. I found that this wasn't intrusive; it was supportive to both of us. It was a way of saying, "I'm here, no matter where you are or where you've been," a way of crossing the divide to the present moment, a place to meet. I have tremendous gratitude for this meeting place, which offers itself to us on any given day.

CHAPTER 11

V = THE "V"s!—VISION, VOICE, VILLAGE, JOIE DE VIVRE, VICTORY

This chapter concludes the book by providing thoughts and suggestions for discovering meaning and purpose in your journey. Life is in many ways senseless, meaningless, and random; and in other ways, magnificent, beautiful, awe-inspiring, and filled with mystery and wonder. Warriors have experienced the depths of what life has to offer, and have much to give to the world. You and your loved ones deserve to be happy and enjoy life.

The last letter of LANDNAV, "V," evokes five different qualities to consider for yourself: vision, voice, village/community, *joie de vivre* (joy of living), and victory. Each of these words is a gift that you can use as a springboard for thinking about what's most important in your life now, and where you would like to see yourself in the future. They provide encouragement to free-associate, reflect, let go, feel free, and think beyond the limits of what you do on an everyday basis.

VISION

Having vision means being present in the moment to see what is before you. It means accepting who you are now and what goals you would like to consider for yourself. It means having faith in yourself and following your truth, wherever that leads you.

How do you know what your truth is? Your truth is what you are motivated and inclined toward, what excites or interests you, what gives you a sense of contribution or accomplishment, what connects you with others, what makes you happy, what you do in the world, what you value, and what you believe to be true.

Vision is also the ability to connect all of your senses so that you "see" what is happening around you more clearly. It's the strength of intuition. It's knowing something that you don't remember ever learning. It's the ability to feel what's happening in others, which is empathy and compassion. It's the ability to offer just what someone needs. It's the ability to know your limits. It's the knowledge of what might happen, and the ability to let go and accept not being able to control what will happen.

VOICE

Voice is how you express yourself in the world, how you communicate, what you wish to share with others, and how you share yourself with others. Your voice is what comes out of you unexpectedly and spontaneously, what rises up from within when you allow it. Voice is an expression of your creativity, of who you are.

Your voice is when you speak your truth. Your voice is your message for the world, your soft touch on humanity, the gift of memories you leave in others, your laughter, your radiance, your warmth, your caring, the healing words you give your children, and your breath on the face of your lover.

VILLAGE/COMMUNITY

There is no greater purpose than the love we share with others. Our capacity to give and receive love and to show compassion and caring for others is what sustains us and lasts beyond our individual lives. Meaning lies in the connections we make in the world.

Biologically we are animals that depend on our family and community for survival. We have progressed because of our ability to live together and work collectively toward common goals, with each member serving a unique role and function in the larger effort.

Our ability to grow, evolve, develop, and transcend depends on the feedback we receive in a myriad of ways from everyone around us. We all have hopes, dreams, and fears that we share. We are all as crazy and as sane as everyone else. We all live and die. We all mourn and grieve. We all laugh. We all hurt. We're all different. We're all the same. We are individuals connected and inseparable from each other. No matter how strongly we adhere to one faith, every great religion carries the same message of love, compassion, forgiveness, transcendence, and hope.

The meaning of life is the time that we share with the ones we love, the stillness of gratitude for their presence in our lives, and the gifts we bring to make the world a better place and do what is right.

JOIE DE VIVRE (JOY)

Happiness and joy are impermanent and ever-present at the same time. Amid everything we do and every pain we suffer, we all have the unalienable right, stated even in our Constitution, to the pursuit of happiness. We all carry the hope of happiness inside us, no matter how much suffering we may encounter in our lives, and only have to look beneath the surface to discover it in this moment. We experience it in moments, like rays of sunshine appearing through the clouds. The spirit of happiness is spontaneous, free, playful, creative, curious, present, warm, and filled with love and gratitude. Playing with your puppy or kitten, watching your infant breathe, lying in the sun, dancing, making love, hanging out, taking in what's around you, paddling in a canoe, or finding the humor and absurdity in life. Happiness is the song we dance to for our entire lives.

VICTORY

Sometimes victory is achieved in loss. Sometimes we must invest in losing in order to gain. Sometimes we must move right to go left or down to go up. Sometimes we must yield to overcome. Softness overcomes hardness, like water gradually etching away stone, or the tears of a child bringing us back to our purpose. As long as we're alive, we're victorious. As long as we give to others and strive to create a better world, we're whole. This is grace.

First Sergeant Mike Schindler:

There is not much in life that equals the camaraderie, courage, sacrifice, love, and devotion shared between brothers and sisters in arms. Your combat buddies "go all the way everyday" for you as you do for them, and the most difficult part of the transition home is the sense of disconnect and loss because you are not with them.

The good news is that you can find a way to fill the void through veterans groups and clubs, team sports, community volunteering, or any activity that gets you engaged with people and life. The world is loaded with wonderful people and lots of challenges that allow you to use your combat talents in a positive manner.

In 2006 I was introduced to the sport of Hawaiian outrigger canoeing, involving one- to six-man crews. In paddling I have found a sense of camaraderie, community involvement, and competitive excitement that I missed when I was no longer with my combat brothers. Paddling is a way of life for me and all involved.

The best aspect of six-man Hawaiian outrigger canoeing for fun or racing is the brotherhood of paddling. Some of the main paddling rules are: shut up and paddle, paddles in together—out together, maximum power with every stroke.

In essence, we must depend on each other to get an 1,100- to 1,500-pound canoe and paddlers up and running smooth. This task must be done with a 100 percent positive attitude. All negative energy must be kept out of the canoe at all times. The crew must paddle hard, trust each other, and depend on each other for survival. Sometimes we paddle in ten- to twenty-foot swells over long distances in the deep blue Hawaiian ocean. Talk about a tiger on the loose, get-down, kick-ass experience! This is it for me, brothers and sisters.

My suggestion is to find a positive physical activity with people who all have a common goal. You will find this type of activity to be a great experience—not to mention that it will keep you in high physical conditioning.

Outrigger canoeing, which involves open-ocean, long-distance racing or voyaging, allows me to use my quick reflexes, physical and mental train-

ing, and stamina. The sound of crashing waves, the feel of ocean spray, enduring the physical demands over long distances, plus the dependency on your fellow crewmates in challenging situations, is truly outstanding.

Outrigger canoe paddling saved me from doom and gloom. Paddling is part of my blueprint to live life. Sometimes you need to be the lone paddler whose quiet power and purpose leads the way for others. Most times life takes a crew, working as one, to reach out as far as you can, digging in and pushing for glory.

Laughter is another design feature in my blueprint. Live life with a smile; laugh at yourself. Give yourself a break and turn your brain off sometimes. Humor and calmness are a must-have tool.

Learn all there is to know about your reflexes and reactions and why you act and feel the way you do after combat. Use your combat skills, loyalty, honor, quickness, physical strength, mental awareness, etc., to accentuate the positive. Just imagine the good energy we combat veterans can give to each other, our families, communities, and ourselves. Combat skills are life. Life is good. Live, love, and laugh.

REFERENCES

The following is a partial list of the books, medical journal articles, and reports considered in preparing this book.

MENTAL HEALTH IMPACT OF DEPLOYMENT, COMBAT, AND MILITARY SERVICE (INCLUDING PTSD, BARRIERS TO CARE, STIGMA)

Adler, A. B., P. B. Bliese, D. McGurk, C. W. Hoge, and C. A. Castro. "Battlemind debriefing and battlemind training as early interventions with soldiers returning from combat: randomized by platoon." *Journal of Consulting and Clinical Psychology* 2009; 77: 928–40. 2009.

Brandi, Sgt. PTSD. *The warrior's guide to insanity: traumatic stress and life.* Self-published. www.warriorsguidetoinsanity.com.

Britt, T. W., T. M. Greene-Shortridge, S. Brink, Q. B. Nguyen, J. Rath, A. J. Cox, C. W. Hoge, and C. A. Castro. "Perceived stigma and barriers to care for psychological treatment: implications for reactions to stressors in different contexts." *Journal of Social and Clinical Psychology* 2008; 27: 317–35.

Dohrenwend, B. P., J. B. Turner, N. A. Turse, B. G. Adams, K. C. Koenen, and R. Marshall. "The psychological risks of Vietnam for U.S. veterans: A revisit with new data and methods." *Science* 2006; 313: 979–82.

Friedman, M. J. "Post-traumatic stress disorder among military returnees from Afghanistan and Iraq." *The American Journal of Psychiatry* 2006; 163: 586–93.

Grieger, T. A., S. J. Cozza, R. J. Ursano, C. Hoge, P. E. Martinez, C. C. Engel, and H. J. Wain. "Post-traumatic stress disorder and depression in battle-injured soldiers." *The American Journal of Psychiatry* 2006; 163: 1777–83.

Hoge, C. W. "Deployment to the Iraq war and neuropsychological sequelae [Letter]." *JAMA* 2006; 296: 519–29.

Hoge, C. W., J. L. Auchterlonie, and C. S. Milliken. "Mental health problems, use of mental health services, and attrition from military service after returning from deployment to Iraq or Afghanistan." *The Journal of the American Medical Association (JAMA)* 2006; 295: 1023–32.

Hoge, C. W., and C. A. Castro. "Post-traumatic stress disorder in UK and U.S. forces deployed to Iraq [Letter]." *Lancet* 2006; 368: 837.

Hoge, C. W., C. A. Castro, S. C. Messer, D. McGurk, D. I. Cotting, and R. L. Koffman. "Combat duty in Iraq and Afghanistan, mental health problems, and barriers to care." *New England Journal of Medicine* 2004; 351: 13–22.

Hoge, C. W., J. C. Clark, and C. A. Castro. "Commentary: Women in combat and the risk of post-traumatic stress disorder and depression." *International Journal of Epidemiology* 2007; 36: 327–29.

Hoge, C. W., H. E. Toboni, S. C. Messer, N. Bell, P. Amoroso, and D. Orman. "The occupational burden of mental disorders in the U.S. military: Psychiatric hospitalizations, involuntary separations, and disability." *The American Journal of Psychiatry* 2005; 162: 585–91.

Iversen, A. C., N. T. Fear, A. Ehlers, J. Hacker Hughes, L. Hull, M. Earnshaw, N. Greenberg, R. Rona, S. Wessely, and M. Hotopf. "Risk factors for post-traumatic stress disorder among UK Armed Forces personnel." *Psychol Med.* 2008; 38:-511–22.

Jacobson, I. G., M. A. K. Ryan, T. I. Hooper, T. C. Smith, P. J. Amoroso, E. J. Boyko, G. D. Gackstetter, T. S. Wells, and N. S. Bell. "Alcohol use and alcohol related problems before and after military combat deployment." *JAMA* 2008; 300: 663–75.

Kang, H. K., B. H. Natelson, C. M. Mahan, K. Y. Lee, and F. M. Murphy. "Post-traumatic stress disorder and chronic fatigue syndrome–like illness among Gulf War veterans: A population-based survey of 30,000 veterans." *American Journal of Epidemiology* 2003; 157: 141–48.

Killgore, W. D. S., D. I. Cotting, J. L. Thomas, A. L. Cox, D. McGurk, A. H. Vo, C. A. Castro, and C. W. Hoge. "Post-combat invincibility: Violent combat experiences are associated with increased risk-taking propensity following deployment." *Journal of Psychiatric Research* 2008; 42: 1112–21.

Killgore, W. D. S., M. C. Stetz, C. A. Castro, and C. W. Hoge. "The effects of combat experience on the expression of somatic and affective symptoms in deploying soldiers." *Journal of Psychosomatic Research* 2006; 60: 379–85.

Milliken, C. S., J. L. Auchterlonie, and C. W. Hoge. "Longitudinal assessment of mental health problems among Active and Reserve Component soldiers returning from the Iraq war." *JAMA* 2007; 298: 2141–48.

Prigerson, H. G., J. G. Johnson, and R. A. Rosenheck. "Combat trauma: Trauma with highest risk of delayed onset and unresolved post-traumatic stress disorder symptoms, unemployment, and abuse among men." *The Journal of Nervous and Mental Disease* 2001; 189: 99–108.

Seal, K. H., D. Bertenthal, C. R. Miner, S. Sen, and C. Marmar. "Bringing the war back home: Mental health disorders among 103,788 U.S. veterans returning from Iraq and Afghanistan seen at Department of Veterans Affairs facilities." *Archives of Internal Medicine* 2007; 167: 476–82.

Self, Nate. *Two Wars: One Hero's Fight on Two Fronts—Abroad and Within.* Carol Stream, IL: Tyndale House, 2009.

Shay, Jonathan. *Achilles in Vietnam: Combat Trauma and the Undoing of Character.* New York: Scribner, 1994.

Smith, T. C., M. A. K. Ryan, D. L. Wingard, D. J. Slymen, J. F. Sallis, D. Kritz-Silverstein, and Millenium Cohort Study Team. "New onset and persistent symptoms of post-traumatic stress disorder self reported after deployment and combat exposures: Prospective population-based U.S. military cohort study." *BMJ* 2008; 336: 366–71.

Tanielian, T. and L. H. Jaycox, eds. *Invisible Wounds of War: Psychological and Cognitive Injuries, Their Consequences, and Services to Assist Recovery.* Santa Monica, CA: RAND Corp., 2008.

Thomas, J. L., J. E. Wilk, L. A. Riviere, D. McGurk, C. A. Castro, and C. W. Hoge. "The prevalance of mental health problems and functional impairment among active component and National Guard soldiers 3 and 12 months following combat in Iraq." Archives General Psychiatry, 2010.

Vasterling, J. L., S. P. Proctor, P. Amoroso, R. Kane, T. Heeren, and R. F. White. "Neuropsychological outcomes of Army personnel following deployment to the Iraq war." *JAMA* 2006; 296: 519–29.

Warner, C. H., J. E. Brietbach, G. N. Appenzeller, V. Yates, T. Grieger, and W. G. Webster. "Division mental health in the new brigade combat team structure: Part II. Redeployment and postdeployment." *Military Medicine* 2007; 172: 912–17.

Workman, Jeremiah. *Shadow of the Sword: A Marine's Journey of War, Heroism, and Redemption.* New York: Presidio, 2009.

Wright, K. M., O. A. Cabrera, A. B. Adler, P. D. Bliese, C. W. Hoge, and C. A. Castro. "Stigma and barriers to care in soldiers postcombat." *Psychological Services* 2009; 6: 108–16.

IMPACT OF DEPLOYMENTS ON FAMILIES

Eaton, K. M., C. W. Hoge, S. C. Messer, A. A. Whitt, O. A. Cabrera, D. McGurk, A. Cox, and C. A. Castro. "Prevalence of mental health problems, treatment need, and barriers to care among primary care seeking spouses of military service members involved in Iraq and Afghanistan deployments." *Military Medicine* 2008; 178(11): 1051–56.

Elizabeth, Quynn. *Accepting the Ashes: A Daughter's Look at Post-Traumatic Stress Disorder,* 2004. Self-published. www.acceptingtheashes.net.

Gibbs, D. A., S. L. Martin, L. L. Kupper, and R. E. Johnson. "Child maltreatment in enlisted soldiers' families during combat-related deployments." *JAMA* 2007; 298: 528–35.

Jakupcak, M., D. Conybeare, L. Phelps, S. Hunt, H. A. Holmes, B. Felker, M. Klevens, and M. E. McFall. "Anger, hostility, and aggression among Iraq and Afghanistan War veterans reporting PTSD and subthreshold PTSD." *Journal of Traumatic Stress* 2007; 20: 945–54.

Sayers, S. L., V. A. Farrow, J. Ross, and D. W. Oslin. "Family problems among recently returned military veterans referred for a mental health evaluation." *Journal of Clinical Psychiatry* 2009; 70: 163–70.

KEY DOD REPORTS

Bray, R. M., L. L. Hourani, and K. L. R. Olmstead, et al. 2005 Department of Defense Survey of Health-Related Behaviors Among Active Duty Military Personnel, RTI International, 2006. (This survey is conducted every three years.)

Department of the Army Field Manual FM 6-22.5. Combat and operational stress control manual for leaders and soldiers, March 18, 2009. Recently revised field manual based in part on extensive research conducted during the wars in Iraq and Afghanistan.

Department of Defense Task Force on Mental Health: An achievable vision: Report of the Department of Defense Task Force on Mental Health. Defense Health Board, Falls Church, VA, 2007.

Deployment Health Clinical Center Web site, www.pdhealth.mil. This is one of the best sources of information for DoD reports, clinical practice guidelines, education material, and policies related to PTSD, mTBI, and postwar health concerns.

Mental Health Advisory Team (MHAT) Reports. A series of reports involving soldiers and marines deployed to Iraq and Afghanistan since the beginning of the wars. Methods involved surveys, focus groups, and assessments of combat stress care conducted by researchers from

Walter Reed Army Institute of Research as part of Land Combat Study. Available at www.armymedicine.army.mil (reports link).

CONCUSSION/MILD TBI

Belanger, H. G., T. Kretzmer, R. Yoash-Gantz, T. Pickett, and L. A. Tupler. "Cognitive sequelae of blast-related versus other mechanisms of brain trauma." *Journal of the International Neuropsychological Society* 2009; 15: 1–8.

Boake, C., S. R. McCauley, and H. S. Levin, et al. "Diagnostic criteria for post-concussional syndrome after mild to moderate traumatic brain injury." *The Journal of Neuropsychiatry and Clinical Neurosciences* 2005; 17: 350–56.2.

Boake, C., S. R. McCauley, and H. S. Levin, et al. "Limited agreement between criteria-based diagnoses of post-concussional syndrome." *The Journal of Neuropsychiatry and Clinical Neurosciences* 2004; 16: 493–99.

Borg, J., L. Holm, P. M. Peloso, J. D. Cassidy, L. J. Carroll, H. von Holst, C. Paniak, and D. Yates. "Non-surgical intervention and cost for mild traumatic brain injury: Results of the WHO Collaborating Centre Task Force on mild traumatic brain injury." *Journal of Rehabilitation Medicine* 2004; 43: 76–83.

Bryant, R. A. "Disentangling mild traumatic brain injury and stress reactions." *New England Journal of Medicine* 2008; 358: 525–27.

Carroll, L. J., J. D. Cassidy, P. M. Peloso, J. Borg, H. von Holst, L. Holm, C. Paniak, and M. Pepin. "Prognosis for mild traumatic brain injury: Results of the WHO Collaborating Centre Task Force for mild traumatic brain injury." *Journal of Rehabilitation Medicine* 2004; 43: 84–105.

Fear, N. T., E. Jones, M. Groom, N. Greenberg, L. Hull, T. J. Hodgetts, and S. Wessely. "Symptoms of post-concussional syndrome are non-specifically related to mild traumatic brain injury in UK Armed Forces personnel on return from deployment in Iraq: An analysis of self-reported data." *Psychological Medicine* 2008; 23: 1–9.

Ferguson, R. J., W. Mittenberg, D. F. Barone, and B. Schneider. "Post-concussion syndrome following sports-related head injury: Expectation as etiology." *Neuropsychology* 1999; 13: 582–89.

Hoge, C. W. "Screening for mild TBI in returning U.S. troops: Invalid results [Letter]." *Journal of Head Trauma Rehabilitation* 2009; 24: 299.

Hoge, C. W., H. M. Goldberg, and C. A. Castro. "Care of veterans with mild traumatic brain injury: Flawed perspectives." *New England Journal of Medicine* 2009; 360: 1588–91.

Hoge, C. W., D. McGurk, J. Thomas, A. Cox, C. C. Engel, and C. A. Castro. "Mild traumatic brain injury in U.S. soldiers returning from Iraq." *New England Journal of Medicine* 2008; 358: 453–63.

Iverson, G. L., M. Gaetz, R. T. Lange, and N. D. Zasler. "Mild TBI," in: Zasler, N. D., D. I . Katz, and R. D. Zafonte, eds. *Brain Injury Medicine: Principles and Practice.* New York: Demos Medical Publishing LLC, 2007, 333–71.

Iverson, G. L., N. D. Zasler, and R. T. Lange. "Post-concussive dissorder," in: Zasler, N. D., D. I. Katz, and R. D. Zafonte, eds. *Brain Injury Medicine: Principles and Practice.* New York: Demos Medical Publishing LLC, 2007, 373–403.

Kashluba, S., J. E. Casey, and C. Paniak. "Evaluating the utility of the ICD-10 diagnostic criteria for post-concussion syndrome following mild traumatic brain injury." *Journal of the International Neuropsychological Society* 2006; 12: 111–18.

Landre, N., C. J. Poppe, N. Davis, B. Schmaus, and S. E. Hobbs. "Cognitive functioning and post-concussive symptoms in trauma patients with and without mild TBI." *Archives of Clinical Neuropsychology* 2006; 21: 255–73.

Marx, B. P., K. Brailey, and S. Proctor, et al. "Association of time since deployment, combat intensity, and post-traumatic stress symptoms with neuropsychological outcomes following Iraq War deployment." *Archives of General Psychiatry* 2009; 66: 996–1004.

McCrea, M. A. *Mild Traumatic Brain Injury and Post-Concussion Syndrome.* New York: Oxford University Press, 2008.

Meares, S., E. A. Shores, and A. J. Taylor, et al. "Mild traumatic brain injury does not predict acute post-concussion syndrome." *Journal of Neurology, Neurosurgery & Psychiatry* 2008; 79: 300–306.

Mickeviciene, D., H. Schrader, D. Obelieniene, D. Surkiene, R. Kunickas, L. J. Stovner, and T. Sand. "A controlled prospective inception cohort study on the post-concussion syndrome outside the medicolegal context." *European Journal of Neurology* 2004; 11: 411–19.

Mittenberg, W., G. Tremont, R. E. Zielinski, S. Fichera, and K. R. Rayls. "Cognitive-behavioral prevention of post-concussion syndrome." *Archives of Clinical Neuropsychology* 1996; 11: 139–45.

Ponsford, J., C. Willmott, A. Rothwell, P. Cameron, A. M. Kelly, R. Nelms, and C. Curran. "Impact of early intervention on outcome following mild head injury in adults." *Journal of Neurology, Neurosurgery & Psychiatry* 2002; 73: 330–32.

Schneiderman, A. I., E. R. Braver, and H. K. Kang. "Understanding the sequelae of injury mechanisms and mild traumatic brain injury incurred during the conflicts in Iraq and Afghanistan: Persistent post-concussive symptoms and post-traumatic stress disorder." *American Journal of Epidemiology* 2008; 167: 1446–52.

Suhr, J. A., and J. Gunstad. " 'Diagnosis threat': The effect of negative expectations on cognitive performance in head injury." *Journal of Clinical and Experimental Neuropsychology* 2002; 24: 448–57.

Suhr, J. A., and J. Gunstad. "Further exploration of the effect of 'diagnosis threat' on cognitive performance in individuals with mild head injury." *Journal of the International Neuropsychological Society* 2005; 11: 23–29.

Wang, Y., R. C. K. Chan, and Y. Deng. "Examination of post-concussion-like symptoms in healthy university students: Relationships to subjective and objective neuropsychological function performance." *Archives of Clinical Neuropsychology* 2006; 21: 339–47.

Whittaker, R., S. Kemp, and A. House. "Illness perceptions and outcome in mild head injury: A longitudinal study." *Journal of Neurology, Neurosurgery & Psychiatry* 2007; 78: 644–46.

Wilk, J. E., J. L. Thomas, D. M. McGurk, L. A. Riviere, C. A. Castro, and C. W. Hoge. "Mild traumatic brain injury (concussion) during combat: Lack of association of blast mechanism with persistent post-concussive symptoms." *Journal of Head Trauma Rehabilitation* 2010.

POSTWAR PHYSICAL, COGNITIVE, AND BEHAVIORAL SYNDROMES—GENERAL

Donta, S. T., D. J. Clauw, and C. C. Engel, Jr., et al. "Cognitive behavioral therapy and aerobic exercise for Gulf War veterans' illnesses: A randomized controlled trial." *JAMA* 2003; 289: 1396–1404.

Engel, C. C., and W. J. Katon. "Population and need-based prevention of unexplained symptoms in the community," in: Institute of Medicine, Strategies to Protect the Health of Deployed U.S. Forces: Medical Surveillance, Record Keeping, and Risk Reduction. Washington, DC: National Academy Press, 1999, pp. 173–212.

Hunt, S. C., R. D. Richardson, and C. C. Engel, Jr. "Clinical management of Gulf War veterans with medically unexplained physical symptoms." *Military Medicine* 2002; 167: 414–20.

Hyams, K. C., F. S. Wignall, and R. Roswell. "War syndromes and their evaluation: From the U.S. Civil War to the Persian Gulf War." *Annals of Internal Medicine* 1996; 125: 389–405.

Jones, E., N. T. Fear, and S. Wessely. "Shell shock and mild traumatic brain injury: A historical review." *American Journal of Psychiatry* 2007; 164: 1641–45.

Jones, E., R. Hodgins-Vermaas, and H. McCartney, et al. "Post-combat syndromes from the Boer War to the Gulf War: A cluster analysis of their nature and attribution." *BMJ* 2002; 324: 1–5.

Office of Quality and Performance and the Veterans Affairs and
   Department of Defense Development Work Group, Veterans
   Health Administration, Department of Veterans Affairs. *Clinical
   practice guideline for post-deployment health evaluation and management.*
   Washington, DC, February 2001, OQP publication 10Q-CPG/PDH-01.

PTSD AND PHYSICAL HEALTH (NEUROBIOLOGY, NEUROPHYSIOLOGY, COEXISTENCE WITH PHYSICAL HEALTH PROBLEMS, AND TREATMENT)

Boscarino, J. A. "Post-traumatic stress disorder and mortality among U.S.
   Army veterans 30 years after military service." *Annals of Epidemiology*
   2006; 16: 248–56.

Boscarino, J. A. "Post-traumatic stress disorder and physical illness:
   Results from clinical and epidemiological studies." *Annals of the New
   York Academy of Sciences* 2004; 1032: 141–53.

Boscarino, J. A. "Psychobiological predictors of disease mortality
   after psychological trauma: Implications for research and clinical
   surveillance." *Journal of Nervous and Mental Disease* 2008; 196: 100–107.

Bremner, J. Douglas. *Does Stress Damage the Brain?* New York: W. W. Norton
   & Co., 2002.

Friedman, M. J., T. M. Keane, and P. A. Resick, eds. *Handbook of PTSD:
   Science and Practice.* New York/London: Guilford Press, 2007.

Hoge, C. W., A. Terhakopian, C. A. Castro, S. C. Messer, and C. C. Engel.
   "Association of post-traumatic stress disorder with somatic symptoms,
   health care visits, and absenteeism among Iraq War veterans."
   American Journal of Psychiatry 2007; 164: 150–53.

Nemeroff, C. B., J. D. Bremner, E. B. Foa, H. S. Mayberg, C. S. North,
   and M. B. Stein. "Post-traumatic stress disorder: A state-of-the-science
   review." *Journal of Psychiatric Research* 2006; 40: 1–21.

Van der Kolk, B. A. "Clinical implications of neuroscience research in PTSD." *Annals of the New York Academy of Sciences* 2006; 1071: 277–93.

Yehuda, R. "Advances in understanding neuroendocrine alterations in PTSD and their therapeutic implications," *Annals of the New York Academy of Sciences* 2006; 1071: 137–66.

PTSD CRITERIA AND DIAGNOSIS

Adler, A. B., K. M. Wright, P. D. Bliese, R. Echford, and C. W. Hoge. "A2 diagnostic criterion for combat-related post-traumatic stress disorder." *Journal of Traumatic Stress* 2008; 21: 301–308.

American Psychiatric Association. *Diagnostic and Statistical Manual for Mental Disorders*, 4th ed., text revision: DSM-IV-TR. Arlington, VA: American Psychiatric Association, 2000.

Terhakopian, A., N. Sinaii, C. C. Engel, P. P. Schnurr, and C. W. Hoge. "Estimating population prevalence of post-traumatic stress disorder: An example using the PTSD checklist." *Journal of Traumatic Stress* 2008; 21(3): 290–300.

PTSD TREATMENT: REVIEWS AND META-ANALYSES

American Psychiatric Association. Practice Guideline for the Treatment of Patients with Acute Stress Disorder and Post-Traumatic Stress Disorder. Arlington, VA: American Psychiatric Association, 2004.

Benish, S. G., Z. E. Imel, and B. E. Wampold. "The relative efficacy of bona fide psychotherapies for treating post-traumatic stress disorder: a meta analysis of direct comparisons." *Clinical Psychology Review* 2008; 28: 746–58.

Bisson, J., and M. Andrew. "Psychological treatments of post-traumatic stress disorder (PTSD) (review)." *The Cochran Collaboration.* Cochran Library 2009; issue 2.

Foa, E. B., T. M. Keane, M. J. Friedman, and J. A. Cohen. *Effective Treatments for PTSD: Practice Guidelines from the International Society for Traumatic Stress Studies.* New York: Guilford Press, 2009.

Institute of Medicine. *Treatment of Post-Traumatic Stress Disorder: An Assessment of the Evidence.* Washington, DC: National Academies Press, 2008.

Stein, D. J., J.C. Ipser, and S. Seedat. "Pharmacotherapy for post-traumatic stress disorder (PTSD) (review)." *The Cochran Collaboration.* Cochran Library 2009; issue 2.

VA/DoD Clinical Practice Working Group. "Management of post-traumatic stress." Department of Veterans Affairs and Health Affairs, Department of Defense, Office of Quality and Performance publication 1O0-CPG/FTSD-04. 2003.

PTSD TREATMENT: SPECIFIC TREATMENT APPROACHES

Bisson, J., J. P. Shepherd, D. Joy, R. Probert., and R. G. Newcombe. "Early cognitive-behavioural therapy for post-traumatic stress symptoms after physical injury. Randomised controlled trial." *British Journal of Psychiatry* 2004; 184: 63–69.

Bryant, R. A., M. L. Moulds, R. M. Guthrie, S. T. Dang, J. Mastrodomenico, R. D. V. Nixon, K. L. Felmingham, and S. Hopwood. "A randomized control trial of exposure therapy and cognitive restructuring for post-traumatic stress disorder." *Journal of Consulting and Clinical Psychology* 2008; 76: 695–703.

Bryant, R. A., M. L. Moulds, R. M. Guthrie, S. T. Dang, and R. D. V. Nixon. "Imaginal exposure alone and imaginal exposure with cognitive restructuring in treatment of post-traumatic stress disorder." *Journal of Consulting and Clinical Psychology* 2003; 71: 706–12.

Foa, E. B., C. V. Dancu, E. A. Hembree, L. H. Jaycox, E. A. Meadows, and G. P. Street. "A comparison of exposure therapy, stress inoculation training, and their combination for reducing post-traumatic stress disorder in female assault victims." *Journal of Consulting and Clinical Psychology* 1999; 67: 194–200.

Foa, E. B., E. A. Hembree, S. P. Cahill, S. A. M. Rauch, D. S. Riggs, N. C. Feeny, and E. Yadin. "Randomized trial of prolonged exposure for post-traumatic stress disorder with and without cognitive restructuring: Outcome at academic and community clinics." *Journal of Consulting and Clinical Psychology* 2005; 73: 953–64.

Foa, E. B., E. A. Hembree, B. O. Rothbaum. "Prolonged exposure therapy for PTSD: Emotional processing of traumatic experience." *Therapist Guide,* Oxford University Press, 2007.

Friedman, M. J., C. R. Marmar, D. G. Baker, C. R. Sikes, and G. M. Farfel. "Randomized, double-blind comparison of sertraline and placebo for post-traumatic stress disorder in a Department of Veterans Affairs setting." *Journal of Clinical Psychiatry* 2007; 68: 711–20.

Monson, C. M., P. P. Schnurr, P. A. Resick, M. J. Friedman, Y. Young-Xu, and S. P. Stevens. "Cognitive processing therapy for veterans with military-related post-traumatic stress disorder." *Journal of Consulting and Clinical Psychology* 2006; 74: 898–907.

Neuner, F., P. L. Onyut, V. Ertl, M. Odenwald, E. Schauer, and T. Elbert. "Treatment of posttraumatic stress disorder by trained lay counselors in an African refugee settlement: a randomized controlled trial." *Journal of Consulting and Clinical Psychology* 2008; 76: 686–94.

Pitman, R. K., S. P. Orr, B. Altman, R. E. Longpre, R. E. Poire, and M. L. Macklin, et al. "Emotional processing during eye movement desensitization and reprocessing (EMDR) therapy of Vietnam veterans with post-traumatic stress disorder." *Comprehensive Psychiatry* 1996; 37: 419–29.

Resick, P. A., T. E. Galovski, M. O. Uhlmansiek, C. D. Scher, G. A. Clum, and Y. Young-Xu. "A randomized clinical trial to dismantle components of cognitive processing therapy for post-traumatic stress disorder in female victims of interpersonal violence." *Journal of Consulting and Clinical Psychology* 2008; 76: 243–58.

Resick, P. A., and M. K. Schnicke. "Cognitive processing therapy for sexual assault victims." *Journal of Consulting and Clinical Psychology* 1992; 60: 748–56.

Rothbaum, B. O., M. C. Astin, and F. Marsteller. "Prolonged exposure versus eye movement desensitization and reprocessing (EMDR) for PTSD rape victims." *Journal of Traumatic Stress* 2005; 18: 607–16.

Schnurr, P. P., M. J. Friedman, C. C. Engel, E. B. Foa, M. T. Shea, B. K. Chow, et al. "Cognitive behavioral therapy for post-traumatic stress disorder in women." *JAMA* 2007; 297: 820–830.

Shapiro, F. "Eye movement desensitization: A new treatment for post-traumatic stress disorder." *Journal of Behavior Therapy and Experimental Psychiatry* 1989; 20: 211–17.

Taylor, S., D. S. Thordarson, L. Maxfield, I. C. Fedoroff, K. Lovell, and J. Ogrodniczuk. "Comparative efficacy, speed, and adverse effects of three PTSD treatments: Exposure therapy, EMDR, and relaxation training." *Journal of Consulting and Clinical Psychology* 2003; 71: 330–38.

SLEEP DEPRIVATION

Belenky, G., N. J. Wesensten, D. R. Thorne, M. L. Thomas, H. C. Sing, D. P. Redmond, M. B. Russo, and T. J. Balkin. "Patterns of performance degradation and restoration during sleep restriction and subsequent recovery: A sleep dose-response study." *Journal of Sleep Research* 2003 Mar; 12(1): 1–12.

Kahn-Greene, E. T., D. B. Killgore, G. H. Kamimori, T. J. Balkin, and W. D. S. Killgore. "The effects of sleep deprivation on symptoms of psychopathology in healthy adults." *Sleep Medicine* 2007; 8: 215–21.

Killgore, W. D. S., T. J. Balkin, and N. J. Wesensten. "Impaired decision making following 49 hours of sleep deprivation." *Journal of Sleep Research* 2006; 15: 7–13.

Killgore, W. D. S., E. T. Kahn-Greene, E. L. Lipizzi, R. A. Newman, G. H. Kamimori, and T. J. Balkin. "Sleep deprivation reduces perceived emotional intelligence and constructive thinking skills." *Sleep Medicine* 2008; 9: 517–26.

Killgore, W. D. S., D. B. Killgore, L. M. Day, C. Li, G. H. Kamimori, and T. J. Balkin. "The effects of 53 hours of sleep deprivation on moral judgment." *Sleep* 2007; 30: 345–52.

Lieberman, H. R., G. P. Barthalon, C. M. Falco, M. Kramer, C. A. Morgan III, and P. Niro. "Severe decriments in cognition function and mood induced by sleep loss, heat, dehydration, and undernutrition during simulated combat." *Biological Psychiatry* 2005; 57: 422–29.

Lieberman, H. R., P. Niro, W. J. Tharion, B. C. Nindi, J. W. Castellani, and S. J. Montain. "Cognition during sustained operations: Comparison of a laboratory simulation to field studies. *Aviation, Space, and Environmental Medicine* 2006; 77: 929–35.

OTHER MENTAL HEALTH

Bryson, Debra R., and Charise M. Hoge. *A Portable Identity: A Woman's Guide to Maintaining a Sense of Self While Moving Overseas.* Glen Echo, MD: Transition Press International, 2005.

Hanna, Judith Lynne. *Dancing for Health: Conquering and Preventing Stress.* New York: AltaMira Press, 2006.

Hightower, Newton. *Anger Busting 101: New ABCs for Angry Men and the Women Who Love Them.* Houston, TX: Bayou Publishing, 2005.

HERB M. GOLDBERG AREAS OF CONTRIBUTION

1) Feedback, facilitator's/psychotherapist's personality attributes, and their effect on students'/clients' self-awareness and personal development

2) Survivor's guilt, self-punishment, and forgiveness of self

3) "Fault" and the "Illusion of choice"

4) The impact of "fault" on individuals and society

5) The impact of the "illusion of choice" on individuals and society

6) The impact of "fault" on responsibility and accountability

7) The relationship between "fault" and responsibility/accountability

8) Student-centered educational principles focused on learning rather than teaching

9) Client-centered psychotherapy

10) The distinction between anger and rage and its basis and implications

11) The nature of nonsensical/irrational (stupid) questions and their relation to irreconcilable thoughts/emotions

12) Humor and absurdity and their application in psychotherapy

OTHER READING

Albom, Mitch. *Tuesdays with Morrie.* New York: Random House, 1997.

Cleary, Thomas, and J. C. Cleary. *The Blue Cliff Record.* Boston: Shambala, 1977.

Frankl, Viktor E. *Man's Search for Meaning.* Boston, MA: Beacon Press, 1959.

Fromm, Erich. *The Art of Loving.* New York: Harper and Row, 1956.

Heller, Joseph. *Catch-22.* New York: Scribner, 1955.

Kopp, Sheldon B. *If You Meet the Buddha on the Road, Kill Him!* New York: Bantam Books, 1972.

Kushner, Harold S. *When Bad Things Happen to Good People.* New York: Anchor Books, 2004 (1981).

Rimpoche, Chokyi Nyima, and David R. Shlim. *Medicine and Compassion: A Tibetan Lama's Guidance for Caregivers.* Boston, MA: Wisdom Publications, 2006.

Tillich, Paul. *Dynamics of Faith.* New York: Harper Collins, 1957.

Viorst, Judith. *Necessary Losses.* New York: The Free Press, 1986.

INDEX

ABOUT THE AUTHOR

Charles W. Hoge, MD, Colonel, U.S. Army (Retired) is regarded as a leading authority on the mental health impact of war. He graduated from Sarah Lawrence College (BA) and the University of Maryland School of Medicine (MD). He completed an Internal Medicine residency at Johns Hopkins Baltimore City Hospital, an Infectious Diseases–Geographic Medicine fellowship at University of Maryland, and a Psychiatry residency from Walter Reed Army Medical Center (WRAMC). His twenty-year active-duty military career began as a Public Health Service Officer at the Centers for Disease Control where he led investigations of communicable disease outbreaks. After two years, he transferred to the Army. For six years he directed field studies to prevent tropical diseases in deployed troops, and for twelve years served as an Army psychiatrist.

Between 2002 and 2009, Colonel Hoge directed the Defense Department's premier research program to mitigate the psychological and neurological consequences of the Iraq and Afghanistan wars, including PTSD, TBI, and sleep deprivation. He served as an attending psychiatrist at WRAMC, providing treatment to warriors and family members. He deployed to Iraq in 2004 and traveled throughout the country to improve combat stress control services.

Dr. Hoge's expertise spans psychiatry, trauma, public health, health policy, and infectious diseases. He has authored more than one hundred peer-reviewed articles in international journals. His groundbreaking studies on PTSD, mTBI, and stigma published in the *New England Journal of Medicine* and *Journal of the American Medical Association* are the most cited medical articles from the Iraq and Afghanistan wars. Dr. Hoge has testified several times to Congress and appeared frequently on national television and radio news shows. His work has contributed to significant increases in congressional funding for programs to help service members and veterans, and he continues to devote his career to promoting evidence-based interventions to improve warrior care.

He lives in the Washington, D.C., area with his wife, Charise, and daughters, Alex and Amelia.